AF770706

Foreign and Domestic Investment in Argentina

Political economy scholarship suggests that private sector investment, and thus economic growth, is more likely to occur when formal institutions allow states to provide investors with credible commitments to protect property rights. This book argues that this maxim does not always hold for infrastructure privatization programs. Rather, differences in firm organizational structure better explain the viability of privatization contracts in weak institutional environments. Domestic investors – or, if contracts are granted subnationally, domestic investors with diverse holdings in their contract jurisdiction – work most effectively in the volatile economic and political environments of the developing world. They are able to negotiate mutually beneficial adaptations to their contracts with host governments because cross-sector diversification provides them with informal contractual supports. The book finds strong empirical support for this argument through an analysis of fourteen water and sanitation privatization contracts in Argentina and a statistical analysis of sector trends in developing countries.

Alison E. Post is Assistant Professor of Political Science and Global Metropolitan Studies at the University of California, Berkeley. Prior to joining the Berkeley faculty, she was a Postdoctoral Fellow with the Committee on Global Thought at Columbia University, a Visiting Researcher at the Centro de Estudios de Estado y Sociedad in Buenos Aires and the UN Economic Commission for Latin America and the Caribbean (ECLAC) in Santiago, and a Researcher at the London School of Urban Research in London. Her doctoral dissertation won the 2009 William Anderson award from the American Political Science Association for the best dissertation in the general field of federalism, intergovernmental relations, state or local politics.

Advance Praise

"What explains variation in the sustainability of private investments in politically volatile environments? This groundbreaking book addresses the question by illuminating the informal mechanisms that protect investors in the absence of formal legal safeguards in developing countries. Building on Vernon's analysis of the 'obsolescing bargaining' and Williamson's notion of 'relational contracting,' Alison Post not only documents but explains the conditions that make private investment more (or at times less) resilient to regulatory capture in the water and sanitation sectors. Her insightful contributions improve our understanding of the political conditions that shape the definition of property rights, while pointing to the vulnerability of institutions and treaties that require third-party enforcement. This book is a must-read for any scholar of economic development and comparative political economy more generally."

– M. Victoria Murillo, Columbia University

Foreign and Domestic Investment in Argentina

The Politics of Privatized Infrastructure

ALISON E. POST

University of California, Berkeley

CAMBRIDGE
UNIVERSITY PRESS

CAMBRIDGE
UNIVERSITY PRESS

32 Avenue of the Americas, New York, NY 10013-2473, USA

Cambridge University Press is part of the University of Cambridge.

It furthers the University's mission by disseminating knowledge in the pursuit of education, learning, and research at the highest international levels of excellence.

www.cambridge.org
Information on this title: www.cambridge.org/9781107048041

© Alison E. Post 2014

This publication is in copyright. Subject to statutory exception and to the provisions of relevant collective licensing agreements, no reproduction of any part may take place without the written permission of Cambridge University Press.

First published 2014

A catalog record for this publication is available from the British Library.

Library of Congress Cataloging in Publication Data
Post, Alison E.
Foreign and domestic investment in Argentina : the politics of privatized infrastructure / Alison E. Post, University of California, Berkeley.
pages cm
Includes bibliographical references and index.
ISBN 978-1-107-04804-1 (hardback)
1. Investments, Foreign – Argentina. 2. Public works – Argentina – Finance. I. Title
HG5312.P67 2014
332.67′30982–dc23 2013030439

ISBN 978-1-107-04804-1 Hardback

Cambridge University Press has no responsibility for the persistence or accuracy of URLs for external or third-party Internet Web sites referred to in this publication and does not guarantee that any content on such Web sites is, or will remain, accurate or appropriate.

Contents

Figures and Tables

FIGURES

TABLES

Abbreviations

ACS	Actividades de Construcción y Servicios S.A. (Construction Activities and Services, a Spanish construction group)
AGBA	Aguas del Gran Buenos Aires S.A. (Buenos Aires provincial water company)
AR$	Argentine pesos
BIT	Bilateral investment treaty
EPAS	Ente Provincial del Agua y de Saneamiento (Water and sanitation regulator for Mendoza Province)
ETOSS	Ente Tripartito de Obras y Servicios Sanitários (Tripartite regulatory agency for water and sanitation, Buenos Aires metropolitan area)
FCC	Fomento de Construcción y Contratas S.A. (Construction and Contract Promotion, a Spanish construction group)
FDI	Foreign direct investment
ICSID	International Centre for Settlement of Investment Disputes
IDB	Inter-American Development Bank
INDEC	Instituto Nacional de Estadística y Censos (National Statistics and Census Institute)
MNC	Multinational corporation
OECD	Organisation for Economic Cooperation and Development
OSM	Obras Sanitarias de Mendoza (Water concessionaire for Mendoza Province)
OSN	Obras Sanitarias de la Nación (National Water and Sanitation Services)
SAMSA	Servicio de Aguas de Misiones S.A. (Water concessionaire for Misiones Province)
UNCTAD	United Nationals Conference on Trade and Development

Acknowledgments

For David

Many individuals and organizations generously supported the development of this book. For financial support for fieldwork, research assistance, and writing, I would like to acknowledge the following organizations and programs. At Harvard University, research and writing were supported by the General Committee on Scholarships; the Foreign Language and Area Studies fellowship program of the U.S. Department of Education; the Project on Justice, Welfare, and Economics; an Eliot Dissertation Completion Fellowship; the Westengard program; the Real Estate Academic Initiative; the David Rockefeller Center for Latin American Studies; and the Institute for Quantitative Social Science. A postdoctoral fellowship from the Committee on Global Thought at Columbia University allowed me to make initial revisions to the dissertation and financed additional fieldwork. Finally, the Institute for International Studies at UC Berkeley funded a book manuscript conference, research assistance, and additional fieldwork.

This book grew out of a doctoral dissertation completed while I was a student in the Government Department at Harvard University. I am indebted to my dissertation committee members, Jorge I. Domínguez, Jeffry Frieden, and Steven Levitsky. Their guidance sharpened my thinking and ensured that I was engaging with disciplinary debates while researching a topic rarely studied by political scientists. Outside the Government Department, fellow infrastructure scholars José (Tony) Gómez-Ibañez, Henry Lee, and Louis Wells provided encouragement and important feedback.

I am indebted to many individuals and institutions in South America. In Argentina, I am indebted to the community of individuals who have devoted their lives to improving water and sanitation services in their country. I would first like to thank members of the different institutions in the sector that supported my research: AIDIS Argentina (Asociación Argentina de Ingeniería Sanitaria y Ciencias del Ambiente), FENTOS (Federación Nacional de

Trabajadores de Obras Sanitarias), AFERAS (Asociación Federal de Entes Reguladores de Agua y Saneamiento de la República Argentina), COFES (Consejo Federal de Entidades de Servicios Sanitarios), and ENOHSA (Ente Nacional de Obras Hídricas de Saneamiento). I also am grateful to all of the individuals who set aside time for interviews, in many cases on multiple occasions, and who put me in touch with their colleagues. I will refrain from mentioning most of these names, as I do in the text, in order to avoid associating the conclusions of this piece – which are entirely my own – with anyone in particular. I would, however, like to acknowledge a few individuals who contributed greatly, and for whom an association with this project would not pose professional difficulties: Emilio Lentini, Román Ghio, Alexandre Brailowsky, Jean-Bernard Lemire, Carlos Ben, Norberto Nevani, Daniel Nallar, Federico Qüerio, the late Alejandro Bidegain, Rodrigo Castillo, Wylian Otrera, Lucía Mercado, and Rúben Pereyra.

I also would like to acknowledge the support of members of the Argentine academic community. Gustavo Herrero and Alexandre de Royere of the Harvard School of Business's Buenos Aires center were very supportive, particularly as I was starting the project. At CEDES (Centro de Estudios del Estado y Sociedad) in Buenos Aires, Valeria Serafinoff, Oscar Oszlak, and Mario Roitter offered important support. I am particularly thankful to Gustavo Ferro, Sebastián Galiani, and Ernesto Schargrodsky for their willingness to share data and source materials, and for Bronwen Morgan and Carolina Fairstein's willingness to share sources on Tucumán. I also thank Alberto Föhrig, Santiago Urbiztondo, Carlos Acuña, Sebastian Etchemendy, Marcelo Leiras, Pablo Sanguinetti, Juan Sanguinetti, Miguel de Luca, and Juan Carlos Torre for making time for very helpful conversations. I am particularly indebted to Valeria and Alberto for their friendship and long conversations about Argentine politics. I am also grateful to Alicia de la Fuente and Román and Giselle Ghio for taking me into their homes in Buenos Aires, and to the Puyó family for their friendship.

In Chile, I would like acknowledge the institutional support of ECLAC, where Miguel Solanes and Andrei Jouravlev provided guidance. Staff members at the David Rockefeller Center in Santiago, Steven Reifenberg in particular, were also extremely supportive. Pablo Serra and Andrés Gomez-Lobo provided helpful advice. I am particularly grateful to Sonia Gómez Urrestarazu and Germán Lorenas Kramer for providing me with a home away from home in Santiago and to Alexia Peyreire for her friendship. Meanwhile, several individuals helped me establish contacts in Brazil: John Briscoe, Jennifer Sara, and Thadeu Abicalil. Lincoln Noronha provided important on-site assistance during my stay.

Completing the dissertation and transforming it into a book manuscript would not have been possible without feedback from many friends and colleagues. I would first like to thank Lewis Bateman at Cambridge University Press, who has offered encouragement since the book proposal stage. Two reviewers for the Press also offered immensely helpful suggestions for improving the manuscript. Members of the Comparative Politics and Political Economy research workshops at Harvard, the Comparative Politics Seminar at Columbia, and the Junior Faculty Workshop at the Institute for International Studies at UC Berkeley provided helpful feedback as well. I would particularly like to thank the following individuals, who read and commented on the entire manuscript: Katerina Linos, Vicky Murillo, Veronica Herrera, Marcus Kurtz, Erica Simmons, and Kurt Weyland. For comments on specific book or dissertation chapters, I am grateful to Jim Alt, Robert Bates, David Collier, Ruth Berins Collier, Peter Evans, Robert Fannion, Magnus Feldmann, Eugenia Giraudy, Stephan Haggard, Peter Hall, Michael Hiscox, Dan Hopkins, Torben Iversen, Robert Kaufmann, Jason Lakin, Jonah Levy, Pauline Jones Luong, Sebastián Mazzuca, Shannon O'Neil, Wendy Pearlman, Susan Pharr, Paul Pierson, Megan Rithmire, James Robinson, Valeria Serafinoff, Ken Shepsle, Jiyeoun Song, Matthew Taylor, and Steven Vogel. I would also like to thank Gary King, Kevin Quinn, Patrick Lam, and Justin Grimmer for advice on specific analytic points. I am also grateful for the supportive environment UC Berkeley provides for its junior faculty members, and for mentoring from Ruth and David Collier in particular; this made the process of turning the dissertation into a book much more enjoyable.

Several young scholars provided me with invaluable research assistance at different points in the project. I would like to thank Benjamin Allen, Bernardo Deregibus, Ignacio Deregibus, María Belén Fernández, Hernán Flom, Eugenia Giraudy, Lindsay Mayka, Pedro Peterson, Ivanna Travaini, and Guadalupe Tuñon. Leslie Kriesel provided excellent assistance with line editing. I am particularly grateful to Bernardo Deregibus for accompanying me through the majority of the fieldwork portion of the project and to Ben Allen for patiently helping me finalize the manuscript.

Friends and family were also incredibly helpful in bringing this book to fruition. I would like to thank my brother and parents for their support. My mother proofread the dissertation and one draft of the manuscript at moments when I could not afford or find editors. David Martin, my partner, has provided invaluable emotional support and humor along the way. Our son, Maxwell, was born a few weeks after I submitted the manuscript for review. I would also like to thank Vibeke Christensen and Maryam Modjaz for their friendship and support over the years.

All errors are my own.

Introduction

The 1990s witnessed a massive influx of foreign funds into the infrastructure sectors of the developing world. Foreign direct investment (FDI) in infrastructure and construction leapt from US$1.9 billion in 1989 to US$27 billion in 1997.[1] Although infrastructure had for decades been seen as a core state responsibility, this view shifted as a new policy paradigm, the Washington Consensus, became dominant. International institutions, academics, governments, and large swaths of the population came to view transnational corporations as more capable than governments of modernizing and extending infrastructure systems. Through their access to international finance and new technology, it was argued, multinationals (MNCs) would transform the aging systems whose services in many cases failed to reach large portions of the population and suffered from severe quality deficits. Infrastructure improvements, in turn, would help spearhead faster rates of economic growth and improvements in living standards.

Eager to expand outside of their home markets and reassured by a new set of international property rights protections designed to protect their investments, European and North American MNCs vied for contracts to invest in and manage infrastructure systems in the developing world (Wells and Ahmed 2007). Historically, investments in infrastructure and natural resources have been plagued by what Vernon classically defined as an "obsolescing bargain" (Vernon 1971: 46–53).[2] The term refers to the temptation and tendency of governments to expropriate foreign investors' assets once up front expenditures have been made, thereby depriving them of income they expected projects to generate over their lifetimes. Vernon's formulation was borne out during the

[1] Total of FDI in electricity, gas, water, construction, transport, storage, and communications. Figures from United Nationals Conference on Trade and Development (UNCTAD) (1999: 421; 2009: 220).

[2] In an earlier depiction of the same phenomenon, Kindleberger (1969: 149–151) focused on the tendency of governments to push foreign investors to renegotiate the terms of their original contracts.

1970s, which witnessed expropriation in sectors such as oil, mining, and utilities (Kobrin 1980, 1984). The demonstrated vulnerability of infrastructure assets made property rights protections – believed to be important prerequisites for economic growth in general – particularly important for private investment in infrastructure. During the 1990s, states attempted to assuage investor fears that history could repeat itself by entering bilateral investment treaties under which investors could lodge grievances and obtain compensation through international arbitration. By 2008, states had signed 2,676 bilateral investment treaties.[3] In entering these agreements, they tied their own hands, thereby providing substitutes for domestic institutions such as independent courts, which would normally safeguard property rights in other contexts.

Privatization contracts now exist throughout the developing world. Between 1990 and 2009, 133 low- and middle-income countries privatized state enterprises in the telecommunications sector, 107 in the energy sector, 82 in transportation, and 61 in water and sanitation (PPIAF-World Bank 2011). These contracts are typically long term – many spanning decades – so that initial project costs can be amortized over a long period. More than twenty years into this privatization wave, it is both possible and necessary to examine the results of this major policy experiment, especially because a new wave of enthusiasm for privatization is taking hold as states face tightening budgets and reduced growth prospects.[4]

"Credible commitments" approaches to the study of property rights and development, including applications to investment in regulated industries, offer a set of concrete predictions regarding the likely fate of contracts entered during the 1990s privatization wave. A first set of analyses suggests that where domestic political institutions do not provide checks and balances on one another, property rights protections will be weak (e.g., North and Weingast 1989; Levy and Spiller 1994, 1996; Montinola et al. 1995; Weingast 1995; Henisz 2002; Acemoglu et al. 2003; Beazer 2012). Regulatory agencies and judiciaries, for example, will not be in a position to resist pressures from heads of state to issue or sanction regulatory rulings that amount to unilateral changes in contractual terms. Anticipating expropriation, firms will be reluctant to invest. As a result, contracts are likely to yield few benefits for local populations, the firms providing infrastructure will become unpopular, and contracts will be vulnerable to cancellation by governments.

A second set of analyses suggests that countries without strong systems of checks and balances can improve their credibility with investors by turning to

[3] UNCTAD International Investment Agreements Database.

[4] On Russian, Indian, and Brazilian plans, see: "Macquarie Joins Recap in Russia." *Global Investor*. Oct. 1, 2008; "Russia: VEB Joins Macquarie in Infrastructure Fund." *Euromoney*. Sept. 1, 2009; "Infrastruggles: One of India's Most Important Industries Has a Knackered Balance Sheet." *The Economist*. Dec. 31, 2011; Brazil Launches $66bn Stimulus Plan." *Financial Times*. Aug. 16, 2012.

treaties that impose financial or reputational costs on governments if they renege on their commitments (Neumayer and Spess 2005; Elkins et al. 2006; Büthe and Milner 2008; Kerner 2009). Bilateral investment treaties, which typically allow investors to take states into international arbitration, are a prime example of this type of alternative commitment mechanism. This means that governments' hands are tied when interacting with MNCs, which enjoy supplemental protections unavailable to their domestic peers. Extending this line of reasoning, it could be argued that MNCs would be more likely to invest than domestic firms working in similar industries, and less likely to see their contracts cancelled prematurely. This implies that treaty protection would also increase MNCs' leverage with host governments during contract renegotiations, so that they would not follow the logic of the obsolescing bargain.

Patterns of investment and contract durability in the water and sanitation sector do not conform to these predictions. Levels of contract durability and investment vary dramatically among countries with weak checks and balances, and even within individual countries.[5] Moreover, contracts held by domestic firms are proving to be more viable politically and financially in the long run than those held by MNCs. Between 1990 and 2008, water and sanitation investment contracts held by MNCs in low- and middle-income countries were cancelled prematurely at almost four times the rate of contracts held by consortia led by domestic investors.[6] The stark difference in cancellation rates is striking given that MNCs often won what were perceived to be the most lucrative contracts because award processes tended to privilege capital requirements, expertise, and experience. Developing-country companies working in their home market, in contrast, maintained smoother relationships with host governments while achieving similar rates of service improvements as foreign firms did. The most comprehensive large-N study conducted to date on factors contributing to privatization success did not find evidence suggesting that foreign firms improved services more consistently than domestic investors did.[7] Moreover, the continuing eagerness of developing-country investors to enter contracts in their home markets in the 2000s suggests they have managed to make water projects

[5] On varied results within the developing world and Latin America, see Gassner et al. (2009: 4, 42) and Andrés et al. (2008: chapter 7). On across-country and within-country variation, see Harris (2003: 23) and Marin (2009).

[6] The rate of premature contract cancellation for concession contracts and divestitures with majority foreign ownership is 19%, whereas the cancellation rate for projects with majority domestic ownership is 5%. Host governments or firms can initiate contract cancellations. Cancellation data are from the Private Sector Participation in Infrastructure database for concession contracts and divestitures entered during the 1990–2008 period (PPIAF-World Bank: data downloaded in May 2008). This is a nearly comprehensive database of private infrastructure contracts in low- and middle-income countries. Criteria used to differentiate between projects controlled by foreign and domestic investors are discussed in detail in Chapter 7.

[7] Analyzing performance data for forty-nine firms in the Latin American water and sanitation sector, Andrés et al. (2008: 215–216) find that increases in network coverage have been, if anything, higher under domestic investors.

work in financial terms whereas MNCs have struggled to earn attractive returns in the medium run. For instance, following the Argentine economic crisis, twenty-seven out of twenty-nine consortia awarded new investment contracts in Latin America were led by domestic firms. Domestic firms bought stakes in existing projects as well.[8] In other words, domestic firms in the sector have been less vulnerable to the obsolescing bargain.

INFORMAL SUPPORTS FOR LONG-TERM CONTRACTS: DOMESTIC INVESTORS' HOME COURT ADVANTAGE

This book seeks to explain variation in contract durability and investment levels in weak institutional environments: settings in which rules may exist on paper but tend not to be followed in practice, or are unstable and frequently subject to change (Levitsky and Murillo 2005, 2009). I develop a general theoretical argument and offer an initial illustration of its explanatory power through an empirical study of long-term privatization contracts in the water and sanitation sector. Long-term contracts between the state and the private sector have been multiplying at an impressive rate as a result of the aforementioned privatization trend in developing countries. Between 1990 and 2008, for instance, low- and middle-income countries entered 4,302 contracts for private sector participation infrastructure (PPIAF-World Bank 2010). The number of long-term contracts between governments and private firms also grew through efforts to "contract out" social and health services.[9] To understand variation in the durability of such long-term contracts, we must shift our focus from institutional to noninstitutional, or informal, supports for property rights.

Long-term contracts with states in weak institutional environments face special challenges. The first is contractual incompleteness, or the failure to address any possible scenario. All contracts are incomplete, but long-term contracts in infrastructure sectors are likely to be less complete than short-term contracts or long-term contracts in many other sectors (Gómez-Ibáñez 2003; Laffont 2005: 3). Economic volatility, which tends to be especially prevalent in emerging markets and weak institutional environments (Gavin 1997; Wibbels 2006), makes long-term contracts even more vulnerable to incompleteness.[10] Moreover, contracts *with the state* in weak institutional environments are particularly difficult to maintain because there is little to prevent new officeholders from changing contractual terms.[11] Informal contractual supports, however,

[8] Data for concession contracts and divestitures calculated from the PPIAF-World Bank (2008).

[9] For a treatment of this trend, see Gough and Wood (2004).

[10] Spiller and Tommasi (2007: 27–28) make these points with respect to public policy more generally.

[11] As Hogan et al. (2010: 2, 19) argue, there are only imperfect ways to appeal to a third party when contracts are held with a state.

can help states and investors negotiate settlements in the wake of changing circumstances.

The central insight of this book is that firms' organizational structure affects their ability to maintain long-term contracts with the state in weak institutional environments. It can help or hinder their efforts to reach mutually acceptable agreements with states about changes in contractual terms following political or economic change. In making this argument, this study combines a political economy emphasis on how firm assets affect corporate preferences and political activity with an economic sociology emphasis on firm cultural and structural embeddedness. I bring these two theoretical traditions together to explain why domestic business groups – particularly those with a long-standing, diversified presence in their contract jurisdiction – are better able to negotiate politically and financially workable adaptations to infrastructure contracts as the preferences and bargaining power of both parties shift over time than are MNCs.[12] My argument not only provides microfoundations for the obsolescing bargain theory but also predicts the circumstances under which it is likely to apply most strongly.

Studies of business organization suggest that while MNCs tend to diversify across countries and specialize in particular sectors, investors based in the developing world tend to diversify across sectors while maintaining a strong presence in their home market through business group or conglomerate structures.[13] Because of their sector focus within particular countries, MNCs have strong incentives to make investment decisions and formulate policy proposals based on the fate of their operations in the sector that comprises their primary investment in a country. Domestic investors with a conglomerate or group structure, however, will view investments in a given regulated sector in the context of a broader, local portfolio because they have sunk costs in their home market. This leads them to exhibit greater patience and entertain a wider set of negotiating outcomes. Aggressive lobbying efforts, after all, may jeopardize their operations in other sectors, and firms may value the regulated asset for returns it can provide at other points in the economic cycle. Overall, a conglomerate structure encourages domestic investors to be more patient and bring more moderate demands to the negotiating table than their MNC counterparts would at any given point in time.

[12] In bringing two research traditions to bear on a substantive problem, this project represents an example of "analytic eclecticism" as described by Sil and Katzenstein (2010).

[13] This is a general characterization, of course. Granovetter (1994, 2005), Guillén (2001), Khanna and Yafeh (2007), and Schneider (2008, 2009) provide excellent reviews of the literature on business groups. The argument proposed in this book should be read as applying to diversified conglomerates and business groups from developing country markets rather than developing country firms that do not resemble the "ideal type." The MNC ideal type is particularly applicable to infrastructure sectors, where multinationals tend to develop strong sector specializations (Scott 2011: 74).

Cross-sector diversification also enables many developing-country business groups to draw on a different and less controversial set of negotiating strategies than those available to MNCs. For domestic investors, negotiations may be facilitated by the opportunity for informal agreements encompassing their operations in multiple sectors. MNCs, in contrast, tend to have access to a different and more formal set of bargaining tactics because of their cross-country organizational structure. In the many countries that have provided for recourse to international arbitration for investors through bilateral investment treaties, domestic investment law, or individual contracts, MNCs can force host governments to the bargaining table by threatening to take them into international arbitration. Recourse to such formal means of pressuring host governments, however, makes conflict more visible and smacks of bullying. Threats to sue, after all, recall long histories of exploitation by foreign firms and colonial powers. The greater and often negative publicity associated with such bargaining tactics can make it more difficult to reach stable settlements. Furthermore, the financial sanctions that could be imposed through international arbitration are far off and therefore unlikely to affect the host government's current officeholders. As a result, the formal negotiating strategies available to MNCs are likely to be less effective than the range of informal strategies available to domestic investors operating in their home market. This is particularly likely when governments come to possess healthy revenue streams, and are therefore less dependent on private capital to supply infrastructure. As a result, domestic investors' contractual relationships with host governments are likely to be more resilient than are those of MNCs.

While this general logic suggests a divergence in the trajectories of utilities and infrastructure contracts held by domestic investors and MNCs, it has a second and very important implication when contracts are granted and regulated by subnational, rather than national, governments. Subnational contracts are very common in infrastructure sectors such as transportation, urban water and sanitation, and electricity. When contracts are regulated at the subnational level, we expect firms with a strong local presence – that is, numerous and diverse operations in the state or municipality in question – to exhibit higher levels of patience, possess more opportunities for linking negotiations with the state in multiple sectors, and maintain more significant ties with the local establishment than domestic firms without diverse local holdings. While all domestic firms may exhibit high levels of cultural embeddedness and be less likely than international firms to initiate legal claims against the governments holding their contracts regardless of the structure of their asset portfolio, they will typically not have opportunities for issue linkage and strong local ties unless they possess a significant set of holdings in the project jurisdiction. Domestic firms without a diverse local presence will also have lower exit costs than firms with long-standing and diverse local operations and are therefore likely to be less patient in negotiations. As a result, domestic investors with significant and diverse local portfolios are more likely to negotiate effectively in the long run with host governments than are domestic investors with few local ties.

ADDITIONAL CONTRIBUTIONS

In addition to critiquing political economy's recent scholarly emphasis on institutional rather than informal supports for property rights, this book also contributes to two relatively new and increasingly important literatures in political economy. First, it provides conceptual innovations to the nascent literature on the politics of public policy in weak institutional environments. Second, it contributes to a new wave of research on the political economy of development that examines the growth and behavior of large firms based in the developing world, as well as the implications of their increasing prominence. In addition, it aims to reframe academic and policy debates on the merits of private sector participation in infrastructure.

Literature on the politics of regulation in developing countries is part of a relatively new and rapidly growing literature on the politics of public policy in weak institutional environments. Although there have been many studies of market reform (e.g., Domínguez 1997; Gibson 1997; Montero 1998; Kingstone 1999; Schamis 1999; Manzetti 1999, 2009; Thacker 2000; Etchemendy 2001; Stokes 2001; Teichman 2001; Corrales 2002; Murillo 2002, 2009; Armijo and Faucher 2002; Madrid 2003; Treisman 2003; Kogut and MacPherson 2004; Weyland 2002, 2005; Arce 2005; Henisz, Guillén, and Zelner 2005; Jordana and Levi-Faur 2005; Victor and Heller 2007; Armijo and Faucher 2008; Brooks 2009), there has been much less scholarship on post-privatization regulatory politics, particularly after the first years following privatizations, and more generally regarding the politics of FDI in infrastructure or utilities. Existing research on regulatory politics has been largely focused on the extent to which policy design and the configurations of institutions and other actors that provide checks and balances on one another together moderate regulatory policy making, thereby protecting firms from unexpected policy changes and producing incentives for investment (Levy and Spiller 1994, 1996; Heller and McCubbins 1996; Henisz and Zelner 2001; Henisz 2002; Shirley and Ménard 2002; Laffont 2005; Krause 2009). Other work examines how institutions providing checks and balances can restrain firm-government collusion (Manzetti 2009). These approaches, while helpful in understanding why there might be more arbitrary regulation in developing countries than in developed ones, offer less analytic leverage for understanding the wide range in investment outcomes in weak institutional environments. This study instead focuses on one of the main interest groups involved in the regulatory process – firms – and argues that variation in firm structure contributes to stark differences in regulatory outcomes. In stepping back from the recent emphasis on institutions to examine interest groups, I join scholars such as O'Rourke (2004), Rhodes (2006), Murillo (2009), and Frye (2010), who examine how citizen pressures, consumer group mobilization, political partisanship and competition, and political polarization affect regulatory politics and enforcement.

Although there has been an outpouring of research on FDI over the last decade, political economy scholars have only recently renewed their interest in developing country firms and their role as influential economic and political actors.[14] Scholars have recently sought to explain why business groups vary across countries (Granovetter 1994, 2005; Guillén 2001; Khanna and Yafeh 2007; Schneider 2009). Scholarship has also probed developing country business groups' motives for international expansion (Ramamurti and Singh 2009), how local institutional environments affect their proclivity to influence politicians through corrupt means (Yadav 2011), their ability to manage oil sector holdings efficaciously (Jones Luong and Weinthal 2010), and the extent to which states turn to them to attain developmental objectives (Wengle 2012). This attention is warranted: developing country firms now operate at a scale and in sectors where they did not forty years ago. This book contributes to the growing body of work through comparative analysis of the respective ability of MNCs and developing country investors to work effectively in the utilities and infrastructure sector.

Perhaps most importantly, this study also suggests we reframe the highly contentious scholarly and policy debates regarding the merits of private sector participation in infrastructure and utilities. A large literature examines the effects of private sector participation in infrastructure, including in the water and sanitation sector specifically.[15] Large- and medium-N studies (Harris 2003; Andrés et al. 2008; Roland 2008; Gassner et al. 2009; Marin 2009) have suggested that it has not had a uniform effect. Given the differing results observed even within individual countries, assessments of sources of *variation* in the performance of privatized utilities within a single sector – water and sanitation – can contribute greatly to the privatization debate. Existing studies have attributed variation to institutional environments, sector policies, contract structure, and firm-specific management decisions but have paid little attention to investor organizational structure.[16] If domestic conglomerates are more likely than MNCs to preside over contracts that remain economically and politically viable in the long run, domestic management should be evaluated as the main alternative to public provision, especially given the dislocations that can occur under failed privatizations.[17]

[14] The preceding wave of scholarship focused on the role of domestic business groups in "late industrialization" in East Asia (e.g., Amsden 1989; Doner 1992; Amsden and Tikino 1994).

[15] Budds and McGranahan (2003), Davis (2005), Lobina (2005), Prasad (2006), Krause (2009), Marin (2009), and Bakker (2010) review the literature on water and sanitation.

[16] Savedoff and Spiller (1999), Shirley (2002), and Krause (2009) examine the influence of the institutional environment as well as sector-specific institutions and regulation on water privatization outcomes. Nickson and Vargas (2002) examine the influence of contract structure and regulatory system features on outcomes. Wu and Malaluan (2008) examine how firm-specific management decisions impact the effects of privatization.

[17] Privatization reversals can have negative, lingering effects: payment rates and public support for systems can plummet and take years to improve again, hence starving systems of resources that could otherwise be used to maintain and improve system infrastructure. Also, major investments in system improvements tend to be deferred during such periods. A prime example of this is the case of Cochabamba, Bolivia: this infamous privatization, which sparked the "water wars," was designed to finance major investments in water supply in a parched region. When the privatization failed, control was returned to the former public provider, which has let system infrastructure fall further into disrepair (Schultz 2008: 35–39).

RESEARCH DESIGN

A Sector Focus on Urban Water and Sanitation

This study follows a venerable tradition of work in political economy that examines variation in single economic sectors (Evans 1995; Bates 1997; Karl 1997; Paige 1997; Snyder 2001). Taking a sector approach offers a number of important advantages. First, it allows us to control for many sources of variation and isolate the principal independent variable: investor organizational structure. Second, given the technical complexity of infrastructure sectors, focusing on a single sector helps ensure that cases are comparable with one another and that case studies devote sufficient attention to the relevant technical background information.

The analysis centers on the water and sanitation sector for several reasons. Investment in water and sanitation is crucial in humanitarian terms. Access to clean water and sanitation yields improved health outcomes, particularly reduced rates of child illness and mortality.[18] There are major coverage deficits in developing countries: according to UN estimates, 46 percent of the world's population currently lacks piped household water connections, and 48 percent lacks access to flush toilets, latrines, or composting toilets.[19] Improving household access to clean water can also contribute to important secondary outcomes, such as improvements in school attendance rates among girls and the ability of all children to learn in school.[20]

The water and sanitation sector also offers excellent variation on the main independent variable: investor organizational structure. The trend toward strong domestic investor participation – not just as a joint venture partner but also as the principal investor – was comparatively strong at the beginning of the privatization wave and grew stronger over time as foreign investors sold their stakes to domestic firms. For this reason, the water sector offers the chance to evaluate over a relatively long period the influence of a set of actors that is becoming increasingly relevant in other infrastructure sectors as foreign investors sell out to domestic firms.

[18] On the link between clean water access and health outcomes, see Merrick (1985); Behrman and Wolfe (1987); Esrey et al. (1991); Lavy et al. (1996); Lee et al. (1997); and Jalan and Ravallion (2003). On the link between improved sanitation facilities and health outcomes, see UNICEF-WHO (2008: 2). Scholars have found that individuals must be educated in personal hygiene and the nature of disease transmission in order for health improvements to be fully realized (Green 2003: 230–231).

[19] Figures from the UNICEF-WHO (2008: 6, 23). An additional 33% of the population obtains access to other "improved sources" of water such as standpipes, boreholes, and protected dug wells or springs.

[20] See "Water, Sanitation, and Hygiene in Schools" and "In Cameroon, Changing Attitudes and Safe Water Mean More Girls in School," www.unicef.org. (Downloaded May 2, 2011).

The water sector is also ideal for analysis because private sector participation has typically occurred at the subnational level. According to 2008 World Bank estimates, subnational governments have granted approximately 87 percent of the water contracts in low- and middle-income countries.[21] This allows for comparisons of a significant number of cases within as well as across countries. The opportunity to conduct within-country comparisons is particularly important because it permits us to control for country-specific influences on privatization outcomes, such as national institutions and privatization program design.

Furthermore, the sector represents a "critical case": business-state relations have been more politicized in water and sanitation than in other sectors because of the fundamental nature of the service *and* the fact that state firms did not charge large swaths of the population for decades, making the transition from operating under deficits to cost recovery particularly political. This being said, as Murillo (2009) and others have demonstrated, many infrastructure sectors attract the attention of politicians and the public. Given that infrastructure contracts are typically long term, tensions are simply likely to surface earlier in water and sanitation. As a result, experiences there can offer important insights regarding tendencies likely to emerge in the long run in other cases.

Within the water and sanitation sector, my analysis focuses on the most popular type of private sector participation. Politicians who sought private investment most often privatized via concession contracts: detailed management and investment contracts that by definition left infrastructure assets under state ownership. This model was generally preferred because large sums were not expected from asset sales and because it allowed governments to establish very specific contractual targets with respect to investment and expansion for particular firms.

Nested, Subnational Comparisons

Within the water and sanitation sector, this book employs a multilevel research strategy: a study of fourteen concession contracts in Argentina is nested within a broader analysis of patterns of premature contract cancellation in low- and middle-income countries.[22] Analysis of the fourteen Argentine contracts takes two forms: medium-N analysis of observed correlations between the main variables of interest and process tracing designed to reveal the ways firm-government negotiations unfolded over time. Focusing on the full sample of cases from a single country allowed me to assemble a broad range of indicators regarding utility performance from primary and

[21] Percentage calculated for all project types (PPIAF-World Bank 2008).

[22] The fourteen include the contract for the Buenos Aires Metropolitan Area, which was granted by the national government and regulated by an agency also including directors from the city and province. It does not include two small city-level contracts from the province of Buenos Aires.

local sources and to ensure that context-specific measures could be developed. It also allowed me to evaluate the respective explanatory power of the firm structure–based argument and explanations focusing on economic nationalism. This comparison would have been very difficult in countries that privatized at the national level.

The Argentine provinces offer particularly appropriate terrain for investigating the sources of variation in contractual outcomes. First, a significant number of provincial governments granted contracts and established regulatory agencies, allowing for the comparison of fourteen contract trajectories while controlling for the effect of overall privatization program design.[23] Decisions made by provincial regulators were likely to be more independent from one another than decisions made by a single, national regulatory entity regarding companies located throughout the country. (Cases are, of course, not completely independent; linkages will be explored in theoretical terms in Chapter 2 and in substantive terms within the case studies.) In spite of these similarities, privatization outcomes differed dramatically. Census figures portray coverage increases in water and sewerage that vary substantially by concession. In the province of Tucumán, where the concessionaire pulled out shortly after the concession award, network coverage stayed at roughly the same level between 1991 and 2001. The province of Corrientes, in contrast, has witnessed substantial coverage increases under privatization. In 1991, 74 percent of the population within the concession area enjoyed access to networked water services and 35 percent to networked sanitation services; these figures jumped to 86 percent and 52 percent respectively by the 2001 census. And although many contracts were cancelled prematurely, four of the original fourteen concession contracts are still in place.

Second, Argentina is uniquely positioned in terms of variation over time. The government began its privatization program in 1991, earlier than other countries,[24] so there have been more years of contract implementation. Argentina has also experienced economic conditions that present wildly different, yet common, contexts for bargaining over investment: a deficit-ridden state (the Menem era), economic crisis (2001–2002), and an economic recovery (2003 onward).[25] Therefore, the Argentine concessions have been subject to many of the conditions that most contracts in developing countries will experience, including periods that cause both governments and firms to desire to revise contractual terms and changes in the economic environment that shift

[23] Murillo (2002) highlights substantial national-level variation in privatization programs in Latin America, which emphasizes the importance of controlling for national-level program design.

[24] The first water and sanitation contracts recorded by the PPIAF-Worldbank database were in 1991, when Argentina and the Central African Republic privatized systems. The Central African Republic only privatized one system, whereas Argentina privatized fourteen provincial and national-level systems starting in that year.

[25] Most provinces in my study moved from deficits to fiscal surpluses between 2002 and 2003; revenues also increased significantly at this juncture.

government leverage vis-à-vis the firms they regulate. Since the privatization program began in 1991, we can observe a large set of contracts unfold before the onset of the Argentine crisis in 2001.

Third, Argentina offers variation on the key independent variable: the type of investor holding a majority stake in the concession. Five of the original fourteen lead investors in the Argentine contracts were subsidiaries of domestic firms. Additional domestic investors bought controlling stakes in contracts over the ensuing fifteen years. These investors varied, however, with respect to whether they held significant portfolios in other sectors within their contract jurisdictions. Foreign investors, on the other hand, all came from Organization for Economic Cooperation and Development (OECD) countries and did not possess significant, diverse portfolios in their contract jurisdiction.[26] Importantly, both foreign and domestic investors entered contracts in provinces that varied significantly in terms of their political and economic environments, which allows us to compare the experiences of different types of investors operating in similar environments.

Finally, Argentina is a quintessential "weak institutional environment" (Levitsky and Murillo 2005) suffering from economic volatility (Albrieu and Fanelli 2008). This makes it particularly appropriate for the development and testing of theories designed to explain variation in regulatory outcomes in weak institutional environments.

The majority of the book analyzes varied contract trajectories within Argentina. The final section then examines these experiences in a broader Latin American and worldwide context, following a tradition of scholarship that aims to place country or regional-level findings in comparative perspective.[27] It includes a statistical analysis of patterns of premature contract cancellation and an examination of patterns of market entry and exit in low- and middle-income countries. This is designed to assess the explanatory power of the argument outside of the country and region that privatized earliest; examine the influence of investor characteristics, such as access to international arbitration and providence from another developing country, that can vary among foreign investors but do not vary among the Argentine cases (e.g., all foreign investors came from OECD countries and enjoyed treaty protection in Argentina); and consider the utility of alternative explanations of the varied effects of privatization that focus on factors difficult to measure or assess in the Argentine context. Because the contract cancellation data fails to capture instances in which foreign (or domestic) investors leave projects through sales of their project shares, I consider additional types of evidence, including patterns of share sales, corporate statements, and patterns of market entry following the Argentine and Asian crises.

[26] As Chapter 1 will clarify, one might expect foreign investors originating from other developing countries to enjoy some, but not all, of the advantages of domestic firms.

[27] See, for example, Gibson (1996), Thacker (2000), and Levitsky (2003).

SOURCES

Piecing together analyses of the evolution of fourteen concession contracts has been a complex process. Other scholars have studied only two of them extensively: the Aguas Argentinas and Tucumán contracts. Reconstructing the trajectories of the others required working almost entirely from interviews and primary sources drawn from provincial regulatory agencies, firms, and archives. This posed a number of potential problems. Although the census data collected by the national statistical agency was better respected prior to 2006 than it is today, many sources have biases: firm-supplied financial and investment data may be misleading, and newspaper articles may be slanted by publication owners – particularly in the least "modernized" and less democratic provinces.

To compensate for potential biases, I triangulated among different types of evidence. I interviewed regulatory officials, legislators, concessionaire owners and employees, union members, representatives of consumer organizations, and ordinary customers – overall, more than 140 individuals in Argentina who had directly participated in the concessions, many of them on multiple occasions.[28] I have used the interview transcripts, however, primarily as an interpretative tool while analyzing other types of documentation. I tend to cite public sources, such as newspaper articles and regulatory resolutions, as this makes it easier for other scholars to replicate my work and respects the wishes of many of my sources for their comments to remain confidential. The empirical chapters examine regulatory resolutions and reports, contracts and concession bidding documents, local press coverage, financial and system data from providers, and interview transcripts alongside one another, and I report results when these various sources are consistent. By consulting and citing multiple types of information, I hope to make clear that the weight of the argument does not rest on any one piece of evidence. Sources are cited in the footnotes, while the book's online appendix contains a full list of interviewees and primary sources grouped by concession contract, as well as a number of other supporting materials.[29]

ROAD MAP

Chapter 1 offers a more rigorous exposition of my theoretical argument. Chapter 2 provides an overview of Argentina's experience with privatization via concession contract in the water and sanitation sector and analyzes the process by which different types of investors entered particular contracts. It also provides a broad-brush assessment of empirical support for the argument

[28] I also interviewed a range of individuals involved with private sector participation in the Chilean and Brazilian markets; these interviews inform the analysis in Chapter 7.

[29] http://www.cambridge.org/apost (see the "resources" tab).

advanced in Chapter 1 and alternative explanations based on aggregate analyses of the fourteen provincial-level contracts granted between 1991 and 2002.

Chapters 3 and 4 are fine-grained examinations of the differing trajectories of contracts held by foreign and domestic investors with and without diverse local holdings in Argentina before the 2001 economic crisis, when the state had relatively little leverage because of its restricted access to capital. The chapters divide the concessions into two groups, those located in more and less contentious political environments, so as to facilitate comparison among contracts held by different types of investors. Chapter 3 examines the divergent trajectories of contracts held by different types of investors in relatively contentious political environments during the pre-crisis period, while Chapter 4 compares the pre-crisis trajectories of contracts held by different types of investors in calmer political settings. These two chapters show that variation in investment levels and the profitability of the concessions emerged during the pre-crisis period. In contentious political settings, domestic investors with strong portfolios in their contract jurisdiction enjoyed important advantages. In relatively calm settings, their advantages were less apparent.

Chapters 5 and 6 then show how differences in concessionaire experiences became more pronounced during the Argentine crisis and in the years thereafter, when the state began to have more resources at its disposal. Chapter 5 examines the respective ability of foreign and domestic investors with and without diverse local holdings to obtain politically and financially viable post-crisis agreements for continuation of privatized service provision in relatively contentious provincial political environments. Chapter 6 compares the respective ability of different types of investors to secure workable post-crisis settlements in calmer provincial political environments. In both types of settings, domestic investors with significant local portfolios proved better able to negotiate effectively with host governments, securing rate increases and relief from investment responsibilities sufficient to help them cope with crisis and subsequent high levels of inflation.

The final section of the book evaluates whether patterns observed in Argentina are visible in a much broader set of countries. Chapter 7 examines patterns of premature contract cancellation and market exit and entry observed in the water and sanitation sector in low- and middle-income countries. Contracts held by domestic investors have been much less vulnerable to premature cancellation, and domestic investors entered contracts at much higher rates than foreign firms after the Argentine and Asian economic crises. The analysis also shows that access to international arbitration is associated with higher rather than lower rates of premature contract cancellation – contrary to expectations from international political scholarship. The conclusion summarizes the book's findings and discusses their theoretical and practical implications.

1

Informal Contractual Supports in Weak Institutional Environments

This chapter outlines the circumstances under which long-term infrastructure contracts between states and private firms endure and facilitate investment in weak institutional environments. It departs from dominant political economy approaches to regulation, foreign direct investment (FDI), and economic development, which stress the importance of institutional safeguards for property rights. Such approaches help explain differences in economic outcomes between the industrialized and developing world but provide less leverage when trying to explain variation among developing countries. For this reason, the theoretical framework presented here foregrounds informal supports for formal contracts. It explains why a diversified organization form – a common characteristic of developing-country conglomerates – endows firms with preferences and negotiating strategies that constitute informal contractual supports in weak institutional environments, especially within their home markets.

This argument applies best to regulated network industries such as utilities and infrastructure services, including highways, urban water and sanitation systems, and fixed line telephony. A number of characteristics set this crucial sector apart and yield particular political dynamics. First, assets are specific and immobile; once firms have made investments, they cannot move them elsewhere, meaning that they are vulnerable to ex post opportunism. Second, their technologies are characterized by economies of scale, and systems tend to be geographic monopolies. In addition, the end product is consumed by masses of individual citizens, ensuring that pricing decisions have political resonance. Finally, the government is associated with prices and service quality via the regulatory process. In other words, while Vernon's original "obsolescing bargain" hypothesis was meant to apply to all sectors characterized by fixed assets – and thereby include sectors such as infrastructure, oil, and mining – the scope of application here is slightly narrower. Most types of mining would not fall within this rubric, as the general population usually does not consume the final product.

A borderline case to which the argument could weakly apply is oil, a sector in which large swaths of the domestic population also tend to consume end products. However, the much larger profit margins in this industry make the pricing-investment trade-offs highlighted by the theory less stark. State ownership in profitable sectors is much more attractive, thereby increasing the government temptation to expropriate once firms have upfront investments.

The chapter begins by defining the outcomes of interest: *resilient* and *brittle* contractual relationships. Differentiating between these two "ideal type" relationships is important not only because they represent very different forms of regulatory politics but also because they result in important policy outcomes. Resilient contractual relationships are associated with incremental yet steady rates of investment and the institutionalization of privatized service provision. Brittle contractual relationships are characterized by uneven patterns of investment and a return to public sector service provision. The chapter then identifies the main actors involved in ongoing negotiations regarding contract compliance and contractual revisions and deduces their preferences on the basis of their political and economic context. It proceeds to analyze the highly political setting within which such negotiations take place following privatization, which puts important constraints on negotiation processes. Against this backdrop, it then explains why domestic business groups' diversified structure and high levels of embeddedness constitute informal supports for their formal contracts, especially in the context of negotiations regarding compliance with and revisions to original contracts. The efficacy of these informal supports contrasts with the weakness of the formal institutional supports typically possessed by multinationals, such as recourse to international arbitration. Political ideology and competition, as well as the respective leverage of host governments and firms, contribute to second-order variation between cases with similar types of lead investors. The chapter closes with a discussion of how the observable implications of the investor type argument advanced in this book differ from those derived from alternative lines of analysis.

THE OUTCOMES OF INTEREST: RESILIENT VERSUS BRITTLE CONTRACTUAL RELATIONSHIPS

Following Kindleberger (1969) and Vernon (1971), this project conceptualizes infrastructure and utilities regulation in weak institutional environments as a bargaining process between two principal actors, the host government and the investor, that have signed a contract for private investment in infrastructure. Negotiations address compliance with existing rules and contractual obligations, as well as formal amendments to contracts and regulatory laws. The outcomes affect firm investment incentives, government willingness to give political cover for the private provider, and the willingness of both parties to continue the contractual relationship. As the Introduction highlighted, existing theoretical approaches to the study of contracts suggest this is a reasonable analytic starting point.

Empirical studies of the infrastructure sector indicate that host governments and firms throughout the developing world indeed negotiate over levels of compliance and changes to contracts themselves. Some degree of contractual noncompliance by both governments and firms is commonplace, which suggests that both parties may be negotiating over *levels* of compliance. The empirical literature examining the effects of infrastructure privatization in low- and middle-income countries shows that while service levels have risen, improvements are in some cases not as significant as had originally been anticipated (Harris 2003: vii; Andrés et al. 2008: chapter 3; Gassner et al. 2009: 4; Marin 2009: 3, 64); the fact that 69 percent of the contract renegotiations examined by Guasch (2004: 18) in Latin America yielded delays or decreases in firms' investment obligations suggests that providers often find means of avoiding meeting original contractual goals. Both academic scholarship and the business press report high levels of government noncompliance with contractual obligations as well.[1] Similarly, studies suggest contract renegotiations are very common in infrastructure and natural resource sectors; empirical work testifies to the prevalence of both "firm-initiated" and "government-initiated" negotiations in a variety of sectors (Guasch et al. 2003, 2005; Woodhouse 2005–2006: 173–174; Zelner et al. 2009; Hogan et al. 2011: 2–4).

Many political economy approaches to firm-government bargaining conceptualize negotiation outcomes as zero sum. International political economy scholarship inspired by Kindleberger (1969) and Vernon (1971) on MNC-government bargaining suggests that ex post negotiations typically prejudice firms and benefit host governments.[2] Other studies of contract regulation suggest renegotiations often benefit firms (Loftus and McDonald 2001; Guasch et al. 2003; Guasch 2004). Meanwhile, much recent scholarship on regulation (Rhodes 2006; Murillo 2009) follows the Chicago School (e.g., Peltzman et al. 1989: 13; Peltzman 1993: 823) in assuming a contest between consumer and corporate interests.

This book instead takes its cue from the game theory literature on bargaining, which starts from the assumption that bargaining can generate surpluses, and parties negotiate over how to divide the surplus. From this perspective, firm-government negotiations represent adaptations to shifting aspects of the contractual environment, including changes in the preferences and leverage of the contracting parties, as well as to unexpected environmental changes or

[1] See Harris (2003: 32, 36), Andrés et al. (2008: 231), and Marin (2009: 92). Instances of government noncompliance that make the headlines or enter international arbitration represent, of course, cases in which investors and governments were not able to reach stable agreements. We can assume that in other cases, parties were able to reach an understanding.

[2] E.g., Henisz and Zelner (2005) and Zelner et al. (2009). Unlike later scholarship on expropriation and creeping expropriation that drew on his work, Kindleberger portrayed bargaining outcomes as nonzero sum (1969: 149–151).

information about the technical or political challenges posed by projects. There are a number of concrete instances under which bargaining would yield outcomes beneficial for both parties. Politicians and firm managers, for instance, could discover that certain means for customer billing provided for in the original contract are more controversial than either party anticipated, and so decide to revise the contract to include a substitute revenue-raising provision. If rates of inflation were unexpectedly high, both politicians and firm managers could find it expedient to delay rate increases triggered under contracts in response to rises in input costs while extending deadlines for certain performance targets. Such agreements would delay the achievement of important long-run goals with respect to improvements, but provide a framework within which both parties are willing to continue the contractual relationship. To the extent that they address unanticipated problems and constitute a net improvement for investors over the status quo, the agreements also provide frameworks for continuing investment and thereby serve as prerequisites for achieving important improvements in service quality and coverage that will benefit consumers, firms, and governments in the long run.[3] We would expect constructive bargaining relationships to correlate strongly with steady, incremental rates of investment and service improvement and associate bargaining impasses with drop-offs in investment in the long run.

Here it is analytically useful to distinguish between two ideal type contractual relationships. Resilient contractual relationships are characterized by constructive negotiations between host governments and investors regarding levels of contractual compliance by both, as well as renegotiations of original contractual clauses, that yield outcomes acceptable to both parties. The ability to reach revised agreements in turn makes it more likely both parties will desire the contract to continue. Productive negotiations in early periods lay the foundations for agreement in future periods. For example, when governments permit firms to follow through with revenue-raising measures included in their original contracts or within sector-specific regulatory laws, the contract becomes financially viable. Firms, reassured by government support, may invest enough to improve services that private sector service provision remains viable in political terms. Should external circumstances change, governments and firms would negotiate corresponding adaptations of their contracts that both parties could accept. They would even be able to reach revised agreements in the wake of major shocks that place contracts under a great deal of stress, such as economic crises. Because of this confluence of mutually reinforcing, supportive actions by both host government and firm, neither would choose to terminate their contract prematurely, nor would investors look for ways of exiting the arrangement. Because both parties possess an exit option, we can interpret their choice to remain in the contract as a sign that the arrangement continues to yield benefits

[3] This study will distinguish between such Pareto-improving renegotiations and those that work to the detriment of either the government or firm.

for them. (This is not to say, however, that one side does not benefit more than the other from negotiations.)

A brittle contractual relationship, in contrast, is one that fails to satisfy both investors and host governments in the short, medium, or long run and as a result is vulnerable to breakdown. Political circumstances, for example, could encourage governments to block important revenue-enhancing measures included in the original contracts or regulatory laws, detracting from the financial viability of the project. Firms could refrain from investing significantly in network expansion or service quality improvement out of opportunism or in retaliation for government actions, thereby making private provision vulnerable to political attacks. If changes in external circumstances made certain contractual provisions obsolete or unworkable for one or both of the parties, host governments and firms would find it difficult to arrive at revised agreements acceptable to both. Negotiating would be particularly difficult in the wake of a major external shock, such as an economic crisis. If mutually reinforcing, consensual dynamics fail to materialize, it is more likely that one or both parties will become dissatisfied with the contractual arrangement. If the contractual arrangement is troubled but still salvageable, disgruntled investors may be able to sell their controlling stakes to another firm; disgruntled governments can pressure investors to sell to new owners with whom they feel they could work more effectively. If a collapse of firm-government negotiations has rendered the infrastructure contract completely unviable in political or financial terms, then the only way out is for one or both parties to cancel the contract, faulting the other party for noncompliance.

The primary characteristics of these contrasting ideal typical contractual relationships are summarized in Table 1.1. While some of these, such as contract cancellation, could be measured in a straightforward manner, measuring others would require viewing multiple indicators in tandem. Assessing whether contract renegotiations yield outcomes satisfactory to both parties, for instance, could involve examining rate increases granted to firms; changes to the size,

TABLE 1.1. *Ideal Typical Contractual Relationships: Central Features*

Resilient contractual relationship	***Brittle contractual relationship***
• Government permits implementation of revenue-enhancing measures	• Government blocks implementation of revenue-enhancing measures
• Ability to negotiate revised agreements satisfactory to both parties	• Inability to negotiate revised agreements satisfactory to both parties
• Steady rate of investment in the long run	• Drop-off in rate of investment in the long run
• Low probability of investor exit via sale to another investor	• High probability of investor exit (usually at a loss) via sale
• Low probability of premature contract cancellation	• High probability of premature contract cancellation

timing, and destination of investments; agreements regarding subsidies; and other factors. Taking any one measure on its own would not give a balanced sense of the contract's trajectory. For example, a government may not grant rate increases, choosing to instead subsidize a provider. By just examining rate increases, we might assume that a provider achieved an unworkable renegotiation outcome. The most tractable summary indicator of whether a contractual relationship is brittle or resilient would be whether the relationship endures in the medium to long run. Continuation, after all, reflects the extent to which both parties find staying in the relationship to confer more advantages than exiting. Even this is an imprecise summary measure: investors, for example, might stay on in contracts in the short or medium run because they worry about the reputational costs of exit, even as renegotiations erode some or even all of their earnings from a project. For this reason, this study conceptualizes the dependent variable in terms of the full set of indicators listed here.

Chapter 2 offers a preliminary empirical illustration of the plausibility of separating contracts into these categories, drawing on data from fourteen Argentine contracts. This being said, not all real-world contracts for private investment in infrastructure fall neatly in the resilient or brittle category. They can fall somewhere in between these two extremes and can switch from one trajectory to another. This chapter offers a theoretical framework outlining the circumstances under which contracts are likely to conform to either the resilient or the brittle model, including cases in which they jump from one pathway to the other.

BILATERAL BARGAINING IN A VOLATILE POLITICAL SETTING

As mentioned previously, this book analyzes negotiations between two principal actors: host governments and firms. There are grounds for treating each party as a unified actor. First, the head of government is the ultimate decision maker in regulatory policy in weak institutional environments. Existing research suggests that in such contexts, regulatory agencies possess little de facto independence from the executive branch, the signatory of the contract; agencies are either formally overruled or influenced through informal channels.[4] Turning to firms, we can make a similar argument. Contracts are typically held by consortia, which often include both foreign and domestic firms. The investor with the largest equity stake in the contract is typically also the "technical operator" of the project, who takes the lead in negotiations and investment decisions and enjoys important

[4] Scholars have documented the frequency with which regulators are overruled by politicians in particular weak institutional environments (Loftus and McDonald 2001; Nickson and Vargas 2002; Bayliss 2003; Manzetti 2009). In addition, privatizations in weak institutional environments typically constrain regulatory agency discretion by placing explicit tariff formulas, performance goals, sanction amounts for specific infractions, etc., in the contracts themselves.

informational advantages over other consortium members. For this reason, the analysis here focuses on the interests and behavior of lead investors.

We can deduce a general set of host government and investor preferences during ongoing negotiations regarding levels of contract compliance and adaptations from the key economic and political features of infrastructure contracts and their context. Investors will desire a combination of respect for "basic rules of the game" and flexibility if circumstances change. They will want governments to allow them to implement cost-recovery policies provided for in infrastructure contracts or within the enabling legislation for the regulatory system and to adjust rates charged to consumers in line with formulas included in their contracts, so that earnings do not erode with inflation or changes in the prices of key inputs such as labor. However, while firms have strong incentives to invest enough to maximize the net present value of their future earnings from a project – which typically entails investing in both basic infrastructure that can improve system capacity and efficacy as well as in network expansion – they desire flexibility regarding the timing and destination of these investments.

Heads of government have somewhat contradictory sets of preferences for the short and medium-to-long run. In the short run, heads of government want to avoid political blame for problems of poor service delivery (especially major service disruptions) and controversial pricing and collections policies that affect large fractions of the electorate and economic actors, especially during electorally competitive periods (Levy and Spiller 1994, 1996; Savedoff and Spiller 1999). Although privatization was viewed as a means of outsourcing the political cost of implementing potentially controversial cost-recovery policies designed to finance long overdue investments, in weak institutional contexts, residential and business consumers will assume that politicians can block firms from implementing controversial measures should they desire to do so. This gives governments a short-run incentive to block such measures and retaliate publicly against providers for service problems during periods when their hold on power is tenuous, even if both actions impede the ability of concessionaires to improve services in the long run, and even if it means forgoing campaign donations or personal payoffs from concessionaires.[5]

When incumbents are not worried about their immediate political survival, they face incentives to pursue policies that encourage concessionaires to deliver medium- and long-run improvements in service quality and network reach.[6] Improving and extending services can increase citizen contentment with the administration and, in the case of new connections, curry favor with particular groups of voters. It can make the sector less a source of political headaches as

[5] Politicians discount future benefits from infrastructure investment heavily during competitive periods. Although politicians also possess a short-run desire for campaign funds, they will be wary of trading donations for policy favors that might jeopardize their reelection prospects.

[6] In some cases, politicians will demand personal payoffs from firms as well. This desire will presumably be balanced against other objectives, and the two are not mutually exclusive.

well. Infrastructure projects also constitute attractive opportunities for local businesses, and encouraging investment by a private service provider allows governments to ensure a flow of contracts to these constituencies, often without drawing on state funds. In addition, providing incentives to invest sends positive signals to new investors (Thomas and Worrall 1994). This distinction between first-order priorities – which take precedence during politically competitive periods – and second-order priorities regarding service improvements comes to the fore during negotiations with firms over the implementation and renegotiation of infrastructure contracts.

The bilateral bargaining process over compliance with and adaptation of original contractual provisions typically takes place in a highly politicized context, particularly when contracts for private sector investment apply to systems previously managed by the public sector. Contrary to the expectations of many reform proponents, this study contends that privatization in the developing world renders the politics of infrastructure and utilities policy both more salient and more volatile, particularly in competitive political contexts. The privatization process sets in motion a contentious post-privatization politics through two institutional changes. First, privatization separates the political establishment and the private provider in the eyes of the public, especially in the case of monopolies (Savedoff and Spiller 1999: 7; Rhodes 2006: 27, 33). Whereas political appointees typically run state companies, voters attribute responsibility for service quality following privatization to the private service provider rather than the government. This offers opportunities for regulatory agency directors, ombudsmen, and legislators (even of the governing party) to gain political prominence by highlighting service problems and noncompliance with contractual goals, especially during periods of intense political competition. Second, individuals and businesses receiving services feel entitled to higher quality services following privatization because of companies' comparatively greater efforts to make consumers pay their bills. This tendency becomes more marked as memories of poor service quality under public provision fade and prices rise (Baker 2009). In addition, the fact that private operators earn profits by delivering services has become increasingly controversial in light of international campaigns advocating a human right to basic services such as water (Conca 2006; Bakker 2010: 96; Morgan 2011: 28, 41). The greater incentives for politicians and other actors to campaign against providers and greater consumer consciousness create a "volatile politics of accountability" in which providers are subjected to high degrees of scrutiny by the mass public, especially during competitive political periods when politicians can attract attention by highlighting service problems.[7]

This volatile context places important constraints on the bilateral bargaining process between host governments and infrastructure investors. First, it makes the policy area much more salient than other regulatory policy areas, where

[7] See Murillo (2009: 43–44) on political competition and utility policy salience.

concentrated beneficiaries exert greater influence than the public at large (e.g., Wilson 1980; Peltzman 1993: 823; Culpepper 2011: 5–6). As a result, firm interests do not always triumph. In addition, high salience creates challenging conditions for firm-government negotiations; if conflict becomes too intense, it is likely to spiral out of control. Salience also provides modest, and undoubtedly imperfect, constraints on firm-government collusion.[8] It encourages firms to live up to at least some of their investment commitments. Because politicians linked to both the government and the opposition have career incentives to highlight firm noncompliance with contractual goals, investors interested in entering future competitions will have incentives to invest under their existing contracts. Contracts yielding few improvements – and particularly those experiencing major service problems – are likely to become difficult for politicians to support.

EXPLAINING DIVERGENT CONTRACTUAL RELATIONSHIPS

This section identifies the main factors driving variation across contracts and over time in weak institutional environments. First and foremost, the *organizational structure* of lead investors in projects greatly affects the probability that contracts will evolve along a durable trajectory characterized by steady investment levels and enduring political support for private sector service provision. Building on important lines of scholarship in political economy and economic sociology, this explanatory framework suggests that domestic investors have access to a range of informal contractual supports largely unavailable to foreign investors. In contrast, foreign investors controlling similar contracts in a wide set of countries are unlikely to negotiate effectively with host governments in the long run – despite their ability to threaten exit and, in most cases, their access to international arbitration. This section also considers how political and economic factors explain variation observed among contracts held by each type of investor.

Investor Organizational Structure and Divergent Contract Trajectories

Differences in firm structure affect their policy preferences as well as their negotiating strategies in the regulatory arena, which in turn influence their ability to bargain effectively with the state. Domestic investors with long-standing, diversified holdings in their contract jurisdiction exhibit greater patience with host governments, are willing to entertain a wider range of negotiating outcomes, and can employ a more informal set of negotiating strategies than foreign multinationals. Higher levels of embeddedness further contribute to domestic investors' interests in maintaining resilient contracts with the state.

[8] This is not to say that collusion does not exist. Delivering a visible and essential service to the public, however, places one in the public eye.

Firm Structure, Preferences, and Negotiating Tactics

Whereas multinationals tend to diversify across countries and specialize in particular sectors, large firms of the developing world tend to diversify across sectors while maintaining a strong presence in their home market (Khanna and Yafeh 2007; Schneider 2008). Diversification within the home market appeals to developing-country firms because it represents an insurance mechanism in volatile political and economic environments. Multinationals instead insure against political risk through cross-country diversification, particularly in infrastructure sectors, where they tend to develop strong sector specializations (Scott 2011: 74).

Political economy scholarship examining corporations' ability to secure favorable policy in capital-intensive sectors, or those characterized by high levels of asset specificity, suggests that the cross-sector diversification so often adopted within home markets by developing-country firms will be associated with lower levels of policy influence (Frieden 1991: 28–31). In contrast, multinationals – because of their ability to manage sector risks through cross-country diversification – will be at a comparative advantage (Shafer 1994: 26–31). I argue that the inverse is actually the case: cross-sector diversification provides a better foundation for resilient contracts than cross-country diversification, as it influences investors' preferences regarding possible negotiating outcomes and determines the negotiating tactics at their disposal in ways that make it easier to reach settlements with the state.

For a number of reasons, developing country investors' diversified portfolio structure in their home market and other organizational adaptations to less-developed-country (LDC) markets lead them to entertain a wider set of negotiating outcomes than foreign multinationals. First, they may be willing to suffer short-term losses in order to preserve stakes in projects that contribute to a diverse portfolio because such assets may yield profits when economic conditions change. This means that domestic investors are likely to exhibit more patience, on average, than would be the case if they did not possess holdings outside the sector.[9] In addition, when firms have long-standing holdings in many industries, owners will weigh the costs and benefits of lobbying for all of the sectors in which they operate, thinking carefully about positive and negative spillovers; they may not want to risk hurting their operations in one sector because they have incurred government wrath through a tough negotiating stance in another. Conversely, investments in infrastructure holdings may benefit their operations in other sectors. Finally, because of their large exposure to the domestic market – a consequence of diversifying across sectors rather than across countries – developing-country firms working in capital-intensive sectors are less likely than multinationals to contract debt in foreign

[9] All other things equal, we would also expect investors operating in more profitable infrastructure sectors to exhibit greater patience in negotiations.

currency to finance upfront investments in infrastructure, preferring to insure themselves against currency volatility and avoid high domestic interest rates by investing out of retained earnings.[10] This leads them to pursue an incremental approach to investment rather than front-loading investment during the initial years of a contract. This graduated approach makes their contracts less vulnerable in periods of economic crisis. Because lower debt levels gives them a more flexible cost structure, they do not need to push for concessions from host governments during post-crisis negotiations as significant as those wanted by multinationals. In sum, domestic business groups, because of the structure of their holdings, are likely to bring more moderate demands to the negotiating table at any given point in time than their multinational counterparts in weak institutional environments.[11] Importantly, the incentives outlined here differ from the factor usually stressed by analysts of business-government relations in the developing world: that cross-sector diversification gives business groups an incentive to support policies that benefit the economy as a whole (Schneider 1998: 110–111; Kingstone 1999; Thacker 2000; Jones Luong and Weinthal 2012: 56).[12]

A diversified structure also enables many developing-country firms or business groups to draw on informal negotiating strategies that keep infrastructure policy out of the newspaper headlines. For domestic investors, negotiations may be facilitated by the opportunity for trade-offs between sectors – what international relations scholars have termed "issue linkage" (Alt and Eichengreen 1989; Eichengreen and Frieden 1993; Lohmann 1995; Davis 2004), rather than the issue-specific lobbying emphasized in much of the political economy literature. Deal elements benefiting firms' operations in other sectors can allow both politicians and firms to avoid controversial measures within the infrastructure sector, such as large consumer rate hikes, strict enforcement of payment, or explicit subsidies for private firms. For instance, politicians might avoid politically costly rate increases by granting investors offsetting measures benefiting their construction or real estate arm. Depending on the legislation in place, such agreements might be illegal. Regardless of their legality or hidden costs, negotiations involving issue linkage can help ensure the infrastructure sector does not become a political liability for elected officials and thereby contribute to the resilience of contractual relationships. Linkages between policy areas also multiply the number of ways that host governments and firms can sanction each other and thereby curb opportunism.

10 In other words, they employ what economists Dixit and Pyndick (1994) call a "real options" approach to investment under uncertainty.

11 Although these demands would be perceived as moderate within a single sector at a particular point in time, they may approach the total demands of multinationals when they are added up over time or across sectors.

12 Thacker (2000) suggests this argument applies best to large economic groups with relatively mobile assets.

Multinationals will not have the same incentives to moderate their claims as domestic firms that diversify across sectors will. They tend to make investment decisions and formulate policy proposals based on the fate of their operations in the sector that comprises their primary investment in a country. Because of this sector focus within particular countries, if an economic shock threatens the profitability of operations in the sector or new officeholders want to revise contractual terms, the multinational investors' patience in renegotiation processes will be based on their sense of the market prospects of investments within that sector.[13]

In addition, multinationals' cross-country diversification gives them access to a different and more "formal" set of bargaining tactics. In the many countries that have provided for recourse to international arbitration for investors through bilateral investment treaties (BITs), domestic investment law, or individual contracts, multinationals can force host governments to the bargaining table through threats to initiate arbitration proceedings, which can eventually trigger sanctions for host governments. A significant international political economy literature emphasizes that these institutions allow governments to make credible commitments to investors for these reasons, and thereby facilitate investment (Ginsburg 2005; Neumayer and Spess 2005; Elkins et al. 2006; Büthe and Milner 2008; Kerner 2009; Schill 2009: 5–6).[14] Although it is not mentioned in this literature, we could imagine a complementary mechanism that would lead contracts protected by BITs to be more durable: investors with BIT protection would possess a more credible exit threat because suits offer investors an opportunity to signal to political risk insurers and equity markets that they are not at fault for conflicts and therefore possess greater leverage in negotiations with host governments than comparable investors without BIT protection.[15] The implication of this line of argument is that multinationals protected by BITs would preside over much more durable contracts in which both parties live up to their commitments.

This book contends, however, that public threats and efforts to lodge international arbitration claims are likely to further politicize negotiations and speed investor exit rather than yield stable settlements. First, initiating arbitration proceedings can make investor-government conflicts more salient, making it more difficult politically for governments to cede ground to investors, especially

[13] Admittedly, multinationals can hedge some or all of their currency risk. This being said, financial markets can also punish multinationals for their exposure to markets in turmoil. Furthermore, multinationals are more likely to be publicly listed companies than developing-country conglomerates and therefore be forced by market pressures to focus on short-term earnings. Nevertheless, this distinction is far from universal and therefore not foregrounded in this analysis.

[14] Hallward-Driemeier (2003) and Tobin and Rose-Ackerman (2003), contrary to the studies cited here, find no link between BIT adoption and FDI flows.

[15] An arbitration award can be a precondition for registering a claim from a political risk insurance policy, while rulings favorable to investors can support claims (Wells and Garcia-Cuellar 2005: 3).

when countries have long histories of exploitation by foreign capital and colonial powers.[16] In addition, initiating proceedings can embitter relations with host governments, given investors' asymmetric access to arbitration and the fact that tribunals are perceived to favor firms (Wells and Ahmed 2007: 10). Given the already volatile and salient nature of politics in the utilities and infrastructure sector, it can be very difficult to salvage negotiations. This leads us to expect that contracts will be less, rather than more, durable when foreign investors have access to international arbitration. This expectation would be particularly strong in the case of subnational privatizations, as subnational governments often do not bear the full financial or reputational cost of international arbitration awards. This expectation has a counterintuitive implication: private sector participation in infrastructure is likely to persist longer in the absence of provisions for international arbitration. Without an arbitration option, foreign investors will be forced to wait for potential private buyers, or for local governments to buy them out, if they do not wish to pull out of the market empty handed. When foreign investors submit suits to arbitration, on the other hand, it increases the probability of contract cancellation amid public recriminations of the private investor, making it politically much more difficult to privatize once again. In stressing the political fallout from pressure tactics that involve attracting popular and international attention to disputes, this argument differs from Markus (2012), who suggests that strategic alliances allowing firms to apply pressure through such means can help them defend their property rights successfully in transition economies.

Investor Organizational Structure and Embeddedness

Differences in negotiating tactics and patience levels between multinationals and domestic firms also stem from the extent to which they possess *structural* and *cultural embeddedness*. Structural embeddedness refers to the "contextualization of economic exchange in patterns of ongoing interpersonal exchange" (Granovetter 1985: 495; Zukin and DiMaggio 1990: 18). Significant literatures within sociology and economics suggest that repeated interactions between economic actors can help build trust and limit opportunism.[17] Repeated interactions are particularly important for limiting opportunism within the context of economic sectors characterized by asset specificity (Williamson 1985). Moreover, membership in broader social and economic networks can facilitate information flow and contribute to norms of reciprocity.[18]

[16] One would expect this effect to be greater when the arbitration venue is public and sponsored by an international financial institution, as is the World Bank's International Centre for Settlement of Investment Disputes (ICSID).

[17] Granovetter (1985: 498) and Gómez-Ibáñez (2003) describe these literatures. Classic studies include Macaulay(1963) and Macneil (1978).

[18] E.g., Granovetter (1985).

Drawing on these insights, we would predict that diversified, domestic firms operating in infrastructure sectors would possess higher degrees of structural embeddedness than multinationals. Because they have long-standing operations in multiple sectors, they would anticipate interacting with the state in a number of capacities over time, within and outside of the infrastructure sector. As a result, negotiations regarding contract compliance and renegotiation would be constrained in such cases by the expectation of ongoing engagement within the context of the contract, and, just as importantly, in other business areas and the social sphere. With this expectation, investors and host governments would be less inclined to engage in brinksmanship-like negotiating strategies. In contrast, investors without substantial local holdings will be concerned that if they do not secure all benefits up front, they might never secure them at all. The constraining effects of structural embeddedness, however, are likely to be most visible *within* particular political administrations. Whereas investors with a long history in a given jurisdiction are likely to know political challengers, new officeholders often have different preferences and therefore may desire to begin contract negotiations afresh.

Integration in local social networks also helps domestic firms negotiate productively with host governments over time. As scholars of business politics have highlighted, network ties can facilitate information flows and thus provide domestic firms with a comparative advantage (Henisz 2002: 110; Schrank 2008; Schneider 2010). In addition, greater integration into local social networks helps prevent opportunism and incendiary behavior by corporate and government actors; knowing that their children may desire to join the same club as members of the political elite, for instance, would constrain the negotiating tactics of a structurally embedded investor. The importance of lead investors themselves – rather than their partners or managers – being network members comes to the fore when we consider how membership affects their incentives as they negotiate with their government contractual partners. This ensures that firm owners suffer both the financial implications of investment decisions *and* the social repercussions of an aggressive (or conciliatory) posture in dealings with the state.

Domestic investors also benefit from cultural embeddedness. As economic sociologists have highlighted, culturally shared beliefs and values tend to influence how economic agents such as firms perceive their goals and the acceptable means by which they might pursue them (Zukin and DiMaggio 1990; Bandelj 2008). A firm's degree of cultural embeddedness, in other words, reflects its understandings of what types of policies and behaviors will elicit particular sorts of reactions – either positive or negative – from government officials and the population at large, as well as the approaches to firm-government relations that are most likely to produce results. Because of their cultural embeddedness, developing-country firms working in their home market will be more likely to recognize the political liabilities associated with lawsuits against the state than will foreign firms and as a result prefer to resolve disputes through informal rather than formal legal channels.[19] They will also be well versed in informal and private means of influencing government officials, including bribery and providing support for political campaigns.[20] Finally, domestic firms will have an understanding of how the way they provide services could present either political problems or opportunities for government officials. Foreign firms may be able to learn about their new context – particularly if they employ local managers, recruit local minority partners, or have long history in the market – but their starting point of reference will be their country of origin.[21]

Investor Organizational Structure and Predicted Contract Trajectories

The political economy and embeddedness logic outlined in the previous section suggests that domestic conglomerates or business groups will negotiate more effectively with host governments over time than foreign multinationals. This would lead us to expect divergent trajectories for utilities and infrastructure contracts held by domestic investors and multinationals, but it is important to make a further distinction to explain cases in which contracts are held by subnational, rather than national, governments. Subnational contracts are very common in infrastructure sectors, particularly in federal countries.[22] This study makes an additional contribution by providing an account of the *circumstances under which subnational contracts are more likely to endure*. When contracts are granted at the subnational level, we expect firms with a strong local presence – that is, numerous, long-standing, and diverse operations in the state or municipality that granted the contract – to exhibit high levels of patience, have opportunities for "issue linkage," and maintain significant ties with the local establishment. Domestic firms without diverse holdings in their contract jurisdiction may have higher levels of cultural embeddedness than do international firms and will be less likely to take legal actions against the governments holding their contracts. Without a significant local presence in the contract jurisdiction, however, they will typically not possess opportunities for issue linkage and strong local ties. They will also have lower exit costs than firms with significant local operations and therefore be less patient in negotiations.

19 The international business literature on the "liability of foreignness" makes similar observations, stressing that multinationals often lack local legitimacy and political intuitions (see Zaheer [1995] for a review).

20 Certainly, multinationals have a long history of engaging in corruption in developing countries. They are, however, increasingly policed by nongovernmental organizations and home governments. They are also less likely to allocate campaign donations effectively because of inferior local knowledge and internal controls. This portion of the argument is analogous to Holburn and Zelner's (2010) argument that investors from emerging markets possess "political capabilities" that provide them with comparative advantages in infrastructure sectors. They do not provide concrete details, however, about what comprises these capabilities.

21 See Morgan and Kristensen (2006) on the management literature about the extent to which firms retain practices from their home markets versus incorporating the practices of new markets.

22 Transportation systems, urban water and sanitation supply, and electricity distribution are commonly privatized at the subnational level.

TABLE 1.2. *Investor Organizational Structure and Contractual Outcomes When Contracts are Granted at the Subnational Level*

	Typical pacing of investment	*Expected level of contract adaptability*	*Expected rate of contract cancellation or exit via share sale*
Multinational	Front-loaded	Low	High
Domestic investor	Incremental	Medium	Medium
Domestic investor with diverse local holdings	Incremental	High	Low

Overall, foreign firms' preferences and negotiating strategies make it more difficult to achieve contractual adaptations that are acceptable to both firms and host governments, thereby contributing to high rates of premature contract cancellation. Domestic firms and – when contracts are regulated at the subnational level – domestic firms with diverse local holdings are better positioned to work with the political establishment to adapt contracts to changed economic and political circumstances. This logic suggests that whereas international investors may be much more willing to contract debt from international financial institutions to fund upfront investments, which can in turn yield impressive improvements in service quality and coverage in the first years of a contract, investment levels are likely to taper off after it becomes clear that governments and firms cannot reach revised settlements that satisfy both parties in the wake of competitive elections or unexpected economic or technical developments. As a result, contracts are more likely to be canceled prematurely. These expectations are summarized in Table 1.2. Ownership by domestic firms with diverse local assets, of course, provides no guarantee of contract survival, but in comparative terms, we would expect their contracts to be more likely to remain in place in the long run, and for these arrangements to incrementally yield important benefits for both firms and host governments.

Variation among Foreign Investors

The preceding analysis grouped all foreign multinationals together, assuming that they all had access to international "substitutes" for formal institutional protections for property rights such as international arbitration, that they all engaged in cross-country diversification and sector specialization, and that the owners were culturally and socially distant from the emerging markets in which they were investing. The assumption that these characteristics typically cluster is realistic. However, it is important to also consider cases that deviate from the ideal types, especially when they offer an opportunity to assess the extent to which particular firm-level attributes lessen the ability of MNCs to maintain durable contracts in infrastructure sectors, or when deviant models, such as multinationals from emerging markets, promise to become more common.

Although many countries signed BITs during the 1990s, such treaties are not universal among the developing countries that launched programs promoting private sector investment in infrastructure. In Latin America, for instance, both Brazil and Colombia largely refrained from ratifying bilateral investment treaties. Multinationals without access to this "substitute" for domestic property rights protections lack the primary formal means of pressuring host governments during contract renegotiations. Without recourse to arbitration, it is also more difficult for them to exit contracts: they do not possess a key means of signaling to international markets their lack of responsibility for problems and of obtaining compensation for their losses. They also lack a key means of escalating conflict with host governments that often precipitates contract cancellation. As a result, we would expect multinationals without arbitration access to be more patient with host governments in negotiations than other foreign investors, and for contractual relationships to endure longer than when recourse to arbitration is possible. This difference is likely to be most pronounced following economic crises, when governments are often tempted to violate contractual agreements with investors in order to help populations cope with their immediate economic difficulties.

Although most MNCs working in infrastructure sectors are based in Organization for Economic Cooperation and Development (OECD) countries and specialize in particular infrastructure sectors, a small but increasing number of firms does not fit this mold. Among this set of investors, the international business literature would lead us to expect multinationals with certain characteristics – commonly held by domestic firms – to be best able to maintain long-term negotiating relationships with host governments in weak institutional environments.[23] Multinationals from other developing countries (Holburn and Zelner 2009), those with significant commitments to the country market in question (Wells and Ahmed 2007: 267; Chan and Levitt 2011: 335), and investors based in home countries that eschew legalism (Wells and Ahmed 2007: 267; Chan and Levitt 2011: 317–319) are likely to be more patient and effective in their negotiations with host governments than the ideal typical MNCs described earlier. This being said, their contractual relationships with host governments are still likely to be more brittle than those between diversified domestic investors and host governments because MNCs are less culturally embedded and unlikely to have significant and diversified operations in their contract jurisdictions.

To summarize, domestic investors with diverse holdings in their contract jurisdiction possess *informal supports* for their infrastructure contracts generally unavailable to foreign multinationals. Their diversified firm structure leads them

[23] Azemar et al. (2012) review the broader literature on the circumstances under which multinationals choose to enter particular country markets.

to exhibit greater patience with host governments, to entertain a wider set of negotiating outcomes, and to employ a wider range of negotiating strategies than their foreign counterparts. This in turn makes it easier for lead investors and host governments to negotiate effectively regarding compliance with original contract terms as well as changes to the formal contract. When investors and host governments are able to negotiate effectively over the long haul, projects are more likely to yield gradual service improvements and remain politically viable. Foreign investors in many cases have access to additional formal protections to their contracts unavailable to their domestic counterparts, but these protections tend not to force governments to honor their commitments to investors, as credible commitments–based approaches suggest; rather, the substitutes for strong domestic property rights protections simply provide investors with an easier exit option. Informal contractual supports, in other words, prove to be more important than formal supports, such as strict property rights laws and access to international arbitration, in weak institutional environments.

Political Sources of Variation

Local political environments vary in the extent to which they are hospitable to negotiation processes. High levels of political competition or instability can shorten politicians' time horizons, making it difficult for them to enter potentially controversial agreements. High levels of political fragmentation or turnover increase the transaction costs associated with ongoing negotiations. Finally, negotiations may proceed less easily if the political incumbent did not originally privatize or is statist in ideological orientation. We can refer to this set of varied circumstances as *political hurdles* to firm-government negotiations.

High levels of political competition, although normatively desirable as an important component of democracy, can force political incumbents to focus on their short-run survival rather than long-run objectives. When incumbent heads of government are electorally vulnerable, they care first and foremost about pleasing consumers (Murillo 2009: 44–45). They will want to avoid blame for major service disruptions and controversial revenue-raising policies such as tariff hikes or service cutoffs. This leads them to prefer private sector service provision but to block controversial cost-recovery policies designed to ensure utilities have sufficient funding to make investments necessary for system improvements in the long run. Intense competition, after all, encourages political incumbents to focus on consumers' short-run interests in low prices and reactions to service problems rather than their long-term interests in basic infrastructure investment, which often does not offer immediate paybacks to individual voters. As a result, we would expect political jurisdictions characterized by very competitive elections – particularly in the initial years after privatization when controversial cost-recovery measures are scheduled for implementation – to be less propitious environments for ongoing negotiations between host governments and infrastructure firms.

In addition, negotiations in political environments characterized by high rates of executive turnover or fragmentation tend to involve high transaction costs. When the head of government changes, negotiations with providers must start afresh.[24] Further, heads of government who did not privatize stand to suffer few reputational consequences if private providers fail to deliver quality services (Murillo 2009: 46). They may even have attacked private providers' performance in the context of their campaigns, weakening the political acceptability of measures seen as concessions to the providers. This may lead new political leaders to hold out for larger gains in negotiations, which in turn may discourage firms from investing. Negotiations following changes in power, then, are likely to be slower and more intermittent than negotiations with political incumbents who privatized or who have been in power for some time. High levels of political fragmentation can also make it difficult to conclude agreements. This logic follows directly from scholarly arguments stressing the extent to which political systems with more veto players present barriers to new legislation (Tsebelis 2002). It will, for instance, be harder on average to secure legislative approval for a revised privatization contract under divided government. It will be similarly difficult for the government to present a single negotiating position when the governing party is highly fragmented.

The ideology of the head of government will also affect the extent to which governments and firms are able to maintain a stable negotiating relationship over time.[25] Heads of government who are statist in orientation will be naturally less inclined to negotiate constructively with private providers, particularly during competitive periods (Murillo 2009: 46). They will be less supportive of private providers on average, particularly if they have sufficient fiscal resources to fund politically opportune infrastructure investments on their own; the tendency will be toward "creeping expropriation." Statist heads of governments, however, are only likely to nationalize infrastructure services that are not major income sources under extreme circumstances. Even when severe problems with service continuity or quality prompt strong public reactions, governments will be hesitant to cancel contracts or take back services unless firms refuse to continue operating under terms acceptable to the public and governments have sufficient resources to be able to take over and make investments sufficient to deal quickly with the problems at hand.[26] Because of their higher levels of patience and the wider set of negotiating strategies available to them, domestic investors with diverse local holdings would be better placed to negotiate effectively with the state even in these less propitious political contexts than multinationals.

[24] The arrival of new officeholders with preferences distinct from their predecessors can also serve as a prompt for renegotiation, as Guasch (2004: 23) highlights.

[25] If services are privatized at the subnational level, subnational heads of government may face financial or career incentives to adopt the ideological positions of the central administration.

[26] Governments will face stronger incentives, however, to take over services that could provide important sources of revenue.

Financial Resources and Changing Leverage over Time

For infrastructure contracts to endure, both investors and host governments need to find continuation more attractive than exit. Both parties, after all, have exit options. While both need to perceive the benefits of staying in the contract as greater than the costs of exit, the extent to which each benefits from ongoing negotiations will vary with shifts in government and firm bargaining power. As Vernon (1971) stressed, firms possess the highest amounts of leverage before market entry; leverage declines over time as immobile investments are made, and as a result, their initial bargains obsolesce. Drawing on a subsequent tradition of scholarship on the obsolescing bargain, Wells and Ahmed (2007) stress the importance of technology: firms that maintain a continuing technological advantage will possess greater leverage vis-à-vis host governments.[27] For most types of infrastructure projects, however, the most important leverage is financial; the technology used in electricity and water systems, as well as for toll roads and airports, is relatively well known. As long as firms have superior access to funding for infrastructure investment, they will have better leverage during negotiations with host governments. Governments usually privatized during periods of capital scarcity, and one of the primary motivators was to secure finance for investment in system expansion and maintenance. During periods when governments have little leverage and levels of political competition are low or moderate, negotiations with firms are likely to produce agreements regarding levels of compliance and contractual revisions that can be seen as particularly favorable to firms. Multinationals, because of their willingness to assume debt to finance upfront investment, will exert particularly strong leverage during periods when governments have scant access to investment capital, provided high levels of political competition or contestation do not bring their privileges to the public eye. Indeed, political science and economics research on regulatory politics in the first years following privatization testifies to strong corporate leverage during periods of capital scarcity (Manzetti 1999, 2009; Basañes and Willig 2002; Guasch 2004: 15–17; Murillo 2009; Serafinoff 2010).

Governments, however, have the upper hand when they gain (or regain) access to international finance or rapidly growing revenue streams, such as taxes from commodities or other exports. They then have the ability to fund infrastructure investment on their own, which increases their bargaining power with investors.[28] Governments can offer firms subsidies in exchange for investments or price decreases they desire. They can even take over systems if they are unhappy with the service levels achieved by private providers because they actually have the resources required to invest sufficiently to restore services to

[27] Haggard (1989: 192–193) reviews this literature.

[28] Haslam (2010) observes that Latin American governments regained some leverage during the 2000s. Serafinoff (2010) argues that the Argentine government preferred to finance infrastructure itself after it regained access to revenue as commodity exports took off following the 2001 crisis.

TABLE 1.3. *Secondary Sources of Variation in Contract Trajectories*

	Level of contract adaptability	*Extent to which negotiation outcomes favor government in short run*	*Expected rate of investor exit*
Political competition	–		+
Political turnover	–[a]		+
Statist ideology	–	+	+
Government financial leverage		+	+

[a] Political turnover brings a new government partner to the negotiating table, which can serve as a prompt for contract renegotiations given that new officeholders often possess preferences different from those of their predecessors. Negotiations may be more difficult to *conclude*, however.

acceptable levels following takeover.[29] (In game theoretic terms, they enjoy a more attractive "outside option.") As a result, negotiating outcomes will tend to favor governments more than firms during such periods.

Overall, then, while firm-government negotiations must yield informal or formal agreements workable for both parties for private provision to continue, the actual terms of these agreements will tend to vary over time with changes in government access to finance. Firms will secure a larger fraction of the benefits during periods when governments do not have good access to finance. Because of their diversified industrial structure, domestic investors will tend to be more patient with host governments and willing to entertain a broader set of negotiating outcomes during periods of high government leverage. The high probability of large changes in the respective leverage of firms and governments over the course of a long-term infrastructure contract is therefore another reason domestic investors are better positioned to maintain stable negotiating trajectories in the long run. The predicted effects of these political and financial sources of variation are summarized in Table 1.3.

SCOPE CONDITIONS FOR THE ARGUMENT

Although the general relationships identified here should be visible in a wide range of countries with weak institutions, they are likely to be strongest in a certain subset. First, the relationship between diverse local holdings and

[29] When privatization occurs at the subnational level, a host government's access to finance will depend at least in part on its relationship with the central government. (Both unitary and federal states typically employ discretional transfer programs, and national governments fund a large portion of large infrastructure projects.)

contract resilience is likely to be strongest in countries with contested elections. Citizens can exert pressure on their leaders even in authoritarian settings, but their ability to punish politicians for rate increases or service problems will be higher when elections – evenly if unfairly administered – exist. Politicians will face electoral incentives to villainize private companies that do not meet their obligations and harry firms into compliance. Fierce electoral competition, political turnover, and other political hurdles discussed earlier in this chapter will also be likely to arise at more regular intervals in such contexts, prompting politicians to desire changes in contractual terms. Domestic investors with diverse local holdings are more likely to reach mutually acceptable settlements with host governments following such episodes.

The relationship between domestic ownership, diverse local holdings, and regular investment rates over the long haul is also more likely to be strong when contracts have been structured to assign firms investment obligations and bring investors in direct contact with consumers accustomed to state provision. If contracts do not assign firm investment obligations, governmental failure to comply with commitments will not cause firms to curtail their investments. Also, it is more likely that contractual provisions designed to move utilities to cost recovery, such as stricter enforcement of bill payment and tariff adjustments to compensate for inflation, will become politicized when private investors have direct contact with consumers (Wells and Gleason 1995: 9). This means that the argument is most likely to apply to sectors that remain *bundled* – that is, when vertically integrated firms handle both production and distribution to consumers.[30] Within the water sector, it also applies most directly to particular types of privatization contracts: *divestitures*, or outright sales of state utility companies to private investors, and *concession contracts*, which assign investment and maintenance responsibilities to private operators for twenty- to thirty-year periods but leave assets under state ownership. (Both types of privatization typically place investors in direct contact with consumers that were accustomed to state-managed utilities, which often did not enforce payment.) We would be less likely to see major differences in contractual resilience for *management and lease contracts*, which leave investment responsibilities with the state, or *greenfield projects*, contracts for new facilities that typically do not bring the mass public in direct contact with private sector operators.[31]

In addition, the association between domestic ownership, diverse local holdings, and healthy rates of investment is likely to be stronger when the lead investors in a project do not completely dominate the local economy. When

[30] Electricity is the prime example of an "unbundled" sector: generation has often been separated from distribution during privatization. Some rail privatizations took a similar approach, separating responsibility for networks from service administration.

[31] Gómez-Ibáñez (2008: 13) makes a related point, arguing that greenfield projects are less prone to political problems because there is no incumbent workforce that resents changes in working conditions and layoffs.

lead investors have a stranglehold on the economy, they tend to wield a great deal of political power as well. Popular political pressures to expand coverage or improve service quality would tend to have less weight, attenuating the pressure for investment observed in more economically diverse jurisdictions.

Having made these qualifications, we would expect many of the dynamics outlined in the preceding pages to be at work in a wider set of sectors and regime types. Contract renegotiation is likely to occur, for instance, in many political environments and infrastructure sectors, given the inevitable incompleteness of long-term contracts in capital-intensive sectors, especially in the wake of crises. Public service provision is likely to become more politicized following privatization even in the developed world. And domestic ownership and a strong local presence are likely to ease relationships with local governments in the many sectors characterized by long-term contracts and asset specificity.

ALTERNATIVE EXPLANATIONS

The explanation of divergent contractual outcomes proposed in this book emphasizes firm structure and highlights the influence of political incentives and government access to financial resources. It suggests that we would observe patterns of contractual resilience in the wake of shocks different from those proposed by a number of competing lines of argument. Although my argument is intended to account for divergent contract trajectories in weak institutional environments, it could be instead argued that variation even in weak institutional environments is driven primarily by differences in local institutions or differences in sector-specific institutions or policies. Institutionalist approaches to regulation suggest that the strengths of checks and balances in the political environment affect the ability of regulatory agencies to commit credibly to contracts and regulatory laws (Levy and Spiller 1994, 1996; Henisz 2002; Krause 2009). Approaches focusing on sector-specific institutions and design emphasize that regulatory institution and policy design can affect contractual outcomes (Laffont and Tirole 1993; Estache et al. 2001; Johnstone and Wood 2001; Groom, Halpern and Ehrhard 2006; Franceys and Gerlach 2008; Krause 2009). These alternative explanations are assessed systematically through analyses of the divergent trajectories of provincial contracts in Argentina as well as cross-nationally in Chapters 2 and 7.

Another literature attributes variation in the effects of private sector participation to differences in state capacity. These theories suggest that better-endowed and more technically competent regulators will be better prepared to police contracts and pressure firms to comply with their commitments. Social scientists and policy scholars have tended to blame poor outcomes on weak regulation (Chong and López-de-Silanes 2005; Haglund 2010). Brown et al. (2009), for instance, find that Russian states with larger bureaucracies have presided over more effective privatization programs than states with small governments. The observable implication of this argument, then, is that there will be more successful privatization contract trajectories in jurisdictions with greater state capacity. This alternative explanation is considered in the Argentine case studies as well as in the context of statistical analyses of varying levels of contract durability in low- and middle-income countries.

Building on a recent outpouring of scholarship on the "Latin American Left," it could be argued that much of the variation in contract trajectories can be explained with respect to the partisan affiliation of the head of government, and the extent to which this leftist head of government is constrained by a well-institutionalized party system, historical experience with failed radical policies, or financial constraints (Flores-Macías 2010; Luna 2010; Weyland 2010; Kaufman 2011; Levitsky and Roberts 2011; Murillo et al. 2011). While the theoretical framework advanced in this book suggests that contracts will fare less well when presided over by heads of government with a statist orientation, it places a greater emphasis on investor organizational structure. Domestic business groups or conglomerates stand a reasonable chance of reaching agreements with statist officials given the costs of nationalizing services or stalling on negotiations and thereby allowing services to deteriorate.[32] This being said, I evaluate the extent to which arguments putting ideology in a primary rather than supporting role account for variation in contract durability. Chapters 2 through 6 examine support for these alternative explanations in Argentina – a country with fairly weak levels of party system institutionalization and high degrees of financial flexibility during the post-crisis commodity boom.

Finally, we might attribute the greater frequency with which international investors have exited their contracts to a selection effect. Following studies of business-government relations that emphasize the informational advantages available to domestic investors (Henisz 2002: 110; Schneider 2010), we might suppose that domestic firms would be able to draw on their networks to obtain information regarding the favorability of different contracts. This would lead them to identify and obtain more remunerative contracts than would foreign investors. Or it could be argued that MNCs with access to international guarantees might take on riskier contracts than domestic investors because of the moral hazard problem created by such insurance policies (Wells and Ahmed 2007: 7, 290). Finally, MNCs could secure better contracts, but these would be more attractive to governments interested in taking over services once economic conditions or the ideological climate changed. These three "selection" arguments are considered and discounted in Chapter 2, which provides an overview of the Argentine privatization program.

The full set of alternative explanations considered in the book is summarized in Tables 1.4 and 1.5. The first three explanations suggest that independent

[32] Governments will have stronger incentives to take over services in sectors that are more profitable and that do not require contact with individual consumers, as running a service with direct customer contact can prove to be a political liability if service quality is poor.

TABLE 1.4. *Alternative Explanations Emphasizing Different Independent Variables*

Independent variable	*Effect on contract resilience*
Checks and balances in institutional environment	+
State capacity	+
Statist ideology and weakly institutionalized party system	–

TABLE 1.5. *Alternative Explanations Emphasizing Same Independent Variable*

Category of explanation	*Mechanism*
Selection effect	Domestic investor access to superior knowledge MNC moral hazard problem Host governments nationalize better contracts held by MNCs

variables other than investor organizational structure drive variation in contractual outcomes. The last three alternative explanations still suggest that domestic investors will preside over contracts that are more resilient but attribute this to selection effects.

CONCLUSION

This chapter has argued that domestic investors – and, when contracts are regulated at the subnational level, domestic investors with a significant presence in their contract jurisdiction – are better able than multinationals to adapt contracts over time in ways that satisfy both politicians and firms in weak institutional environments, particularly in the wake of economic crises and commodity booms that greatly increase state leverage. When institutions are weak and regulatory agencies unlikely to have de facto independence, political and economic volatility will inevitably affect the regulatory sphere. Long-term contracts are bound to be incomplete. Domestic investors with diverse local holdings possess greater access to informal contractual supports through their industrial organization, cultural understandings, and local ties for their highly detailed, formal contracts. They will be more patient when negotiating with host governments and enjoy a wider range of bargaining outcomes than will foreign firms or domestic firms with few local ties. Their industrial organization, cultural understandings, and local ties provide informal supports for the maintenance and adaptation of formal contracts.

This greater negotiating ability tends to facilitate more contractual and policy adaptation, which can ensure that both firms and governments find the contractual relationship attractive in the long term. This translates into a greater likelihood not only that private sector participation will endure but also that service quality and access will gradually improve. (While negotiations over compliance and changes in contractual terms often involve backtracking relative to original commitments, they help circumvent the sudden stops in investment prompted by negotiating impasses.) Although foreign and domestic investors without diverse portfolios in their contract jurisdiction may invest heavily in the short term – particularly in times of political and economic stability – their relationships tend to be knocked off track when politicians' time horizons shorten or state leverage increases.

In other words, the argument advanced in this study turns the conventional wisdom regarding the benefits of sector specialization and cross-country diversification on its head. When working in the developing world, focusing on particular country markets and building a diversified presence may be a more effective strategy than expanding cross-nationally. This approach will likely provide stronger protection against the obsolescing bargain than external legal guarantees or other formal property rights protections.

2

Water and Sanitation Privatization in Argentina: An Overview

This chapter takes us to Argentina, the first large country in the developing world to privatize urban water and sanitation services during the 1990s reform wave. Under the leadership of Carlos Menem in 1989, Argentina embarked on a far-reaching market reform program that included efforts to liberalize trade, improve macroeconomic stability, and privatize large portions of its economy. Spurred by domestic economic problems, Menem and his allies launched headlong into its reform program – ahead of Washington Consensus admonishments to developing countries to reform along similar lines. As an upper middle–income country with a sizable population (33 million in 1991), and one of a growing set of new democracies in the region, its efforts captured a great deal of international attention.[1] Given the country's early start and the significant income disparities among provinces, the results of its policy experiment can inform efforts to analyze post-privatization regulatory politics in a wide range of developing countries with weak institutions.

This chapter provides an overview of the Argentine experience with privatization and regulation of private service provision in the urban water and sanitation sector. As a federal country, Argentina granted contracts at the provincial level and established provincial regulatory agencies. Provincial contracts and regulatory institutions resembled each other closely, yet the pathways traveled by the fourteen provincial concession contracts diverged dramatically over the ensuing fifteen- to twenty-year period. This chapter first reviews of the antecedents to privatization and important contextual factors. It then describes the privatization wave in the sector, highlighting its reasonably uniform character in the provinces that chose to follow central government directives. This sets the stage for an analysis of the "selection process" by which investors acquired particular contracts, showing that MNCs secured more desirable contracts; the analysis helps establish that MNCs

[1] Argentina became a democracy in 1983.

did not perform poorly because of selection effects. The chapter then assesses whether Argentina's experience with provincial water and sanitation is consistent, in general, with the argument that domestic investors with diverse holdings in their contract jurisdiction possess distinct advantages in negotiating contractual revisions acceptable to both governments and firms and therefore preside over more stable contractual relationships in the long run. It finds that domestic investors with diverse local holdings indeed maintained more resilient contracts. The chapter concludes with a preliminary assessment of the extent to which alternative explanations drawn from the literature on regulatory politics and market reform can account for variation among the Argentine cases.

THE SETTING FOR PRIVATIZATION: A DECENTRALIZED AND DEFICIT-RIDDEN SYSTEM

Argentina's water and sanitation system, once a model emulated throughout Latin America, faced serious challenges by the 1990s. The national government assumed responsibility for urban systems throughout the country in 1900, following a period of local public provision and city experiments with long-term franchise contracts with foreign firms during the nineteenth century, a typical progression in the region (Gilbert 1998: 108; Hardoy 1988: 109).[2] After receiving operational and budgetary independence in 1912 (Rey 2003: 61), Obras Sanitarias de la Nación (OSN) began an ambitious public works program on a national scale. Because urban systems outside Buenos Aires typically had lower-income consumers and less significant economies of scale, OSN found it necessary to subsidize investments in the interior more heavily than those in the capital region (Brunstein 1986: 154; Rey 2003: 82). The state company prioritized building new infrastructure to meet increasing demand for water and sanitation rather than "managing demand" through price increases because water metering (Rey 2003: 62) and raising consumer rates in line with inflation proved politically contentious (Brunstein 1986: 155–156). Water network coverage for the Argentine population increased from 17 percent in 1910 to 57 percent in 1970 largely thanks to OSN investments, while sewerage network coverage increased from 11 percent to 29 percent (Rey 2003: 117).[3] These increases are particularly

[2] Franchises were awarded for systems in Buenos Aires (Bordi de Ragucci 1997) and Córdoba (Boixadós 2000) in Argentina. See Rey (2003: 54) regarding the establishment of national responsibility in the sector. Foster (2005) documents the national-level administration of water and sanitation service provision in six Latin American countries prior to 1990.

[3] Part of this expansion was accomplished by SNAP (Servicio Nacional de Agua Potable), the national government agency responsible for rural water and sanitation. In some middle-income provinces (e.g., Entre Rios, Chubut), user-controlled cooperatives provided services in small towns (Ordoqui Urcelay 2006: 7). Brunstein (1986: 157) argues that the impetus to expand services was strongest during the first half of the twentieth century.

impressive in light of the fact that the population grew from approximately 8 million to 23 million over this same period.[4]

By the 1970s, however, OSN encountered increasing difficulties. Facing daunting economic challenges, the national government pushed state-owned enterprises such as OSN to operate more efficiently and wean themselves from central government subsidies (Rey 2003: 109–110). Meanwhile, OSN received declining revenues from consumers as inflation eroded the real value of residential rates; by 1979, household water rates had fallen to 33.7 percent of their 1961 base (Rey 2003: 119). Investment tapered off as a result (Rey 2003: 114). As the system's infrastructure aged, service quality deteriorated (Brunstein et al. 1988: 22–25; Stillwaggon 1998: 105–106). Those outside the formal network relied on household wells, which often drew on contaminated sources of groundwater, or informal providers who frequently charged rates several times higher than the public firm.[5] Against this backdrop, the military government chose to decentralize responsibility for service provision to the provinces in 1979, thereby joining a region-wide trend.[6] Most provinces resisted the decree because their systems *all* ran deficits but were not successful in blocking the transfer[7]; the provinces were forced to take on OSN water systems within their territories by 1982, with the exception of the Buenos Aires metropolitan area, which OSN continued to service (Rey 2003: 119–121; Ordoqui Urcelay 2006: 8).[8]

The state of the country's urban water and sanitation systems further deteriorated during the 1980s under decentralized management. With the onset of the Latin American debt crisis in 1982 and the sudden halt in lending to the region, the financial constraints on system management became yet tighter. Provincial governments, suddenly responsible for managing their loss-making water and sanitation systems, invested far less in infrastructure maintenance and expansion than OSN had done during the 1970s – already a period of low investment in comparison with preceding decades. Whereas OSN and provincial entities invested on average US$303 million annually throughout the country between 1970 and 1981 (the vast majority of this by OSN), they together

[4] Instituto Nacional de Estadística y Censos (INDEC).

[5] Brunstein et al. (1988: 16–17) describe the use of contaminated well water in the Buenos Aires metropolitan area. Estache et al. (2001: 1185) describe the prevalence and cost of water from water vendors and other informal providers in Latin America.

[6] By 2008, municipalities and states were individually or jointly responsible for drinking water provision in Argentina, Bolivia, Brazil, Colombia, the Dominican Republic, Ecuador, Guatemala, Honduras, Mexico, Nicaragua, Paraguay, Peru, Uruguay, and Venezuela (United Cities 2009: 187).

[7] Rey (2003: 119) presents collections and expenditures by province for Obras Sanitarias in 1979. Only in the federal capital did income exceed expenditure. Income was less than 50% of expenditures in nineteen of the twenty-three provinces and usually was equivalent to roughly 20% of expenditures.

[8] In a few cases, such as Entre Rios and Córdoba, provinces chose to further decentralize services to the municipal level.

invested US$101 million annually between 1982 and 1991.[9] Projects realized during the 1980s tended to emphasize network expansion without complementary investments in basic system capacity (Rey 2003: 125). While network expansion was an important objective in humanitarian terms, and made sense in political terms following the return to democracy in 1983, the lack of attention to basic system investments meant that overall service quality deteriorated.

Admittedly, more affluent provinces tended to manage their systems more effectively within this difficult economic context than poorer provinces – sometimes by managing state providers more efficiently and in other cases through subsidies. Comparative data on provincial systems during the 1990s portrays this variegated landscape of service provision. The data, ordered by provincial income per capita in Table 2.1, shows that poorer provinces often emphasized patronage employment at the expense of investment – even in network expansion to new users. The third column presents data on the number of employees per thousand connections, a standard measure used to benchmark water utilities with respect to their operational efficiency. While we would expect small provinces not to enjoy large economies of scale and thus need more employees per connection, the difference between two small provinces such as Catamarca, at thirty-four employees per thousand connections, and the more prosperous Tierra del Fuego, with 3.6 employees per connection, is striking.

The fourth column of Table 2.1 presents comparative data on collection efficiency, or the percentage of revenue levied that is actually collected, for the early 1990s. With some important exceptions, peripheral and poorer provinces such as Formosa and Santiago del Estero again failed to collect the majority of the revenue from services they were due, which greatly affected their operations and investment budgets. Provinces such as Santa Fe and Santa Cruz placed greater emphasis on commercial management. These figures underestimate levels of uncollected revenues; one of the most common forms of low-level corruption in the sector involved officials asking for kickbacks from consumers in return for connecting them to the network while failing to add them to central databases, thus ensuring they would not receive bills.[10]

The final two columns testify to the provinces' varied achievements with respect to network coverage by the early 1990s. Poor provinces such as Santiago del Estero and Chaco clearly had significant coverage gaps, whereas higher income provinces such as Tierra del Fuego and Santa Cruz had achieved almost universal coverage for water.[11] The challenges for service provision

[9] Figures are in 1991 dollars and represent averages based on annual expenditure data from Rey (2003: 131). Banco Interamericano de Desarrollo (BID) (1996: 40) presents comparable figures.

[10] *El Arreglo* (1983), a classic Argentine film directed by Fernando Ayala, portrays these practices.

[11] The province of Jujuy is an obvious outlier in Table 2.1. The utility in this province, controlled by an excellent set of directors, managed to achieve an unusual degree of operational autonomy during the 1980s and early 1990s.

TABLE 2.1. *Condition of Provincial Water and Sewerage Utilities Prior to Privatization (Includes Provinces That Did Not Privatize)*

Province	*Provincial income per capita*[a] *(1992; historic dollars/pesos)*	*Employees per 1,000 connections (1993)*	*Collections as % of sales (paid by deadline)*	*% population with household water connection (1991)*	*% population with household sewerage connection (1991)*
Argentina average	$6,703			66%	34%
Santiago del Estero	$1,667	9.3	37% (1994)	51%	14%
Formosa	$1,881	9.2	44% (1993)	51%	19%
Jujuy	$2,777	4.0	80% (1994)	73%	35%
Chaco	$2,697	7.8	59% (1998)	49%	13%
Corrientes	$3,124	N/A	N/A	60%	29%
Tucumán	$3,149	5.1	87% (1993)	77%	33%
Catamarca	$3397	34.4	36% (1997)	80%	22%
Salta	$3,477	6.9	60% (1993)	70%	43%
Mendoza	$3,950	4.6	59% (1992)	77%	37%
San Juan	$4,161	4.4	67% (1992)	80%	12%
Entre Rios	$4,269	5.8	49% (1997)	72%	34%
Misiones	$4,381	8.2	66% (1997)	34%	7%
Córdoba	$5,912	6.3	75% (1992)	75%	14%
Buenos Aires province[b]	$6,258	3.5	76% (1992)	54%	31%
Santa Fe	$6,367	6.0	96% (1992)	68%	28%
Rio Negro	$6,768	5.7	65% (1997)	80%	34%
La Pampa	$6,883	8.7	67% (1998)	66%	31%
La Rioja	$7,279	10.3	10% (1999)	83%	22%
Neuquén	$8,074	12.7	56% (1993)	87%	33%

TABLE 2.1. (*cont.*)

Province	*Provincial income per capita*[a] *(1992; historic dollars/pesos)*	*Employees per 1,000 connections (1993)*	*Collections as % of sales (paid by deadline)*	*% population with household water connection (1991)*	*% population with household sewerage connection (1991)*
Chubut	$9,133	4.7	89% (1993)	90%	49%
Santa Cruz	$12,532	4.9	94% (1992)	92%	48%
San Luis	$12,742	4.0	57% (1997)	76%	27%
Tierra del Fuego	$15,115	3.6	46% (1997)	90%	78%
Capital Federal[c]	$18,654	N/A	85% (1992)	98%	95%

Sources: Provincial income per capita from the Ministry of the Interior. Connection percentages for each province calculated from municipal-level data on the population served through the public network either within one's dwelling or on one's property. Municipal totals taken from INDEC, 1991 Census (Table V6, series B). Employees per thousand connection data from BID (1996: 38). Collection efficiency data from BID (1996: 37) for the 1992–1994 period, except Misiones (ENOHSA-COFES 1999: 173; 1997 figures for percentage of billings collected over year), La Rioja (ENOHSA-COFES 1999: 223; 1999 estimate), Catamarca (ENOHSA-COFES 1999: 231; 1997 figure for percentage of billing collected over year), Entre Rios (ENOHSA-COFES 1999: 183; 1997 data for city of Paraná), Rio Negro (ENOHSA-COFES 1999: 162; 1997), La Pampa (ENOHSA-COFES 1999: 190; data for Santa Rosa for Oct. 1997–Sept. 1998), San Luis (ENOHSA-COFES 1999: 270; data for Villa Mercedes for 1997), Tierra del Fuego (ENOHSA-COFES 1999: 197; figure for city of Rio Grande for 1997), Chaco (ENOHSA-COFES 1999: 280; data for Dec. 1997–July 1998), and the Buenos Aires Metropolitan Area (Artana et al. 1999: 203; figure reflects cumulative delinquency rather than collections in a particular year).

[a] The Argentine peso was pegged to the dollar in 1992.

[b] Outside Buenos Aires metropolitan area.

[c] Service quality indicator for the Buenos Aires metropolitan area.

were certainly greater in provinces with lower population densities, but there were discrepancies between levels of service provision even in the least populated provinces. While low performers such as Formosa, Catamarca, and Chaco are sparsely populated, for instance, so were high performers such as Santa Cruz and Tierra del Fuego.

By the early 1990s, the Argentine water and sanitation system was in poor shape. Although based on its per capita income figures Argentina would have been considered an upper middle–income country, its access rates to water and sanitation had lagged, placing the country in the same category as those with much lower per capita incomes, including Ecuador, Peru, India, and Malawi (Stillwaggon 1998: 98). As the data presented in this section illustrates, however, some provincial services performed better than others a decade following decentralization.

A RELATIVELY UNIFORM PRIVATIZATION PROGRAM WITH PARTIAL UPTAKE

After inheriting the presidency during a period of hyperinflation and crisis in 1989, President Carlos Menem embarked on a far-reaching market reform program that included trade liberalization, deregulation, a large-scale privatization program, and a currency board that effectively fixed the value of the Argentine peso to the dollar. The privatization of state-owned companies, Menem and his advisers reasoned, would help the country address its financial problems by raising funds from asset sales and eliminating subsidies for loss-making public enterprises. Officials also reasoned that privatizing utilities and infrastructure services through divestitures or long-term management and investment contracts (concessions) would facilitate access to international finance. Foreign investors, after all, had excellent access to international capital markets, and multilateral banks were increasingly steering loans to countries that followed their public sector reform recommendations.

The decision to decentralize urban water and sanitation services during the 1980s greatly influenced the Menem administration efforts to privatize service provision. Economy Minister Domingo Cavallo and other technocrats within the administration cited the profligate spending of provincial governments as one of the primary sources of economic instability in the country; provincially owned banks, they argued, granted loans based on political rather than economic criteria and then required bailouts, while provincial state-owned companies ran persistent deficits. Argentine governors, in other words, faced a moral hazard problem: the consequences of their individual fiscal decisions affected the economy at large rather than just their own jurisdiction (Jones et al. 2000; Wibbels 2004: 214). Moreover, the revenue-sharing arrangements reached in 1987 obliged the federal government to transfer roughly 60 percent of its revenues to the governors, placing great strain on the national budget (Eaton 2004: 147). Menem's negotiations with the provinces over revenue sharing culminated in two new fiscal pacts in 1992 and in 1993. Menem required provinces signing the 1993 Fiscal Pact to privatize many public services administered at the provincial level, including provincial banks, electricity distribution systems, and water and sanitation services.[12]

The Argentine national government had two, albeit somewhat limited, means to enforce provincial compliance with its privatization prescriptions. Menem could pressure governors from his own Peronist Party through channels such as party control over political career trajectories. Governor Ramón Ortega of Tucumán, for instance, embarked early on a provincial privatization process as he jockeyed for the vice presidential slot in Menem's reelection campaign. The federal government could also apply fiscal pressure. For example, it steered World Bank and Inter-American Bank loans to fund water and sanitation system upgrades to provinces that adhered to the national "institutional reform" program.[13] The government could also utilize discretionary transfers and federal bailouts of particular provinces to pressure for provincial reforms such as privatization (Wibbels 2004: 222, 2006: 141–150). This meant that provinces with more severe revenue constraints faced greater pressures to privatize as they had fewer funds with which to subsidize loss-making systems, and particularly, to fund large-scale infrastructure improvements.[14]

Although privatization was more likely under Peronist governments and tight fiscal conditions, two provincial-level factors made adherence to requirements to privatize under the Fiscal Pact less likely: union resistance and the decentralization of services to the municipal level during the 1980s. While the national federation of the sanitation workers' union decided to support privatization in the sector once it had secured an agreement that governments would set aside 10 percent of the shares in concessions for local union chapters, provincial chapters controlled by factions not aligned with the national organization often resisted attempts to privatize.[15] Meanwhile, a handful of provinces that had decentralized services to the municipal level – including Entre Rios, Chubut, La Pampa, and San Luis – did not privatize, as they could not do so without coordinating with a large number of actors to create a concession area large enough to attract private investors.[16]

[12] See article 9 of the Pacto Federal para el Empleo, la Producción y el Crecimiento, signed August 12, 1993. Eaton (2004: 147–150) and Wibbels (2004, 2006) describe these negotiations.

[13] World Bank and Inter-American Development Bank loans for the sector were administered by the national government through a program called PRONAPAC.

[14] Galiani et al. (2005) model water and sanitation privatization in Argentina and find local economic conditions and Peronist gubernatorial control to be strongly associated with privatization. They model the decision to privatize as a municipal decision, yet decisions regarding the privatization of provincial water companies were actually made by governors in almost all cases.

[15] This occurred in the province of San Juan (interview with Daniel Canone, general secretary of the Water and Sanitation Union, Mendoza Province, August 1, 2006).

[16] Sanguinetti (2001: 107).

Because of these varied local incentives and disincentives to comply with federal directives, only a subset of the Argentine provinces privatized their water and sanitation services. Although twenty-one out of twenty-three provinces signed the 1993 Fiscal Pact, only thirteen of the twenty-four provinces actually privatized in the sector. The national government, meanwhile, oversaw the privatization of OSN, which had remained under its control following the military government's decentralization of services in the sector. Figure 2.1 shows the geographic distribution of privatizers. The map makes clear that the southern provinces of Patagonia, many of which received revenues from special taxes on minerals extracted within their borders, privatized less enthusiastically than their central and northern colleagues. The resulting subset of provinces that privatized occupied a wide spectrum from very poor provinces in the northeast and northwest, such as Formosa and Misiones, to more industrialized (but not mineral rich) provinces of the central plains and Andes, such as Córdoba and Mendoza.

Governors who chose to privatize their water and sanitation systems tended to follow a common template, following the format used by the national government in 1993 to privatize OSN, which had come to only service Greater Buenos Aires. This makes cross-provincial comparisons more feasible.[17] All jurisdictions that privatized did so via concession contract, or management and investment contracts of twenty to thirty years that left asset ownership in state hands.[18] Concessions encompassed both water and sanitation services.[19] Contracts provided for local union chapters to own 10 percent of concessionaire shares.[20] They also retained a remarkable number of features from existing provincial systems, which had in turn been inherited from OSN's tenure as the national provider. For the vast majority of the privatizations, the geographic boundaries of the area for private sector management closely matched the remit of the provincial utility that was privatized.[21] Contracts also required investors to hire a large fraction of the provincial companies' existing workforce and

[17] The criterion used to choose the winning bid varied, with the lowest multiplier of the existing tariff formula being the most common.

[18] La Rioja first privatized via a management contract when there was insufficient private-sector interest in the concession contract it offered, but then converted this contract to a concession after three years.

[19] The Córdoba concession, which only includes water services, is a notable exception. During the 1980s, the province had chosen to decentralize sewerage services to the municipal level and retain responsibility for the capital city's water system. This meant that when the provincial water company was privatized, it only included water services.

[20] The exception was Corrientes, which only granted the union 2% of the shares. This situation was subsequently changed so that the union came to enjoy the usual 10% (interview with Ramón Santacruz, Aguas de Corrientes, August 2006).

[21] Cooperatives, small entrepreneurs, small municipalities, and private vendors continued to cater to the portion of the population not served by the provincial company or service provider both inside and outside of the concession area boundaries. In the remaining cases, households relied on well water.

FIGURE 2.1. Argentine Provinces That Privatized Their Water and Sanitation Systems, 1991–2000

respect long-standing labor agreements.[22] Finally, the detailed rate (i.e., tariff) calculation formulas used to determine charges for individual households bore very close resemblance to – and often mirrored exactly – progressive rate formulas employed by the state companies inherited from OSN.[23]

The model contracts drafted by the provincial public works or economy ministries and their consultants also contained *very specific and ambitious targets* for the expansion of the water and sanitation networks within concession area boundaries, which usually coincided with the urban areas attended by the state companies or agencies to be privatized. To cite just one example, the contract for the province of Santa Fe required the concessionaire to expand water coverage from 74 percent to 100 percent of the population by the eighth year of the concession and sewerage coverage from 30 percent to 100 percent by the tenth year the concession.[24] Contracts also included explicit quality, service continuity, and water pressure standards that grew more demanding over time, as well as expectations regarding the time frame within which customer complaints should be resolved. In addition, the contracts typically specified the type of fine or sanction the provincial regulator could impose if the concessionaire failed to meet any of its contractual obligations.

The Argentine contracts also contained common provisions for adjustment to consumer rates, investments, and other key features of the concessions. They detailed a variety of specific circumstances under which concessionaires could file for rate increases, including high rates of inflation that dramatically affected input costs, and the removal of Argentina's exchange rate peg to the dollar. These increases would be implemented through adjustments to a coefficient in the formula used to calculate consumer rates. Investment targets for coverage and quality were included in the contracts, and concessionaires were required to submit investment plans detailing how these goals would be met every several years. Given this general framework, a *contract renegotiation* involved formal agreements to change key features of the contract, such as the formula used to calculate tariffs, adjustments to the contractually defined quality or coverage targets, the introduction of state subsidies beyond what was included in the original contract, or changes in the magnitude of fines that could be levied for particular violations. The similarity among the Argentine contracts should not be surprising: provincial ministers worked closely with a small group of consulting firms, national government officials from the Ministry of Water

[22] A subset of the former provincial company's employees was typically transferred to the new regulatory agency.

[23] These characterizations are based on examination of the contracts. Bimonthly charges for individual households were based on proxies for household income.

[24] See appendix X of the "Pliego de Bases y Condiciones Generales y Particulares para la Concesión del Servicio Público de Agua Potable y Desagües Cloacales en el Ámbito de la Dirección Provincial de Obras Sanitarias," December 1994. All eleven Argentine contracts examined contained explicit, ambitious coverage targets with the exception of the Salta contract, which contained peso-denominated investment goals.

Resources, and World Bank advisors as they prepared provincial privatization processes.[25] A survey of concession contracts in Latin America across a range of infrastructure sectors suggests that these features are characteristic of those adopted elsewhere in Latin America, with one exception: contracts in other countries sometimes contained explicit "triggers" for contract renegotiation (Guasch 2004: 28–34), whereas the Argentine contracts did not.

Legal frameworks for the privatization process and the post-award regulatory process were also very similar across provinces. Bidding pre-qualification procedures effectively privileged large foreign investors because they awarded points to firms based on the number of customers served and established large minimum thresholds for capital.[26] Provincial laws and decrees issued at the time of privatization also established formally independent regulatory agencies charged with monitoring firm compliance with their contracts.[27] Although some of these agencies did not get off the ground until a few months after privatization, the vast majority of the provinces had their agencies up and running by the end of the first year of the contract.[28] The agencies were similar in their funding sources and remit.[29] The main difference was that smaller provinces often chose to establish multi-sector agencies to monitor all privately provided public services so as to pool expertise and resources, whereas larger and more affluent provinces tended to establish single-purpose agencies focused on particular sectors. In addition, some regulatory frameworks allowed firms to appeal decisions to the executive branch, which limited agencies' de facto independence. (This difference between agencies is analyzed in the final section of this chapter.)

In summary, it is fair to say that contracts and regulatory institutions across the Argentine provinces resembled each other reasonably closely, thus allowing comparisons across cases to examine the influence of non-contractual features, such as investor organizational structure. Some provinces chose not to privatize, but this is immaterial for an examination of the uneven effects of privatization;

[25] Three engineering consultancies prepared the vast majority of the draft model contracts and bidding conditions used by the provinces: Halcrow, HYTSA, and CETI. Provincial governments worked closely with the subsecretary for water resources, Jorge Raís, who in turn worked closely with World Bank sector specialists.

[26] This generalization is based on the bidding conditions for eleven of the fourteen provincial contracts. The exception to this statement is Santiago del Estero, which awarded points for a strong presence in the local economy. This concession, however, located in one of Argentina's poorest provinces, was uninteresting to foreign investors.

[27] In legal terms, they were all *autarquías*.

[28] Azpiazu et al. (2008: 119) report the dates by which the provincial regulatory agencies had commenced their day-to-day operations. In the cases of Córdoba and Buenos Aires Provinces, agency functions were performed by a segment of the provincial administration for several years before being handed over to an independent agency.

[29] Review of the enabling laws for regulatory agencies does, admittedly, highlight some small differences between the provincial institutions. Agency directors' formal length of term and the regulations regarding director salaries, for instance, varied. The case studies in subsequent chapters, however, will show that such formal rules tended not to constrain the executive branch.

what matters is that the process was relatively uniform across cases. Otherwise, we might attribute different privatization outcomes to variation in privatization program design. Moreover, the fact that privatization took place in a set of provinces with per capita income levels ranging from those of an upper middle–income country to those of the poorest countries in the region suggests that the patterns observed in the Argentina case can inform analyses of privatization in a wide set of developing countries.

THE "SELECTION PROCESS": INVESTOR ENTRY INTO PARTICULAR CONTRACTS

As the Argentine provincial privatization programs unfolded during the 1990s, two main types of investors exhibited strong interest in entering concession contracts for local water and sanitation systems: large MNCs from Europe and North America with a strong sector focus, and domestic business groups interested in obtaining a foothold in a new market. Both types of investors bid for concessions throughout the country. Large MNCs, however, led the consortia that won the most coveted contracts in larger and more affluent provinces. A mix of domestic investors and MNCs secured the remaining contracts in less affluent and peripheral markets.

Large European and North American firms competed aggressively for water and sanitation concessions in Latin America during the 1990s. Their interest constituted part of a significant wave of enthusiasm for infrastructure investment during this period, foreign investor confidence being buoyed by a new set of international property rights guarantees, including international arbitration provisions contained in bilateral investment treaties between developed and developing countries. Moreover, the attractiveness of emerging markets such as Latin America to European utility firms grew as the European Union began to deregulate its internal market, thereby exposing infrastructure firms to greater competition within their home markets (Guillén 2005: 71–75; Clifton et al. 2007: 5, 221; Fridenson 2007: 65–68). In the water and sanitation sector, a small set of European players led the charge into emerging markets: Lyonnaise des Eaux (later Suez), Compagnie Générale des Eaux (later Vivendi), Thames Water, and RWE. Later, Spanish and Italian firms such as Fomento de Construcción y Contratas (FCC), Actividades de Construcción y Servicios (ACS), and Impregilo entered the fray. Argentina, as an early privatizer, became a major focus of interest for the large European and American players, particularly after Menem and his economy minister Cavallo had stabilized the economy. They assembled bidding consortia that placed them in the role of lead investor and technical operator of services but also included the banking and construction arms of Argentine business groups as minority partners.

Argentine business groups also perceived a new market opportunity in water and sanitation and bid for contracts. When pre-qualification criteria emphasized previous sector experience and firm financial capacity, they partnered with MNCs in the manner previously described, particularly for contracts in relatively affluent metropolitan areas. Minority stakes in projects led by MNCs were seen as opportunities to secure lucrative construction contracts or as arbitrage opportunities (stakes, it was presumed, could be sold later at higher prices). In poorer provinces where the competition was more lax, Argentine business groups formed their own consortia to submit bids. Submitting these bids constituted explicit decisions to experiment with a new business model.[30] While domestic firms had traditionally competed for contracts granted by the state to build specific infrastructure projects, and system management was historically handled by the public sector – or in the nineteenth century, by foreign investors. Heads of business groups realized that concessions would offer them a monopoly source of revenue at times when the state had few resources to devote to construction contracts and therefore would constitute a nice addition to portfolios designed to ensure revenues at different points in the economic cycle.[31] Prequalification criteria for previous experience and technical capabilities in the sector could be addressed, for instance, through advisory contracts with European firms in provinces where MNC-led consortia had chosen not to compete.[32]

Provincial decisions to privilege sector expertise and capital in bidding processes, as well as the eagerness of both MNCs and Argentine firms to secure contracts, led to a particular pattern of contract allocation between different types of investors. Consortia led by MNCs focused their efforts on contracts in higher-income provinces with large metropolitan areas, where most consumers paid their utility bills. They viewed such contracts as less risky politically because they would not have to convince a large fraction of the population to start paying for a service they had previously received for free, and considered social protests against periodic rate adjustments provided for in contracts to be less likely. Even though competition for such contracts tended to be fiercer, leading firms to propose smaller multipliers on the existing tariff or larger lump-sum payments in order to obtain the contract, many firms anticipated that these entry conditions could be renegotiated ex post.

As a result, as Table 2.2 shows, consortia led by European and American investors won contracts in the wealthier jurisdictions with larger markets.

[30] In this sense, the Argentine experience in the water sector is consistent with arguments made regarding domestic investor support for market reform programs in other sectors and Latin American countries once governments ensured they could receive a slice of the pie. See, for instance, Corrales (1998), Manzetti (1999), Schamis (1999), Etchemendy (2001), Teichman (2001), Treisman (2003), and Armijo and Faucher (2008).

[31] Multiple not-for-attribution interviews with domestic investors.

[32] Prequalification requirements were usually stricter in markets considered to be more lucrative. The large and relatively prosperous province of Córdoba, for example, required that at least one member of the consortium have significant experience providing services in a similar-sized market and that the consortium possess US$200 million in net assets and positive balances over the preceding three years. In contrast, the poorer and smaller province of Corrientes only required that consortium members possess US$15 million in net assets.

TABLE 2.2. *Contracts Secured by Particular Types of Investors*

Province	*Provincial GDP per capita (1992/historic dollars/pesos)*	*Population in concession area*[a]	*Collections as% of sales (paid by deadline)*[b]	*Year contract granted*	*Recipient*[c]
Santiago del Estero	$1,667	410,315	37%	1997	Argentine firm (Sagua)
Formosa	$1,881	245,078	44%	1995	Argentine firm (Sagua)
Corrientes	$3,124	601,403	N/A	1991	Argentine firm (Sideco)
Tucumán	$3,149	862,594	87%	1995	MNC (Vivendi)
Catamarca	$3,397	174,065	36%	2000	MNC (FCC/ Vivendi)
Salta	$3,477	1,079,051	60%	1998	Argentine firm (J.C.R.)
Mendoza	$3,949	1,191,380	59%	1998	MNC (Saur/ Enron)
Misiones	$4,381	279,961	66%	1999	MNC (ACS)
Córdoba	$5,912	1,267,521	75%	1998	MNC (Suez)
Buenos Aires Concession I	$6,258	2,067,275	76%	1999	MNC (Enron)
Buenos Aires Concession II	$6,258	1,686,332	76%	2000	MNC (Impregilo)
Santa Fe	$6,267	1,762,060	96%	1995	MNC (Suez)
La Rioja	$7,279	184,968	10%	2002	Argentine firm (Latinaguas)
Buenos Aires metropolitan area[d]	$18,654 (for Capital Federal)	9,200,000	85%	1993	MNC (Suez)

[a] Data from Azpiazu et al. (2008: 54), which draws on the 2001 census. Figures include households that do not yet have connections and therefore represent a measure of market potential.
[b] For sources, see Table 2.1. The Tucumán figure is for 1993, the year in which the province actively improved the management of its provincial provider to make it more attractive to investors. The payment rate for 1992 was 72% according to a report commissioned from CETI consulting to inform the privatization process (table 8.1).
[c] Primary documentation regarding recipients is included in the case study chapters.
[d] Contract granted by national government.

Contract awards were mixed in the remaining concessions in poorer provinces with smaller systems and historically lower payment rates; consortia led by MNCs secured contracts where they submitted bids, while consortia led by domestic investors obtained contracts in the remaining cases. Bidding processes were competitive in all but one province, Tucumán. The average number of bids per concession was 2.4.[33] The lack of competition for the Tucumán concession reflected an unusually ambitious contract design, as will be explained in Chapter 3.

The selection process of investors into particular contracts is inconsistent with two alternative explanations for the observed correlation between domestic investor management and more stable contract trajectories in the long run described in the Introduction and Chapter 1. One alternative explanation, inspired by arguments stressing informational and political advantages available to domestic investors (Henisz 2002: 110; Schneider 2010), would attribute the observed correlation to domestic investors' ability to secure more favorable contracts. As Table 2.2 and the preceding description of the contract award process suggest, however, domestic investors obtained what were considered to be the least desirable contracts at the time of privatization. Moreover, the consortia led by MNCs included domestic investors, who would have found it in their own interest to pass on any additional information they could obtain regarding the greater favorability of particular contracts. A second alternative explanation focused on selection processes would suggest that because foreign investors enjoyed international arbitration protections, they would be willing to bid for riskier contracts; in other words, access to international arbitration creates a moral hazard problem. Again, the Argentine experience does not indicate that this occurred; consortia led by MNCs secured what were generally considered to be the most promising contracts.

A BROAD-BRUSH TEST OF THE BOOK'S ARGUMENT IN THE ARGENTINE WATER SECTOR

The Argentine privatization process created a new institutional landscape for water and sanitation service provision. In thirteen provinces, as shown in Table 2.2, legally independent regulatory agencies were charged with monitoring the performance of private monopoly service providers.[34] In the Buenos Aires metropolitan area, a regulatory agency directed by appointees from the national, provincial, and city government supervised Aguas Argentinas, the regional concessionaire. Private service providers, regulators, and government ministers found themselves adapting to new roles and a changed politics surrounding service provision. This section assesses the extent to which Argentine business groups with diverse holdings in their contract jurisdictions were better

[33] Calculated on the basis of provincial press coverage of each privatization process and BID (1996).

[34] Services were divided among three concessions in the province of Buenos Aires (including the national contract for the Buenos Aires metropolitan area), yielding a total of fourteen contracts.

placed than other domestic or international investors to work effectively with provincial governments to adapt their contracts to changing circumstances in ways acceptable to both parties.

It is important to analyze Argentine water and sanitation concession contracts in two periods: prior to and following the Argentine crisis of 2001–2002. The argument predicts that negotiating outcomes would differ between the two periods. Prior to the crisis, the political and economic environment was more hospitable for private providers. Although the Tequila Crisis triggered a short recession in 1995, and economic growth rates tapered off toward the end of the decade, there were no major economic shocks that endangered the main financial assumptions included in the contracts. Because the national and provincial governments were financially quite constrained, and the national political climate remained fairly supportive of private service provision through the 1990s because President Menem – who had launched the privatization program – remained in power for most of the decade, private providers exercised a fair amount of leverage in their ongoing negotiations with host governments.[35] Moreover, multilateral banks and central government agencies offering to help finance investments in local water and sanitation systems made access to low interest loans contingent on institutional reform in the sector.[36] As a result, we would expect negotiations between host governments and firms to be confined to relatively modest issues, and outcomes – when achieved – to be workable for both parties but more favorable to investors. As the case studies examined in subsequent chapters show, even during this period of relatively high investor leverage, there were important differences in the ability of various types of investors to secure adaptations to contractual arrangements acceptable to both host governments and firms.

Following the Argentine crisis, however, both host governments and firms needed to reach agreements on a broader and much more fundamental set of issues. When the government removed the exchange rate peg in January 2002, the value of the peso plummeted, creating an income shock for both consumers and providers. For providers, the cost of imported inputs increased between three- and fourfold, and an ensuing period of significant inflation triggered increases in key domestic inputs such as labor. Consumers struggled to pay their bills as the economy contracted by 16 percent, unemployment levels reached 25 percent,

[35] Of the eleven provinces discussed in Chapters 3 and 4, only Santiago del Estero and La Rioja ran surpluses during the pre-crisis period. Although budget deficits provide only a rough indication of the leeway governments had to finance infrastructure on their own, combined with the presence of conditionality attached to borrowing, it makes sense to categorize most of the provinces as "capital poor" with respect to infrastructure finance. Provincial budget data for 1990–1999 compiled by the Economics Department of the University of La Plata.

[36] The national government's PRONAPAC loan program, which administered loans from international financial institutions for the water and sanitation sector, promoted the institutional separation of service provision from provincial governments, the establishment of regulatory agencies, and privatization.

and the middle class saw their savings decimated when accounts were frozen. The same public emergency law (25,561) that ended the exchange rate peg to the dollar also stipulated that all concession contracts would be renegotiated and that consumer rates could no longer be pegged to the dollar. Provincial governments quickly issued laws and decrees confirming their adherence to the national law. Opening up contracts for renegotiation was justified on a number of grounds, perhaps the most important being that adjusting consumer rates to compensate concessionaires for the effects of the crisis in the manner specified in most contracts – which would have kept investment commitments intact and raised consumer rates sufficiently to compensate for the new cost structure – would have been politically impossible in the post-crisis context.

Post-crisis renegotiation proceedings resembled one another closely because they addressed a common set of concerns: they focused on finding a way to balance providers' concerns about profitability with politicians' interests in keeping rate increases lower than those provided for in the original contracts in the event of a devaluation or high inflation rates, placating unions lobbying for wage increases and maintaining reasonable rates of investment. Government leverage grew steadily throughout the post-crisis period. Demand for Argentine agricultural exports increased dramatically, and export taxes replenished national government coffers. Much of these funds made their way to governors in the form of financial assistance with infrastructure projects. This changed situation offered provincial governments the possibility of funding infrastructure investment on their own rather than relying on private service providers. Starting in May 2003, the political context grew less favorable to negotiations as well. Presidents Néstor Kirchner and Cristina Fernández de Kirchner came from a more left-wing branch of the Peronist Party than ex-president Menem, and they were fickle supporters of private provision. These financial and political shifts greatly weakened investor leverage.

Choice and Measurement of the Key Dependent and Independent Variables

In assessing the extent to which the Argentine contracts controlled by different types of investors were characterized by brittle or resilient contractual relationships in the pre- and post-crisis period, it is necessary to focus on a few indicators obtainable and comparable across the fourteen concessions. The analysis in this section is of three indicators, often occurring in conjunction with one another. First, in resilient contractual relationships, firms and host governments are able to successfully conclude contract renegotiations, especially following major upheavals such as the Argentine crisis. Second, contract renegotiations should yield benefits for both parties. In the post-crisis period, when investors possessed low leverage, new contractual terms should have contained important concessions for firms to ensure that their business models remain viable. One concrete benefit of this type is a tariff increase significant enough to substantially compensate for inflation. Finally, we should observe lower rates of investor exit both pre- and post-crisis from contracts in which investors and host governments are able to negotiate effectively regarding levels of compliance with and amendments to formal contracts. After all, having successfully concluded contract renegotiations or informal negotiations in a fashion that yields important benefits for both parties, there will be little incentive for either to end the contractual relationship prematurely. In other words, there is a tight relationship among these three indicators: they all reflect the ability of host governments and firms to adapt their contractual relationship to a shifting context. Although a range of other indicators, including rates of investment and extent to which rate increase requests are spread out over time, also reflect the ability of firms and host governments to negotiate effectively, it is harder to obtain and compare these measures in a medium-N format given the particularities of the political and infrastructural challenges faced in each province and limitations on data availability. These additional indicators are presented and analyzed in the context of the case studies in subsequent chapters. This section thus explains how three indicators – rates of contract renegotiation, tariff increases, and investor exit – are best measured in the Argentine context. It will also describe how the main independent variable, investor organizational structure, is operationalized in this study.

Conceptualizing and Measuring Investor Organizational Structure

Evaluating empirical support for the argument across the Argentine cases requires distinguishing between different types of investors. As Chapter 1 stresses, analysis should focus on "lead investors," or majority owners of concessionaires that make the main investment decisions and handle everyday management. In the subsequent analysis, a lead investor is treated as foreign if it is majority owned by an economic group or holding company incorporated outside Argentina and if strategic decisions and many management decisions are made outside the country. (An Argentine firm that incorporates in Barbados to avoid domestic taxes, for example, would constitute an Argentine firm according to this definition.) Distinguishing between domestic firms with and without a diverse local presence involves identifying the range of assets held by a given investor in a particular province prior to acquiring their water and sanitation contract. If the investor operates in multiple sectors (i.e., not only in water and sanitation) and its additional holdings are at least as significant in size as its water holdings, the investor is coded as having a diverse local presence.

In practical terms, it is straightforward to place the lead investors in Argentina's water and sanitation sector into one of these three categories after conducting local fieldwork. Drawing on interviews and local press coverage, we can readily distinguish not only between foreign and Argentine investors but also between domestic investors with and without diverse assets in their contract jurisdiction. The coding for each investor utilized in the analysis in this chapter is displayed in Table 2.A.I (chapter appendix), while documentation informing this coding is included in the book's online appendix. Importantly, one observes all types of investors during both the pre- and post-crisis period. Although the majority of the original entrants in the Argentine concessions were either foreign or domestic without significant local holdings, a domestic investor with a diverse local presence won the original bid for the Salta concession in 1998. And the original Buenos Aires–based investors in the Corrientes concession sold their shares to a Corrientes-based investor in 1996. Domestic investors with significant prior local holdings entered two additional concessions following the crisis.

Conceptualizing and Measuring Investor Exit

The analysis of patterns of investor exit reflects two different means by which investors can pull out of contracts with which they – or their government partners – are dissatisfied: sale and contract cancellation. If the contractual arrangement is troubled but still salvageable, disgruntled investors may be able to sell their controlling stakes to another firm; displeased governments can pressure investors to sell to new owners with whom they feel they could work more effectively. Such share transfers usually entail lengthy negotiations with host governments, as contracts typically reserve them the right of approval. If there are interested buyers and an agreement with all parties can be reached, the concession contract itself will continue in the hands of this new private investor.

If a collapse of firm-government negotiations has rendered the infrastructure contract completely unviable in political or financial terms, the only way out is for one or both parties to cancel the contract, faulting the other party for noncompliance. Argentine concession contracts allow both governments and firms to cancel if the other party has flagrantly violated its obligations, and they stipulate that the party at fault will be liable for a cancellation fee. If the private sector provider is deemed to be at fault, this usually means that the provincial government can draw down a sizable guarantee held in a local bank account.[37] If firms believe that the government is at fault, they can file for damages with the local courts or – if their home government has signed a bilateral investment treaty with the host country – through international arbitration. When contracts are canceled amid mutual acrimony, both the host government and investor will receive negative publicity in international markets. Investors can be portrayed as incompetent or negligent of their commitments, whereas host governments can develop reputations as expropriators. Reprivatizing under such circumstances can be very difficult, so a return to state provision is likely.

These two modes of exit are treated together in the analysis presented in this chapter but are disaggregated and treated separately in the case studies in subsequent chapters. In the analysis that follows, exit is defined as an instance in which a *lead investor* with majority control of a concession pulls out of a project at any point in time. Sales of equity stakes by minority partners – because they do not change the day-to-day management of operations – are not the focus of analysis.

[37] The size of the guarantees was roughly proportional to the size of the concession.

This summary of all of the Argentine cases examines all instances of lead investor exit during both the pre- and post-crisis periods because exit provides a summary measure of the extent to which firm-government negotiations in both periods were resolved to the satisfaction of both parties.[38] All instances of exit by lead investors are documented in Table 2.A.I (chapter appendix).

Measuring Successfully Concluded Contract Renegotiations

The analysis in this chapter focuses on the ability of particular types of investors and host governments to conclude contract renegotiations *following* the Argentine crisis. The crisis provided a uniform prompt for renegotiation across the contracts, which makes comparing the successful conclusion of renegotiation across cases more straightforward. Renegotiation following the crisis can be interpreted clearly as an improvement on the status quo for firms, as consumer rates had been frozen and contracts suspended immediately following the crisis. Case studies in following chapters examine contract renegotiations prior to the crisis, which were prompted by less uniform circumstances and thus do not lend themselves as readily to a cursory analysis.

The analysis here differentiates between negotiating outcomes in the post-crisis period according to two criteria: the breadth of issues resolved and whether agreements were legally enforced. Renegotiations, following the model outlined at the national level, addressed topics in a standard sequence. Less controversial topics, such as unpaid fines and unpaid government bills, were addressed in a first round of "partial" accords. Topics such as consumer rate increases and revisions to service quality and expansion targets were left to a second set of "comprehensive" contract renegotiations. (The legislation approving accords clearly identifies whether partial or comprehensive agreements were reached.) Governments varied with respect to whether they obtained formal legislative sanctions for agreements and whether they blocked their implementation. On the basis of regulatory documentation, case histories constructed from local press coverage, and interviews with key participants in renegotiation processes, outcomes achieved by particular investors and host governments in the post-crisis period are placed in one of the following categories: (1) full formal renegotiations concluded and implemented (score of 1); (2) full informal renegotiation concluded and implemented (score of 0.75); (3) partial renegotiation concluded and implemented (score of 0.5); (4) full renegotiation concluded but not implemented (0.25); (5) no progress toward renegotiation (score of 0).[39] The outcomes in each case are documented in Table 2.A.I (chapter appendix).

[38] The prompts for renegotiation varied during the pre-crisis period, so comparing rates of renegotiation during this period would give us a less valid measure with which to compare across cases.

[39] This analysis follows Post and Murillo (2011).

Conceptualizing and Measuring Post-Crisis Rate Increases

The final outcome analyzed in this broad-brush assessment of empirical support for the argument partly captures the extent to which contract negotiations following the Argentine crisis benefited firms as well as host governments. Firm exit decisions, of course, already provide one indication of whether renegotiation outcomes (or a lack thereof) yielded contractual conditions that were workable for investors. It could be argued, however, that domestic investors with diverse local holdings might stay in loss-making contracts because they fear reprisals should they exit; in other words, they persist because they are being held hostage during a period of low investor leverage. To determine whether domestic investors – and particularly those with diverse local holdings – are less likely to exit because they are being held hostage or are able to secure better deals requires analyzing the actual policy concessions made in contract renegotiations.

The type of accommodation granted to private providers that is most readily comparable across the provincial cases is tariff, or consumer rate, increases. Rate increases became increasingly necessary in the years after the crisis due to high inflation: in 2002 alone it was 41 percent, and the total amount of inflation between 2002 and 2010 was roughly 204 percent.[40] Although renegotiation agreements typically included reductions to (and often state assumption of) many investment commitments, these are much more difficult to compare across cases given the particularities of investment programs and the variety of mechanisms utilized by host governments to subsidize them. For each contract, this section examines variation in the total percentage tariff increases granted to residential consumers during the post-crisis period.[41] When one lead investor sold to another lead investor, the analysis considers the total percentage increase granted to each set of investors. Admittedly, this aggregate measure does not capture the extent to which investors staged their requests for rate increases over time; this important difference between the staged requests made by domestic firms and the all-or-nothing demands made by MNCs will be documented in the case studies in subsequent chapters.

Correlations between Investor Organizational Structure and Contractual Outcomes

Turning to the fourteen Argentine contracts, we can first assess whether the three indicators described earlier – concluding contract renegotiations following the Argentine crisis, total tariff increases post-crisis, and investor exit – cluster as the

[40] Inflation estimate calculated from INDEC for December 2001–December 2005 and the province of Santa Fe for December 2005–December 2009. (Official Argentine inflation estimates have lacked credibility since the national government's 2006 "intervention" of INDEC, the statistics agency, whereas the Santa Fe figures are viewed as credible.)

[41] Analysis focuses on residential rates because these comprised by far the largest source of income for concessionaires (ENOHSA-COFES 1999). Estimates of tariff increases based on data from regulatory agencies, providers, and local press coverage.

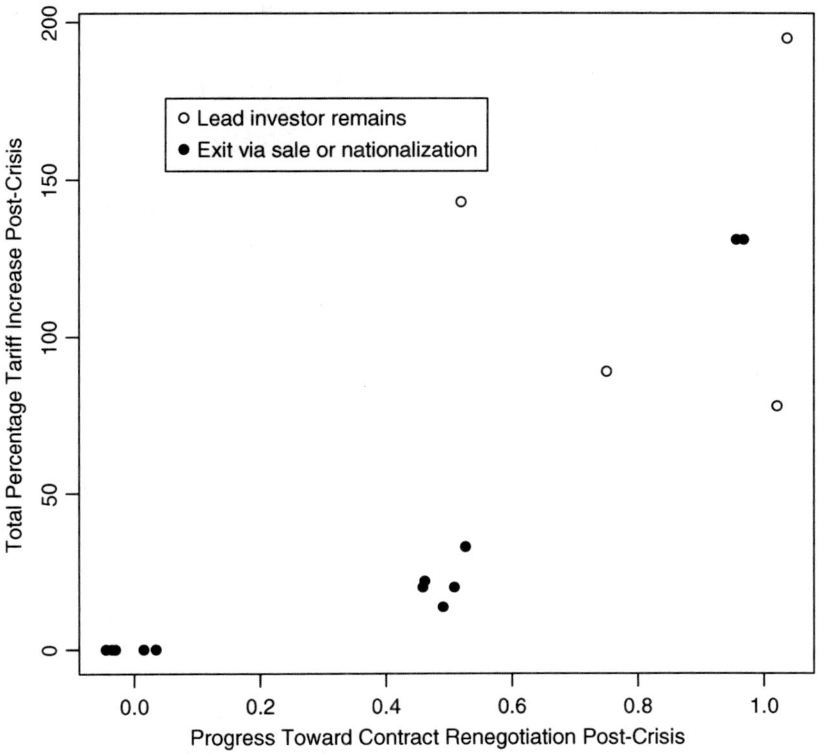

FIGURE 2.2. Clustering of Contractual Outcomes by Concession
Note: Investor status as of May 2011. Observations are for particular "investment regimes," or periods during which a particular lead investor controlled a contract during the post-crisis period. Note that all but two observations in this graph refer to cases in which the same lead investor was in place for the entire post-crisis period, prior to contract cancellation if that occurred. For cases in which ownership is split 50/50 between two types of investors, both set of investors are represented in the scatterplot. Renegotiation scores are jittered, or spread around their real value, for clarity of presentation.

argument predicts. Figure 2.2 examines the relationship among these indicators. The x coordinate for each case reflects the contract renegotiation outcome, the y coordinate the average tariff increase, and the color whether the investor exited its contract. Clustering is clearly evident: investors only chose to remain in their contracts when either an informal or formal negotiation was concluded and actually implemented by the local political authorities. In addition, all investors that received less than a 60 percent tariff increase left the market.

Which types of investors were able to negotiate accords that allowed them to stay in the market? The data on patterns post-crisis contract renegotiations and tariff increases make clear that domestic investors with significant and diverse operations in the same province as their contract exhibited a much greater ability to adapt their contracts to changing political circumstances than consortia led by foreign investors or domestic conglomerates with few local holdings. Table 2.3 analyzes the relationship between investor structure and negotiating outcomes.[42] Domestic investors with diverse local holdings concluded contract renegotiations that reconfigured concessionaire responsibilities following the 2001–2002 Argentine crisis at higher rates (92 percent, compared with 50 percent and 25 percent for domestic firms without local holdings and foreign firms). A one-way analysis of variance for the factor "investor organization" and post-crisis contract renegotiation suggests that these between-group differences are strongly significant ($F(2,13) = 6.24$, $p = 0.01$).[43] We also observe the higher total rate increases received by domestic investors with diverse local holdings following the crisis and the lower rates of exit by local investors from concession contracts via share sales or nationalizations. The fact that concessions led by domestic investors with a strong local presence have been more likely to receive rate adjustments more in line with inflation following the crisis (116 percent compared with 54 percent and 50 percent) suggests that these consortia were not simply being held hostage by provincial governments but actually negotiated more effectively than other types of investors. A one-way analysis of variance for the factor "investor organization" and total tariff increases after the Argentine crisis is also statistically significant ($F(2,13) = 3.00$, $p = 0.08$). Column 3 reports that rates of exit for domestic investors with local holdings were lower than those for domestic firm *without* local holdings and MNCs, though the difference is not statistically significant. The table summarizes all cases of exit for 1991–2010, thus capturing the extent to which contractual relationships were viable both prior to and after the crisis.[44] All in all, these results suggest a general association between investor type and contractual adaptation acceptable to both governments and firms in the Argentine case.[45]

[42] For cases in which an original set of investors sold their holdings to another set of investors, the two different owners are recorded separately. Cases in which ownership is split 50/50 between two types of investors are weighted by 0.5 in each category with results attributable to the relevant investor. This yields a total of 16.5 investors for the analysis of exit between 1991 and 2010, and a total of 13.5 investors for the post-crisis period (three investors exited or decided to exit before the crisis).

[43] Results are comparable if one creates a dichotomous variable for contract renegotiation and conducts a Fisher exact test for the rounded totals. See the online appendix.

[44] While a one-way analysis of variance for factor "investor organization" and investor exit during both the pre- and post-crisis period is statistically insignificant, an analysis of the difference between *domestic investors with diverse local holdings* and other types is statistically significant ($F(1,17) = 4.73$, $p = 0.04$)). A Fisher exact test on rounded totals, however, suggests that the relationship is not statistically significant.

[45] Admittedly, this analysis does not account for the fact some investors were in place for more years than others and hence had more opportunity to secure tariff increases and contract renegotiations. This is why it is important to view the results for the three indicators together; as Chapter 1 stressed, one of the key advantages of firms with significant local portfolios is their greater patience in negotiations.

TABLE 2.3. *Investor Organization and Rates of Post-Crisis Contract Renegotiation, Post-Crisis Tariff Increases, and Investor Exit by 2010*

Lead investor type	*Contract renegotiation rate (2002–2010)*	*Average tariff increase (2002–2010)*	*Investor exit (1991–2010)*
Foreign	25% (1.75/7)	50%	89% (8/9)
Domestic *without* diverse local holdings	50% (1.75/3.5)	54%	78% (3.5/4.5)
Domestic *with* diverse local holdings	92% (2.75/3)	116%	33% (1/3)

Note: This table contains the full set of provincial and national-level privatizations in Argentina in the water and sanitation sector. Provinces that had already decentralized management in the sector to the municipal level conducted additional privatizations at the city level, but these subsume a significantly smaller portion of the population and have been omitted because of a lack of data. Not included: Laprida (approx. 10,000 served; Italian investor), Balcarce (40,000 served, joint Italian-Argentine consortium), Campana (80,000 served, Argentine consortium). The unit of analysis is an "ownership regime," or the window during which a concession is controlled by a particular majority investor. Data analyzed in this table and background information on data sources and measurement is included in the online appendix. The total number of cases is higher for investor exit than for contract renegotiations because investors who exited before the crisis did not have an opportunity to renegotiate their contracts during the post-crisis period.

Three-quarters of investor exits occurred during the administrations of Néstor and Cristina Kirchner (Table 2.A.I, chapter appendix).[46] Both presidents, emboldened by increasing commodity revenues, pressured governors to avoid granting significant rate increases to private providers in a range of utilities sectors. They were not, however, interested in nationalization as an end itself: subsequent chapters document national and provincial government efforts to attract alternative private investors when existing concessionaires had decided to leave. Governments typically only took over services if unable to find a private investor willing to operate under their conditions.[47]

Within this more difficult policy environment, domestic investors with diverse local holdings continued their relationships with host governments at a greater rate than their domestic or MNC counterparts: the rate of exit by investors holding contracts during the Kirchner administrations was 86

[46] In Table 2.3, the total number of exits is reported as 12.5, as Azurix's 50% participation in the Mendoza concession is weighted at half the value of lead investors with controlling stakes.

[47] Cristina Fernández de Kirchner's nationalization of the national oil company YPF in 2012 gave international markets an imbalanced picture of the economic program she and her husband had previously maintained. Prior to this, the Kirchners only nationalized a limited number of firms: YPF, the national postal service, the pension system, the country's flagship airline, and the water company servicing the Buenos Aires metropolitan area.

percent (6/7) for MNCs, 71 percent (2.5/3.5) for domestic firms without local holdings, and 33 percent (1/3) for domestic firms *with* local holdings. While the number of cases is small, the higher rates of contract renegotiation, higher average tariff increases, and lower rates of exit observed for domestic investors with diverse local holdings together suggest that they were best able to adapt to the new circumstances. That consortia led by foreign firms performed so poorly in the context, despite the fact that many possessed domestic junior partners, suggests that preferences and strategies tied to lead investor organizational structure – rather than privileged access to information – is responsible for these differences in performance.

Domestic investors that already possessed diverse holdings in particular jurisdictions actually chose to take over concessions being abandoned by MNCs during this period in the provinces of Mendoza and Córdoba, reflecting a growing confidence in their ability to manage water and sanitation concessions effectively and profitably.[48] As the case studies in subsequent chapters suggest, domestic firms with diverse local holdings also expressed strong interest in additional contracts being abandoned by foreign investors during the post-crisis period but were ultimately unable to reach agreements with the national and provincial governments regarding the terms of ownership transfer. Tellingly, these investors remained interested in acquiring the stakes of foreign investors even after the Argentine crisis and years of stalled contract renegotiation processes, suggesting that they felt confident they could succeed in negotiations where other types of investors had failed. These expressions of interest also demonstrated their confidence that they could manage regulatory politics in more affluent provinces where utilities policy could be more salient because of a stronger independent media and professional organizations.

Overall, the association between investor organizational structure and the ability of firms and host governments to reconfigure their contracts to reflect the changing circumstances and preferences of both parties is strong in the Argentine case. Domestic investors with significant local holdings not only were less likely to exit their contracts prematurely but also concluded contract renegotiations successfully at a greater rate and received larger consumer rate increases following the Argentine crisis. Their willingness to acquire the stakes of both foreign and domestic firms that had failed to make particular contracts work testifies to their confidence in their ability to negotiate effectively. Their continuing interest in controlling stakes in water and sanitation concessions following the crisis is particularly telling, as this was a period of high government leverage when it was much more difficult for firms to exact favorable terms in contract renegotiations.

[48] In Corrientes Province, a local firm also bought the stakes of a domestic investor without local holdings in 1996. In Mendoza, a foreign investor (Azurix, an Enron subsidiary) sold its 50% stake in the concession to a domestic investor with a significant local presence. SAUR, the French firm controlling the other 50%, remained.

AN INITIAL CONSIDERATION OF ALTERNATIVE EXPLANATIONS

This initial analysis of the Argentine experience supports an approach to regulation emphasizing the importance of informal supports for formal contracts derived from cross-sector diversification. Skeptics might argue, however, that the observed relationship between within-jurisdiction diversification and contractual resilience could instead stem from either governor partisan affiliation or ideology or differences in local institutional environments, local state capacity, or regulatory agency design.

It might be assumed that the observed correlation between investor organization and regulatory outcomes actually reflects the partisan affiliation or ideological leaning of the governor presiding over the contract. Murillo (2009), for instance, has argued that while government heads of all stripes are likely to cater to consumer interests during politically competitive periods, at other times left-leaning politicians – particularly if they did not oversee the privatization themselves – are more likely to privilege consumer interests than right-leaning politicians. Flores-Macías (2010) suggests that the ability of left-leaning politicians to actually follow through with nationalization will be greater in more weakly institutionalized party systems – of which Argentina was a prime example following its 2001 crisis. It might be supposed that the election of a left-leaning administration at the national level would still influence provincial-level regulation: national politicians, after all, may pressure governors or mayors of their party to fall in line with their policy preferences.

Following this line of reasoning, it might be supposed that governors aligned with the Kirchners would be less willing to conclude contract renegotiations than would unaligned governors. We might also expect aligned governors to revoke privatization contracts or discourage investors from staying in the market at a higher rate than for nonaligned governors. To see if alignment is actually driving the correlation between investor organizational structure and contractual resilience, I turn to expert survey data compiled by Carlos Gervasoni in each of the Argentine provinces gauging governors' alignment with President Néstor Kirchner. Investors did successfully renegotiate their contracts between 2004 and 2007 – the period covered by Gervasoni's data – at a higher rate in the few provinces run by unaligned governors. This being said, domestic investors – and particularly those with diverse local holdings – concluded negotiations at far higher rates than foreign firms in provinces governed by aligned governors.[49] The respective rates of contract renegotiation for domestic investors with diverse local holdings, domestic investors without diverse local holdings, and international investors were 83 percent, 42 percent, and 23 percent.[50] Furthermore, foreign firms exited their contracts at much higher rates than domestic investors with and without

[49] No contract renegotiations were concluded prior to 2004.

[50] See Tables A.II.1–A.II.3 in the online appendix.

diverse local holdings in provinces governed by both aligned and nonaligned governors. Case studies in subsequent chapters show how governors with different partisan affiliations concluded contract renegotiations with concessionaires.

Institutionalist approaches to regulation suggest that the strengths of checks and balances in the political environment affect the ability of regulatory agencies to commit credibly to contracts and regulatory laws (Levy and Spiller 1996). Although this logic is typically used to explain cross-country variation in investment levels, we could also employ it to differentiate between subnational governments. Despite the fact that scholars have treated Argentina as an emblematic weak institutional environment (Levitsky and Murillo 2005), the Argentine provinces vary somewhat in the extent to which institutions such as the judiciary, public prosecutors' offices, and so forth possess de facto independence. To assess whether the relationship between control by domestic investors with diverse local assets and contractual resilience in fact stems from differences in provincial institutional environments, I employ a proxy measure of provincial checks and balances: Agustina Giraudy's index of "dispersion of authority" (Giraudy 2010). This index weights equally a score reflecting the average tenure of provincial supreme court justices, a measure of government patronage, and a measure of the governor's level of fiscal discretion. The relationship between the average provincial dispersion of authority score for the 1983–2006 period and rates of contract renegotiation, consumer rate increases, and investor exit are statistically insignificant.[51] Moreover, rates of exit and contract renegotiation conditional on the dispersion index generally exhibit a similar association between local ownership and higher rates of contract renegotiation and lower rates of exit. In subsequent chapters, case studies of regulatory processes in provinces with relatively high and low levels of checks and balances provide further evidence that checks and balances are not necessarily associated with more resilient contractual trajectories in Argentina.

Another literature would attribute variation in the effects of private sector participation to differences in state capacity. Weak states, it is argued, will not be able to regulate private sector service providers effectively because of resource constraints and lack of trained personnel, among other difficulties. To assess whether the relationship between control by domestic investors with diverse local holdings and contractual resilience in Argentina actually stems from differences in local state capacity, I calculate measures of sector-specific state capacity for each contract. Provinces that already possessed a technically able set of hydrologic engineers, as well as accountants and lawyers able to exercise considerable influence within the sector, would be better placed to regulate private providers. This would lead us to expect that provinces that had administered their water and sanitation systems more effectively prior to privatization would be better able to regulate providers more effectively post-privatization and that

[51] See Tables A.II.4–A.II.7 in the online appendix for score categories by province and correlation coefficient calculations.

healthy government-firm negotiations would take place. When provinces are grouped according to the level of network coverage and collection efficiency achieved by public sector service providers prior to privatization, there is no correlation between sector-state capacity and rates of investor exit, post-crisis contract renegotiation, and post-crisis tariff increases.[52] Moreover, rates of exit and contract renegotiation conditional on the state-capacity score generally exhibit a similar association between ownership by domestic firms with diverse local holdings and higher rates of contract renegotiation and lower rates of exit: for example, whereas all international and domestic investors without local holdings exited their contracts in provinces with high sector-state capacity, only 50 percent of domestic investors with diverse local holdings did so. This cursory analysis suggests that the association between control by domestic investors with diversified local holdings and more resilient contractual relationships is not an artifact of differences in local state capacity.

Finally, it might be supposed that the divergence in contractual relationships observed between different types of investors in fact stems from differences in regulatory institution design. As already indicated, the legal framework for privatization and regulation was quite similar across provinces. This being said, levels of formal regulatory independence did vary. All provinces that privatized in the water sector created legally independent bodies, but the laws that established some of the provincial agencies allow firms (or other groups) to appeal regulatory decisions to the executive branch.[53] The possibility of conducting such appeals could, in practice, limit regulatory independence because regulators would anticipate the probability that their decisions would be overruled. However, when we compare rates of investor exit from 1991 to 2010, as well as contract renegotiation and average tariff increases following the Argentine crisis, for investors operating in regulatory environments with and without an appeals option, there is no clear association between formal independence (that is, no provision for appeals) and these outcomes.[54] Moreover, rates of exit and post-crisis contract renegotiation conditional on investor organizational structure do not suggest that MNCs' difficulties can be explained by the regulatory institutions they faced. International and domestic investors without diverse local holdings exited their contracts at twice the rate of domestic investors with diverse local holdings, while domestic investors with diverse local holdings renegotiated their contracts at least four times as often as international investors, under both types of regulatory institutions. The discussions of particular cases in later chapters illustrate why such institutional features designed to safeguard regulatory independence mattered little in the Argentine case: regulatory institutions were frequently sidestepped and overruled regardless of their formal powers, particularly in the context of contract renegotiations.

[52] See Table A.II.8, online appendix.

[53] This discussion draws on Post and Murillo (2011). Azpiazu et al. (2008) classifies the provincial regulatory frameworks with respect to whether they allowed for appeals.

[54] See the online appendix.

Overall, this preliminary review of the association between rates of investor exit, as well as post-crisis contract renegotiations and tariff increases, suggests that the main bodies of theory explaining variation in regulatory outcomes provide little analytic leverage in the Argentine case. While the number of cases is small, the trends are clear. Explanations focusing on checks and balances in the local political environment, local state capacity, the ideological orientations of heads of state, and regulatory institution design appear to account for little of the observed variation in contract trajectories. The case studies included in subsequent chapters tackle these alternative explanations in greater detail and, no doubt, to greater satisfaction of the reader.

CONCLUSION

Argentina's experience with private sector participation in water and sanitation, launched during the 1990s ushered in a relatively uniform set of institutional arrangements and contracts at the national level and in thirteen of its twenty-four provinces. In promoting privatization, the national government aimed to reduce provincial deficits and encourage investment in systems that had fallen into disrepair and failed to keep pace with population growth. Although the contracts themselves resembled one another quite closely, the pathways traveled by the provincial concessions diverged substantially during the 1990s and 2000s. In some cases, firms and host governments were able to adapt the concessions to changing circumstances and thereby avoid investor exit via asset sale or contract cancellation; other contractual relationships foundered in the short, medium, or long run.

This chapter provided an overview of the privatization processes in Argentina and introduced three measures that capture the extent to which each of the fourteen water and sanitation contracts followed a resilient or more brittle trajectory. Analyses of the privatization processes, as well as of rates of concluding contract renegotiations following the Argentine crisis, total rate increases granted during the post-crisis period of high inflation, and rates of investor exit help establish a number of facts. First, privatization processes steered contracts in more lucrative markets to MNCs; the remaining contracts, located in poorer provinces, were split between MNCs and domestic investors. This suggests that the poor performance of MNCs cannot be attributed to the process by which firms "selected" into particular contracts. Second, domestic investors with diverse local holdings exited their contracts less frequently, successfully concluded contract renegotiations at a higher rate, and secured significantly larger rate increases following the crisis than domestic investors based elsewhere or foreign firms. Finally, there appears to be no correlation between these indicators of stable contractual relations and factors highlighted by alternative explanations centered on state capacity, checks and balances in the institutional environment, local economic conditions, ideology, and regulatory institution design.

CHAPTER APPENDIX

TABLE 2.A.1. *Investor Organizational Structure and Contractual Outcomes*

Province	*Contract*	*Year contract awarded*	*Lead investor*	*Lead investor type*	*Progress toward post-crisis contract renegotiation*	*Exit date and mode*[a]
Corrientes	*Aguas de Corrientes*	1991	Sideco (Macri Group) (1991–1995)	Domestic	Not applicable	Exit via sale of equity stake in 1996
			Chamas Group (1996–present)	Domestic with diverse local holdings	1 (Formal negotiation concluded and enforced)	Contract continues
Buenos Aires Metropolitan Region	Aguas Argentinas	1993	Suez	MNC	0 (No renegotiation concluded)	Exit in 2006; services transferred to state
Formosa	Aguas de Formosa	1995	Sagua (Sielecki Group)	Domestic	0 (No renegotiation concluded)	Exit in 2008; services transferred to state
Santa Fe	Aguas Provinciales de Santa Fe	1995	Suez	MNC	0 (No renegotiation concluded)	Exit in 2006; services transferred to state
Tucumán	Aguas del Aconquija	1995	Vivendi	MNC	Not applicable	Exit in 1997; services

TABLE 2.A.1. (*cont.*)

Province	*Contract*	*Year contract awarded*	*Lead investor*	*Lead investor type*	*Progress toward post-crisis contract renegotiation*	*Exit date and mode*[a]
						transferred to state
Santiago del Estero	Aguas de Santiago	1997	Sagua (Sielecki Group)	Domestic	0.75 (Informal accord concluded and enforced)	Contract continues
Córdoba	*Aguas Cordobesas*	1998	Suez (1998–2006)	MNC	0.25 (Partial agreement concluded but not enforced)	Exit via sale of equity stake in 2006
			Grupo Roggio (2007–present)	Domestic with diverse local holdings	1 (Formal agreement concluded and enforced)	Contract continues
Mendoza	*Obras Sanitarias de Mendoza (OSM)*	1998	Saur and Enron (1998–2003)	MNCs	0 (No renegotiation concluded)	Enron exits via sale of equity stake in 2003
			Saur and Sagua (2004–2010)	MNC and domestic with diverse local holdings	0.5 (Partial agreement concluded and enforced)	Saur and Sagua exit in 2010; services transferred to state
Salta	Aguas de Salta	1998	Latinaguas and Necon (JCR)	Domestic and domestic with diverse local holdings	1 (Formal agreement concluded and enforced)	Latinaguas and JCR exit in 2009; services transferred to state

Misiones	Servicio de Aguas de Misiones (SAMSA)	1999	ACS	MNC	0.5 (Informal accord concluded and enforced)	Contract continues
Buenos Aires	Azurix	1999	Enron	MNC	Not applicable	Enron exits in 2002; services transferred to state
Buenos Aires	Aguas del Gran Buenos Aires (AGBA)	2000	Impregilo	MNC	0 (No renegotiation concluded)	Exit in 2006; services transferred to state
Catamarca	Aguas del Valle	2000	Vivendi and FCC	MNCs	0 (No renegotiation concluded; agreement concluded provided for firm exit)	Exit in 2008; services transferred to state
La Rioja	Aguas de la Rioja	2002 (begun as management contract in 1999)	Latinaguas	Domestic	0 (No renegotiation concluded)	Exit in 2010; services transferred to state

Note: The "investor type" for each contract are coded based on the characteristics of the owner with the largest percentage of shares in the consortium controlling the concession. In almost all cases, this lead investor also constituted the "technical operator" of the concession, or the firm responsible for everyday operations of the utility. When ownership was split fifty-fifty between two investors, both investors are coded. Lead investors are categorized as foreign if their headquarters are based in another country and they carry out activities in a number of different countries. Investors are coded as domestic if they are based in the domestic market. Investors are coded as domestic with diverse local holdings if they possess significant operations in sectors other than water and sanitation *prior* to securing the concession contract. Specific documentation for the coding for each case is included in case studies in Chapters 3 through 6 and in the online appendix. Contracts in which a first set of owners sold their controlling stakes in the concession to another set of investors are italicized.

[a] Exit dates correspond to the year in which the lead investor formally left the contract. In a few cases, the provincial government "intervened" in the administration of the concession prior to rescinding the contract. If the date of the intervention were to be taken as the exit date, exit from the La Rioja and Mendoza concessions occurred in 2009 rather than 2010.

3

Contractual Fragility Prior to the Crisis: Investors without Diverse Local Holdings Falter

Chapter 2 analyzed the correlation between measures of contractual resilience and investor organizational structure in the Argentine water and sanitation sector. It found a strong association between investor portfolio structure and the extent to which privatization contracts were able to remain viable for governments and firms despite political and economic volatility, as well as changes in the balance of power between the state and firm. The next four chapters provide a more detailed examination of the process through which investor portfolio structure influenced firm preferences and behavior in the context of ongoing negotiations with the Argentine provincial governments and the implications of these behaviors for the durability of contractual relations, as well as improvements in the quality and reach of services. Cases are presented in a narrative format, which helps make common long-run processes visible and also allows for the incorporation of contextual detail necessary to understand particular negotiating outcomes but that lies beyond the book's analytic framework (Büthe 2002: 486). The case narratives also document the many types of legal, financial, and political information utilized to categorize cases for the correlational analysis in Chapter 2.

This finer-grained analysis is broken into two time periods. Chapters 3 and 4 examine the Argentine water and sanitation concessions before the economic and political crisis of 2001–2002. Chapters 5 and 6 analyze firm-government relations and contract trajectories following the crisis. Separating the pre- and post-crisis periods allows for comparison of investor behavior during periods when investor leverage – one of the secondary sources of variation in contract durability discussed in Chapter 1 – did not vary significantly. During the pre-crisis period, investors had high degrees of leverage because of their ability to invest heavily in infrastructure when the state had little access to investment capital. During the post-crisis period, in contrast, increasing state access to funds and a political backlash against privatized utility companies gave provincial governments the upper hand in negotiations.

As Chapter 1 stresses, political hurdles such as turnover, electoral competition, and divided government also affect the necessity and difficulty of firm-government negotiations regarding contractual compliance and revisions. Chapters focusing on the pre- and post-crisis periods therefore compare the performance of different types of investors within similar political environments. Chapter 3 examines the respective ability of different types of investors to maintain constructive negotiations in relatively contentious political environments during the pre-crisis period, whereas Chapter 4 compares investor performance in relatively stable political environments during the same period. Chapters 5 and 6 adopt an analogous approach for the post-crisis period.

This chapter first explains the analytic strategy used to differentiate between political environments that present varying levels of political hurdles for contract renegotiations and categorizes the Argentine provinces for the pre-crisis period. It then outlines expectations for contracts located within jurisdictions characterized by high levels of political hurdles prior to the crisis. The chapter then describes the measurement strategies used to compare governmental compliance with contractual measures designed to improve concessionaires' revenue streams, improvements in concessionaire finances, the extent to which investors employed legalistic pressure tactics against host governments, and the rates at which concessionaires invested in the systems they managed. The final section compares the pre-crisis trajectories of contracts held by different types of investors within political contexts characterized by high levels of political competition and fragmentation.

IDENTIFYING MORE AND LESS CHALLENGING POLITICAL ENVIRONMENTS FOR INFRASTRUCTURE CONTRACTS

To determine which types of investors are better placed to negotiate effectively with host governments over time and thereby preside over more resilient contracts, we need to compare contracts that have unfolded in political environments presenting similar levels of challenges. Environments that shorten politician time horizons or increase the transaction costs associated with firm-government negotiations will be more difficult contexts in which to negotiate, as suggested in Chapter 1. This section develops a strategy for differentiating between political environments presenting high and low levels of political hurdles or challenges for contracts in Argentina that follows from the expectations outlined earlier: a political hurdle index that distinguishes between provinces based on six factors.

The index includes two factors that influence government time horizons: the level of electoral competition in a given year and whether political uncertainty increased because the provincial political party system experienced a breakdown. (Although high levels of political competition would usually be

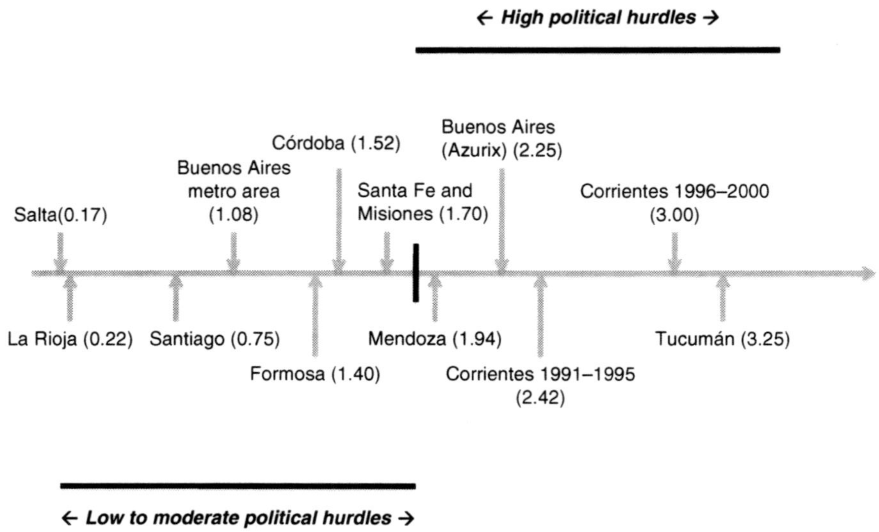

FIGURE 3.1. Provincial Political Hurdle Scores: Averages for Pre-Crisis Period
Note: Scores for Corrientes Province are calculated for two periods corresponding to control by different lead investors.

considered normatively desirable, they make politicians focus on their short-run survival and thus discourage governments from approving policies that help utilities recover their costs in the long run.) The index also incorporates two indicators of the level of transaction costs in a given jurisdiction: whether the provincial government was divided and the lingering effect of political turnover in the executive branch, which often prompts both parties to restart negotiations.[1] Finally, the political hurdle index includes a score indicating whether or not the governor who originally privatized service provision is still in place (and therefore has a reputational stake in the continuing success of the privatized service provision) and whether the governor harbors statist policy preferences. The method used to measure each index component, the formula used to calculate the index, and annual data by contract are included in the chapter appendix. A perusal of the index components by year shows that provinces in the "high-hurdle" category have experienced similar conditions, but of varying intensity and frequency (Table 3.A.I, chapter appendix).

A composite index incorporating all of these factors is used to assess the respective level of political hurdles presented by different provincial political environments during the pre- and post-crisis periods. Figure 3.1 displays the

[1] Because of lack of data, the index neglects another source of fragmentation and transaction costs in Argentina: within-party factionalization. Its role will be discussed in the case studies. The chapter appendix and online appendix present more detail on the index.

pre-crisis average scores for each of the provinces. When different investors controlled concessionaires for a particular subset of the period, investor-specific averages are presented. The case study chapters consider clusters of contracts located in provinces falling in the "low to moderate" or the "high" category in the pre- and post-crisis periods. Chapters 3 and 4 take 1.80 as the cutoff point between low to moderate and high scores for the pre-crisis period. Although the cutoff could be drawn at a number of different points, the case studies will show that starting with the Mendoza case (score of 1.94), political challenges to the concession were so great that foreign investors and domestic firms with few local holdings faced extreme difficulties negotiating effectively with host governments. The chapters group these two clusters of cases together, but process tracing is sensitive to the fact that certain provincial environments were more favorable to concessionaires than others, even within the low to moderate and high categories.

EXPECTATIONS AND MEASUREMENT FOR CONTRACTS IN HIGH-HURDLE POLITICAL ENVIRONMENTS DURING PERIODS OF HIGH INVESTOR LEVERAGE

Chapter 1 suggests that domestic investors with diverse local holdings would be better placed to conclude mutually satisfactory agreements regarding contractual compliance and revisions than other types of firms, resulting in more resilient contractual relationships. We would expect this pattern to be particularly pronounced in the high-hurdle political environments discussed in this chapter – although we would expect differences between the contractual relationships of various types of investors to diverge yet more following the Argentine crisis, when investors lost financial leverage. We would expect the advantages of domestic investors with diverse local holdings come to the fore in high-hurdle environments because they have incentives to exhibit greater patience with host governments that delay the implementation of revenue-enhancing provisions in contracts and are more flexible and less provocative during negotiations regarding substitute, less politically risky policies. They are likely to be willing to entertain a wider set of negotiating outcomes because of their long-standing interests and have access to a range of informal bargaining strategies that avoid open conflict with the government. In the contracts reviewed in this chapter, then, we would expect them to negotiate effectively with host governments and to exit infrequently. Domestic investors without local holdings and foreign investors, however, would be more likely to reach negotiating impasses and exit their contracts prematurely.

We would also expect the *character* of ongoing negotiations between host governments and concessionaires in more volatile and fragmented political environments to vary with investor structure. Observing differences in the way firm-government negotiations unfold over time allows for tracing the causal process – or sequence of steps – through which investor portfolio structure affects the durability of contractual relationships.[2] A first indication that relations are evolving smoothly is that governments do not block the *implementation of contractual measures designed to move utilities to cost recovery.* Governments face strong incentives to delay or even completely block potentially controversial contractual provisions designed to improve firm revenue streams during periods of political competition or uncertainty. Only domestic investors with diverse local holdings, with flexibility regarding the timing of and the form in which governments acknowledge their financial circumstances, and with a different set of negotiating strategies will be positioned to reach workable settlements with host governments regarding the implementation of cost-recovery policies. In other words, we would expect host governments to be more likely to eventually honor original contractual provisions designed to help investors improve concessionaires' financial health – or to eventually agree to compensatory measures if contractual provisions prove politically unviable – with domestic investors with diverse local holdings than with foreign or domestic firms with few local assets. This leads to a second indicator of a resilient contractual trajectory: the *extent to which concessionaire financial health improves over time.*

Because domestic investors with diverse local holdings can access informal negotiating strategies, we would also expect them to rely on legalistic pressure tactics much less frequently than domestic investors without local holdings, and particularly foreign investors. Foreign investors' recourse to courts – and most important, international arbitration – is likely to heighten conflict with host governments, particularly in high-hurdle political environments where utilities policy is likely to be quite salient. Finally, Chapter 1 suggests that higher levels of patience, a greater ability to reach settlements with host governments, and improving finances would also prompt concessionaires controlled by domestic firms with diverse local holdings to invest more regularly over time. In other words, *steady investment rates* also signal that a bargaining relationship is on track. As a result, services are likely improve over time. These various signs of a mutually satisfactory negotiating relationship between host governments and firms are summarized in Table 3.A.II (chapter appendix) under the column corresponding to domestic investors with diverse local holdings.

As the table suggests, concessionaires controlled by domestic firms without local holdings and MNCs are less likely to negotiate productively with host governments in high-hurdle environments. When host governments delay the implementation of contractual measures designed to move systems to cost recovery during periods of high competition or instability, these types of investors have

[2] For definitions of process tracing, causal processes, and causal-process observations, see Seawright and Collier (2010).

less patience and fewer means at their disposal with which to negotiate. We would expect such government delays to prompt foreign firms and domestic firms with few holdings in the contract jurisdiction to revise their expectations regarding the long-run profitability of the arrangement and scale back investments. Withholding investment or other deliverables specified in the contract is one important way, after all, that companies without local assets can exert pressure on the government. Domestic investors are unlikely to retaliate in ways that further escalate conflict; taking the government to court or other such confrontational actions is unlikely to yield favorable judgments and could worsen their reputation nationally. (Once parties to a contract make mutual accusations, it is often difficult to know who is at fault.) Foreign investors, however, are more likely to escalate conflict when they perceive that governments are unwilling to honor their side of a bargain. We would expect multinationals (MNCs) to turn to legal measures – such as filing cases in the local courts and threatening international arbitration, if this is an option – to pressure the government to follow through on its commitments. We would also expect these highly public measures in turn to often contribute to a public and political backlash against privatization rather than actually succeed in forcing governments to comply with commitments.

In order to compare the aforementioned characteristics across provincial cases, this book develops a set of measures appropriate for the Argentine case. To create a rough measure of government support for revenue-raising elements of the contract (henceforth "government compliance"), I count the number of main revenue-enhancing measures included in the original contracts with which it would be reasonable to expect the government to have complied, given how long the contract had been in effect. I then code the level of government compliance with each measure using a value that falls between 0 and 1; usually, a government either complies or does not – yielding either 0 or 1. The ratio between these two figures yields a clear, albeit rough, measure of government compliance that can be used to compare across cases, as the measure reflects the fact that we may fail to observe noncompliance on some counts in cases that terminate early (because inflation adjustments, for instance, are not yet warranted) or that place fewer burdens on governments.[3] Compliance scores for the five cases examined in this chapter are included in Table 3.1.

In the case study chapters, I also rely on indicators of *concessionaire financial health* commonly used by accountants and economists working in the infrastructure and utilities sectors. I ascertain whether after-tax revenues are increasing over time, and if returns are positive and significant. Case studies also compare return on sales and return on equity for the concessionaires. Data on these various indicators has been calculated from firm balance sheets and records, and wherever possible, verified with comparable data from regulatory

[3] More detail regarding the choice of measures and their interpretation is in the online appendix.

TABLE 3.1. *Government Contract Compliance for Pre-Crisis Period (High-Hurdle Provinces)*

	Investor portfolio structure				
	Foreign investors			*Domestic investor* without *diverse local holdings*	*Domestic investor* with *diverse local holdings*
	Mendoza (1998–2001) (1.5/3 = 50%)	*Tucumán (1995–1997) (0/0 = 0%)*	*Azurix (1999–2001) (0/4 = 0%)*	*Corrientes I (1991–1995) (2.5/4 = 62.5%)*	*Corrientes II (1996–2001) (3/4 = 75%)*
Allowing implementation of originally programmed tariff hikes, if scheduled	None scheduled	0 (Negotiated tariff hike, which provided basis for company entry, blocked)	0 (Programmed increases blocked)	Not applicable	Not applicable
Allowing updates to consumer databases, regularization of clandestine connections as specified in contract	0.5 (Agency refusal to allow new property valuations)	Not applicable (Concession did not proceed far enough for this to come up)	0 (Property valuation updates blocked)	1	1
Not blocking efforts to enforce payment	1	0 (Government officials actually contributed to nonpayment campaign)	0 (Governors, mayors encouraging nonpayment)	0.5 (Uncertainty about service cutoffs after judicial ruling in 1994, political flack)	1

Paying promised subsidies or contributions specified in contract, if applicable	0 (Nonpayment of promised subsidies)	None required	0 (Delays in turning over promised infrastructure, due mainly to problems with contractors)	0.5 (Provincial agencies, municipalities were not paying their bills, which stood for half of the amount owed the company)	0.5 (Decree 4289/97, which would have introduced subsidies for poor users and debt forgiveness for debts before 1996, never went into effect)
Following through with inflation adjustments included in contract	None requested pre-crisis	Contract did not progress this far	Not applicable (Azurix applied for a tariff revision toward end of period; the issue was not resolved before contract rescinded)	0.5 (Application for a tariff adjustment in 1993 yielded increase far lower than requested)	0.5 (Applications for inflation-based increases after 1998 unheeded)

officials.[4] Figures are quoted in Argentine pesos, which were equivalent to U.S. dollars in the pre-crisis period because of the country's exchange rate peg.

Investors in particular concessions are also categorized with respect to *the extent to which they employ legalistic or formal retaliatory tactics* to pressure host governments. Tactics coded as legalistic or formal, in order of increasing severity, include: withholding the payment of fines levied by regulatory agencies, appealing regulatory decisions in court, withholding the payment of sums owed to the provincial government according to the contract, and threatening or actually initiating court or international arbitration proceedings against the government.

The final causal process measure is *firm investment levels*, which is measured as the percentage of concessionaire revenues spent on investment in a given year. Measuring investment as a percentage of revenue produces a figure that is fairly comparable across concessions with different goals for coverage expansion and quality improvements. It is also valid for the post-crisis period, when original contractual requirements were suspended. Whenever possible, the case studies also examine realized investment as a proportion of the amount proposed in investors' bidding documents and investment relative to contractual commitments. These investment measures are especially useful when viewed in conjunction with earnings figures; if firms are investing heavily while earning modestly, this suggests a long-term commitment to the market. If they are investing little and paying out large dividends, this suggests a short-term perspective.[5]

FOREIGN-LED CONTRACTS IN PROVINCES WITH HIGH POLITICAL HURDLES

This section examines the evolution of the three concession contracts majority controlled by foreign investors that were located in more politically contentious provinces prior to the crisis: Obras Sanitarias de Mendoza (OSM) (Mendoza Province), Aguas del Aconquija (Tucumán Province), and Azurix (Buenos Aires Province). Regulated by their respective provincial governments and controlled by different foreign firms, the contract trajectories unfolded reasonably independently of one another.[6] We would expect all three contracts to encounter serious difficulties during the pre-crisis period, given that these provinces were characterized by tight elections, executive turnover, and divided government – which prompted governors to focus on short-run concerns regarding reelection

[4] Although there are reasons to treat data supplied by firms with skepticism, the ensuing analysis will show that the variation in reported figures between cases is often so large that it is clear that there are differences. Also, interviews and improvements in service quality and coverage are consistent with the ordering between cases based on financial indicators.

[5] Greater detail regarding the measurement of investment levels and earnings is included in the online appendix.

[6] Contracts, of course, did not evolve completely independently. This being said, they evolved much more independently than they would have had they been regulated by a national agency.

and made it necessary, yet difficult, to negotiate revised accords adapted to the political preferences of new officeholders. Foreign firms would have particular difficulties securing acceptable contractual revisions because of limited patience, a narrow range of acceptable negotiating outcomes, and a preference for formal, legalistic negotiating strategies. Because the political hurdles faced in the provinces of Buenos Aires and Tucumán were much higher than those encountered in Mendoza, we would expect the former contracts to founder more quickly than the latter.

Saur's Faltering Trajectory in Mendoza Province

The French firm Saur, the lead investor and technical operator in the OSM consortium, won a competitive bidding process for the twenty-five-year Mendoza concession and commenced operations in June 1998. Saur, a specialized provider of drinking water services, controlled roughly 10 percent of the concession market in France (Barjot 2011: 792). After being purchased by the French group Bouygues in the early 1980s, it began expanding internationally. As it did so, it maintained its focus on water and sanitation and developed a secondary focus on electricity through joint ventures with France's privatized state electricity firm, Électricité de France (EDF). Latin American investments represented a very small fraction of its international holdings.[7] The Mendoza concession offered a chance to gain a foothold in what was seen as a growing market, thus expanding on its role as a junior partner in several electricity investments in the country.[8] Mendoza, a reasonably well-governed province, was an attractive destination for investors keen on establishing a presence in the Latin American water sector and was therefore able to attract a number of offers from consortia led by foreign firms with significant sector expertise.[9] In preparing its bid, Saur formed a consortium that placed itself in the role of technical operator, involved Azurix (an Enron subsidiary) as an equal equity partner, and included several local investors.[10]

[7] Bouygues Group. *Bouygues 2001*. May 31, 2001. Although Bouygues was active internationally in areas such as construction, almost all of its projects were outside Latin America.

[8] Through its partnership with EDF, Saur had secured a very small (3.3%) participation in the electricity concession for half of Greater Buenos Aires (Azpiazu et al. 2008: 87), a 10.1% stake in the electricity transmission company for the Cuyo region (of which Mendoza is a part), and stakes in two electricity generation firms in Mendoza Province. See "Ganancias más allá de Edenor." *La Nación*. Aug. 18, 1996; "Costará 21% más caro traer energía a Mendoza." *Diario Uno*. July 31, 2005. Two months after securing the Mendoza water contract, it obtained a 7.7% stake in the province's electricity distribution concession.

[9] Mendoza's provincial GDP was AR$3,950 in 1992, compared with AR$6,258 in Buenos Aires Province and AR$3,149 in Tucumán.

[10] Three bids were submitted, two with domestic minority partners. The winning consortium was led by Saur (28.75%) and supported by Azurix (28.75%). A group of Mendoza investors held 10%, Italgas 2.5%, the provincial government 20%, and the union 10%. (Share data from EPAS, the sector regulatory agency.)

Tight electoral competition, turnover in the governor's mansion, and divided government – conditions common to all of the high-hurdle cases discussed in this chapter – prompted the provincial administration to change contractual provisions important for the stabilization of concessionaire finances soon after contract award (Table 3.A.I, chapter appendix; Table 3.1). While relations between the concessionaire and the government of Peronist Arturo LaFalla were relatively amicable during the first year of the contract, his administration delayed the implementation of revenue-enhancing provisions in the contract seen as politically controversial, as his handpicked successor faced a credible challenger from the Radical Party in the fall 1999 gubernatorial race. Facing a budget deficit, LaFalla failed to provide promised financing for subsidized tariffs for low-income households and then asked the firm to delay what he anticipated would be a controversial update to property valuations used to determine household rate levels.[11] Company directors refused, worried that if they didn't proceed before the elections, they might never be able to do so.

Conditions worsened when the Peronists lost the 1999 election. Not having presided over the privatization process, the new governor, Radical Roberto Iglesias, did not face the same reputational incentives as his predecessor to make the concession work. He first consolidated control over the regulatory agency, Ente Provincial del Agua y de Saneamiento (EPAS): the founding head stepped down before the end of his term so that Iglesias could appoint a new president of the body. Two more of the six directors stepped down as well.[12] The agency's new management then failed to provide political cover for the company when its lack of political experience led it to make missteps. After calculating new tariffs bases for one-eighth of its customers based on updated property valuations, the concessionaire's management failed to anticipate that the few customers receiving extremely large rate increases would be likely to complain loudly and erode public support for the concession. EPAS proceeded to block the updates when controversy erupted following their introduction in August 2000.[13] The provincial government also did not pay the subsidies for low-income households promised in the contract, although it had signed an agreement in December 2000 to do so.[14] Meanwhile, EPAS and the company began to dispute whether the firm was simply responsible for meeting contractual goals regarding the percentage of households receiving services, meter installation,

[11] Not-for-attribution interviews with former company directors, June–August, 2006. Provincial law 6044/93 provided for state subsidies for low-income households chosen by state authorities.

[12] José Luis Puliafito, the original head of EPAS, decided to step down because he felt that a director from the Radical Party would better manage relationships with the provincial executive (interview, August 2006).

[13] The contract stated that the company should use up-to-date property registries and descriptions to calculate residential tariffs. Based on an aerial survey and government data, the firm estimated that entries for 40,000 out of 320,000 users needed to be changed. See *Los Andes* August 24–30 and "OSM reclama una deuda al Gobierno." *Los Andes*. July 6, 2001.

[14] "OSM reclama una deuda al Gobierno." *Los Andes*. July 6, 2001.

and quality standards or if it had in fact committed to funding specific projects enumerated in the investment plan submitted as part of their bid for the concession. The agency issued a regulatory resolution in April 2000 rejecting the firm's stated intention to meet the contract's quantitative performance targets rather than construct each piece of infrastructure included in the investment plan, which the firm viewed as "referential" only.[15]

Overall, the government's unwillingness to follow through with revenue-enhancing measures in the contract provided a comparatively unsupportive environment for the concessionaire during its first years. The firm's failure to anticipate publicity problems that might stem from property valuation updates not doubt contributed to this. As shown in Table 3.1, the Mendoza government achieved a compliance ratio of 50 percent (1.5/3). As a result, the concessionaire's financial situation did not improve significantly relative to the time of takeover. After-tax revenues were almost flat during the pre-crisis period, rising 6.5 percent between 1999 and 2001, from AR$52 million to AR$55.4 million.[16] Returns were very modest: the return on sales increased from –3 percent to 10 percent by 2001, while rates of return on equity rose from –2 percent to 3 percent, well below the cost of capital.[17] The vast majority of these returns were reinvested in the business; the firm only paid out dividends once, in 2001.[18] Although Saur and Azurix had anticipated that significant upfront investments would need to be made before the concession would be very profitable, a former company director suggested that these results were far worse than expectations (not-for-attribution interview, July 2006).

Unwilling to provide the provincial government with the specific investments it desired, the company found the government unwilling to negotiate. The foreign-controlled OSM increasingly turned to administrative and court appeals to retaliate against what the primary investors viewed as arbitrary and unfair regulatory rulings. OSM formally requested that EPAS reconsider the decision to reject its investment plan, and when this was refused, filed suit in the provincial supreme court.[19] From then on, the government and firm were unable to agree on investment planning; annual investment program proposals and progress reports submitted by the firm were rejected by the regulatory agency, and the firm in turn appealed these decisions in court, refusing to pay the associated

[15] The investment plan, from a 1994 report drafted by engineering consultancy Halcrow S.A., included estimates for the amount it would be required to spend to reach expansion and quality goals contained in regulatory framework. These figures were updated and included in the concession contract. EPAS rejected OSM's interpretation of this plan as "referential" (Resolución de Presidencia No. 147–00 POE 4/26/00).

[16] AR$ refers to Argentine pesos. Calculated from EPAS data.

[17] For 2004, the weighted cost of capital for the water sector was 13% in Argentina, compared with 2% in the United States. The cost of equity in the water sector in Argentina was 18% compared with 5% in the United States (Sirtaine et al. 2005: 15–16).

[18] Investment levels and dividend payment information from EPAS data.

[19] Autos 69.351, 70.069, 70.073, and 70.455.

fines.[20] In addition, in July 2001, the company stopped paying the "canon," or the lump-sum payment it owed the province on an annual basis in return for market access, in response to the government's continued withholding of the promised subsidies for poor users.[21] As other case studies in this chapter will show, these measures were both legalistic and public compared to those employed by domestic firms in other provinces, but they were not as extreme as those used by the foreign investors in the more contentious political environments of Tucumán and Buenos Aires Provinces. Saur's holdings in the electricity sector were apparently too dispersed and modest for the water concessionaire's management to possess incentives to scale back its complaints out of concerns for other operations. Given the variety of political pressures facing the new governor – including consolidating his support base, working with an opposition-controlled legislature, a recession, and an upcoming tight legislative election in 2001 – OSM's formal pressure tactics were ineffectual. They served mainly to sour relations with regulatory officials and to contribute to a record of mutual contract noncompliance that could be used against the firm, especially in the court of public opinion. Legal threats, in other words, did not give the firm leverage.

Unable to reach a settlement that was both politically palatable for the provincial government and financially workable for the concessionaire as the economic situation worsened, OSM invested modest amounts for an international firm: an average of 26 percent of net revenues during the 1998–2001 period, the initial years, when investment requirements were highest.[22] The consortium also chose not to contract major long-term loans in foreign currency in order to finance its investment program, the strategy usually adopted by MNCs to access lower rates of interest.[23] After much internal debate, the firm's management instead decided to contract a small number of short-term loans at higher interest rates.[24] Debt-equity ratios remained very low as a result, growing from just 0.29 to 0.41 between 1998 and 2001.[25] Because of the concessionaire's reluctance to invest, improvements in the system were modest. According to a regulatory agency evaluation, two-thirds of the investment deficit

20 This pattern continued until the Argentine crisis (EPAS Resolutions No. 057–00, 094–00, 091–01, 153–01, and 182–01). Nonpayment was justified with the legal argument that the fine was not considered "levied" until a court had confirmed its validity.

21 Resumen documento de EPAS, May 2, 2007, and "EPAS, pieza clave con futuro difícil." *Diario UNO*, Nov. 17, 2003. Also, interview with Dario Hernandez, EPAS, August 2006.

22 Calculations by author with EPAS data.

23 Chapter 4 will show that MNCs operating in more favorable political contexts during the pre-crisis period contracted very large loans in foreign currency to fund initial investments.

24 OSM's debt only grew from $49.7 million pesos (dollars) to $73 million between 1998 and 2001. According to an anonymous source, approximately 30% of this debt was contracted outside the country. This compares with 70% in the Aguas Argentinas case. Aguas Argentinas continued to assume long-term debt in dollars up until the crisis, taking on a new US$108 million syndicated loan with ING Barings in 2000 (Aguas Argentinas *Annual Report*, 2001).

25 Calculated from EPAS data.

fell in the areas of new water treatment plants and a failure to make sufficient headway with meter installation.[26] Investment concentrated more on expanding coverage, which could be partly funded out of user fees. In its 2002 report to the regulator, the firm documented an increase from 91 percent to 97 percent coverage for water services between 1996 and 2002; this is slightly lower than the contractual goal of 98.5 percent.[27] In sewerage, the firm documented an improvement from 82 percent to 91.2 percent coverage between 1996 and 2002; this exceeded the contractual target for 2005.[28] In sum, the concession failed to provide the returns that either politicians or investors had expected because of negotiating impasses made insurmountable by the increasingly public nature of the conflict.

The Implosion of Azurix's Contract in Buenos Aires Province

The Azurix concession was located in the province of Buenos Aires, a relatively prosperous portion of the country, somewhat more affluent than the Mendoza case discussed in the previous section.[29] The concession did not include the Buenos Aires metropolitan area, but serviced two of the most important cities of the province as well as much of its suburban territory.[30] The provincial government granted the contract to Azurix, a new water sector specialist, in May 1999. Azurix was a recent spin-off from the American energy firm Enron, and its managers were under pressure to quickly secure additional water contracts following the 1998 acquisition of its core asset, Wessex Water, a British utility.[31] This led the firm to offer a bid of AR$438 million, significantly higher than those of other consortia.[32]

Buenos Aires Province in the late 1990s was not an easy environment within which to launch a water concession, especially for a company whose core management was inexperienced in both the water sector and developing countries. Like the Mendoza concessionaire, Azurix began its contract in a period of electoral

[26] EPAS. Informe Técnico No. 173–02. "Situación Plan de Operación y Expansión de OSM SA." Oct. 2002.

[27] The contractual goal is 98% coverage for all areas for 2000 and 99% for 2005. In its 2002 report, OSM measured its progress against goals for 1996. It reported exceeding water targets (goal 10.1) everywhere (especially in Greater Mendoza) except the most outlying municipalities.

[28] See 2002 OSM annual report on progress with respect to goal 11.1.

[29] See note 9 (this chapter) and Chapter 2, Table 2.1. There is, however, high income inequality in the province.

[30] The concession included La Plata, Bahía Blanca, and numerous smaller municipalities and had approximately 500,000 users. Of the population in the concession area, 58% had access to the water network and 37% to the sewerage network. "OSBA: el consorcio norteamericano Azurix se quedó con cinco de las seis regiones en que fue dividida la empresa al ofertar algo más de 438,5 millones." *La Nación*. May 18, 1999.

[31] Bethany and Elkind (2003: 229–316) and Eichenwald (2005: 249–258).

[32] "OSBA: el consorcio norteamericano Azurix se quedó con cinco de las seis regiones en que fue dividida la empresa al ofertar algo más de 438,5 millones." *La Nación*. May 18, 1999.

competition, divided government, and gubernatorial turnover – a context that led provincial politicians to be very concerned about political backlash against contractual provisions intended to improve utility finances.[33] Azurix assumed control of the system just a few months before the October 1999 presidential and gubernatorial elections. Provincial governor Eduardo Duhalde was competing for the presidency and had picked an ally from his party to run for his position. Concerned about the upcoming elections, his administration failed to defend contractual provisions designed to enhance firm revenues in the first months of the concession, when they elicited criticism.[34] Controversy first erupted when a large percentage of the firm's bills either did not reach customers or contained mistakes. Apparently state company employees had deliberately transferred an old version of the consumer database to Azurix, aiming to sell Azurix a newer version.[35] The regulatory agency instructed the firm to issue new bills to customers at the beginning of September 1999.[36] And when quality problems surfaced in the city of Bahía Blanca, Duhalde announced at a campaign rally that users would not have to pay their bills until the situation improved – essentially setting policy on the campaign trail rather than leaving the determination of sanctions, if applicable according to the contract, to the regulatory agency.[37]

Matters did not improve once power turned over to Carlos Ruckauf, Duhalde's handpicked successor, in December of that year. Ruckauf needed to work with an opposition-controlled legislature and important opposition mayors, and with an increasingly fragmented Peronist Party. He also had little political capital invested in privatization, especially given that the Menemist program was more of a sinking ship than a policy bandwagon by the winter of 1999. Billing problems continued, turning public opinion regarding the concession, leading Ruckauf to become even less supportive of the concessionaire than Duhalde had been.[38] The provincial administration first blocked Azurix's efforts to update consumer rates for 60,000 users to reflect changes to the provincial property valuations used to categorize consumers by income level.[39] Tensions increased most dramatically, however, following an algae bloom in the reservoir serving the city of Bahía Blanca, which led to the delivery of turbid water to city residents during April

[33] These political conditions are reflected in the province's hurdle score of 2.25, slightly higher than the score for Mendoza. See Table 3.A.I.

[34] This discussion has been abbreviated. For more detail, see Post (2008).

[35] "No llegan a los vecinos las facturas de Obras Sanitarias." *El Dia*. July 7, 1999. See also: International Centre for the Settlement of Investment Disputes. 2006. "Laudo en el Procedimiento entre Azurix Corporation y La República Argentina." Caso CIADI No. ARB/01/12, Washington, DC.

[36] ORAB (the regulatory agency). Resolution 1/99, August 4, 1999.

[37] "El Gobernador en Bahía Blanca." *La Nueva Provincial/AIBA Noticias*. Sept. 24, 1999.

[38] See, for example, "Llegan cada vez más facturas de agua con errores." *El Día/AIBA Noticias*. Nov. 30, 1999; "Nuevo abuso de Azurix contra los usuarios." *La Plata Informador*. Jan. 12, 1999.

[39] The provincial regulatory agency, ORAB, issued resolution 7/00 on February 8, 2000, blocking the implementation of the recategorizations. The ICSID award documents the conflict and sides with the company (ICSID 2006: 33–36).

and May 2000.[40] The province had obligated itself under the contract to complete algae-removal facilities for the reservoir and turn them over to the concessionaire. Azurix managers had complained that that they were unsatisfied with the quality of the completed project and refused to assume control. The mayor and other public officials in Bahía Blanca, controlled by the opposition party, warned residents not to drink the water and called on users not to pay their bills until water quality improved.[41] Users protested outside the Azurix branch office, throwing eggs and vegetables at the building.[42] Azurix responded to public attacks by blaming the province for the incident because of its failure to turn over the water treatment plant on time.[43] Put on the defensive, the Ruckauf administration publicly blamed Azurix for the problem, legitimized the nonpayment campaign, and ordered the company to distribute bottled water to affected households, even as independent laboratory test results came back showing the water was potable.[44] Members of the opposition in the legislature then chimed in, blaming the provincial government for failing to complete the algae works, for weak regulation, and for undertaking the privatization process.[45]

Employing the same simple criteria used to assess the level of government compliance in comparison with other cases in Argentina, the Buenos Aires provincial government achieved 0 percent compliance, compared with 50 percent in Mendoza (Table 3.1). As a result of the province's unwillingness to support revenue-enhancing measures, the private utility not only failed to develop a surplus but was actually losing AR$2 million a month by the time it decided to cancel the contract, in October 2001.[46]

Throughout this period of escalating conflict, Azurix adopted a confrontational and legalistic stance vis-à-vis the provincial government, which served to aggravate the situation, similar to the pattern observed in the Mendoza case. The firm's posture stemmed from severe pressures to generate returns from the concession in the short run after its June 1999 public offering, as well as a trust in legal and formal routes of appeal.[47] Azurix not only appealed fines and regulatory rulings that it felt were unjustified,[48] it also defended itself very

[40] See the 2006 ICSID award (cited earlier).

[41] "Escasez de cloro – el agua de red no es segura, dijo Reimers." *La Nueva Provincia*. April 26, 2000; "La responsabilidad es de la Provincia, dijo Linares." *La Nueva Provincia*. April 26, 2000; "Devolvieron 30,000 facturas de agua potable de Bahía Blanca." *La Nación*. May 30, 2000.

[42] "A huevazo limpio contra Azurix SA." *La Nueva Provincia*. April 26, 2000.

[43] "Masiva concurrencia a los surgentes, cunde el malhumor por el tema agua." *La Nueva Provincia*. April 22, 1999.

[44] "La Provincia prometió sancionar a Azurix – no hay que pagar facturas en duda." *La Nueva Provincia*. April 23, 2000; "Ruckauf pidió mayor eficacia y capacitación." *Hoy*. April 27, 1999; "Bahia Blanca sigue sin agua potable." *El Clarín*. April 27, 1999.

[45] "Sigue el debate por el agua." *Hoy*. May 9, 2000; "Domínguez responsabilizó a Duhalde por la baja calidad del agua de Azurix." *Nuevo Día*. May 19, 2000.

[46] Interview with Rodrigo Castillo, Azurix president, June 2006.

[47] McLean and Elkind (2003) and Eichenwald (2005: 272–275).

[48] "El gobernador de Buenos Aires ahora busca un acuerdo con Azurix." *La Nación*. Jan. 19, 2001.

publicly against politicians' allegations, placing full blame for the water quality problems on the provincial government, citing its failure to turn over key pieces of infrastructure.[49] The concessionaire also threatened to take the provincial government into international arbitration well before actually launching proceedings. Rather than developing a constructive negotiating relationship that delivered benefits to both parties, the two sides had become adversaries, embroiled in disputes over contractual responsibilities, especially where any gray area existed in the 200-page contract. This in turn only further disillusioned the public with private sector service provision.

How did the conflictive relationship between the firm and government affect investment rates? The firm focused on emergency-related investments designed to fix immediate problems with the system, spending approximately AR$100 million between July 1999 and October 2001, of which 70 percent was devoted to capital expenditures.[50] According to former directors, much of this went to fixing the newly constructed infrastructure not built to standard by the province's contractors. The firm did not, however, make progress toward long-term objectives. Not only did conflictual relations with the provincial government make the concessionaire wary of investing, but the multilateral and government agencies that usually granted low-interest, long-term loans to private operators in the sector decided that the concession was too risky to fund; the firm and government simply were not getting along well enough.[51]

It quickly became clear to Azurix managers that the situation was getting worse rather than better. Azurix filed its claim with the International Centre for Settlement of Investment Disputes (ICSID) on September 19, 2001, citing contract violations on the part of the provincial government; the province, in turn, rescinded the contract and accused the firm of noncompliance.[52] Parent company Enron's dire financial situation at the time contributed to its quick exit and willingness to take the case into international arbitration.[53] But it is also clear that the company's problems in Buenos Aires began well before Enron's troubles – right from the start in July 1999. Azurix managers' desire for immediate results came into direct conflict with gubernatorial incentives to avoid political

[49] See, for example, "Quiere que el contrato sea analizado en sesiones extraordinarias de la Legislatura." *La Nación*. Jan. 16, 2001.

[50] Ibid. This figure does not include the canon payment of US$438 million. Eduardo Sícaro, former subsecretary for public works and public services, also stressed that the firm did not move beyond investments designed to tackle immediate problems (interview, July 2006).

[51] The 2006 ICSID award describes the refusal of the Overseas Private Investment Corporation (OPIC) to grant a US$100 million loan following a due diligence report that described the concessionaire's difficult political environment (pp. 62–65). According to Azurix, the OPIC refusal made it impossible to obtain loans from other multilateral agencies. The ICSID tribunal ruled in Azurix's favor on this point.

[52] See the 2006 ICSID award, p. 2; "El estado bonaerense se hizo cargo del agua." *La Nación*. March 20, 2002.

[53] Enron's financial problems first became public knowledge in August 2001, and the firm filed for bankruptcy that December. "The Enron Collapse." *The Financial Times*. Feb. 12, 2002.

controversy in a competitive and factionalized political environment. Key provisions of the concession contract became the focus of conflict; the "volatile politics of accountability" described in Chapter 1 took hold, and conflict spread beyond healthy bounds.

The Collapse of the Aguas del Aconquija Contract in Tucumán

Compagnie Générale des Eaux, later renamed Vivendi, submitted the winning (and only) bid for the concession contract in Tucumán province in 1994, alongside a set of junior partners. It was one of the two leading firms in the French water sector and had, since the 1980s, begun to operate a range of local public services within its home market (Barjot 2011: 795; Johnson and Orange 2003: 21). While Générale des Eaux held a small portion of the shares in the Buenos Aires concession, the Tucumán concession represented the company's first entry as a lead investor and technical operator in an Argentine – and for that matter, Latin American – concession contract.[54] Its Tucumán bid represented an effort to gain a foothold and positive reputation in the water sector in developing countries, which it saw as a growing and lucrative market that would contribute to its internationalization efforts.[55] Générale des Eaux's position as a new entrant anxious to prove itself gave the firm an incentive to be somewhat patient in the face of unexpected difficulties. It also meant, however, that the firm had a steep learning curve regarding local political conventions. Its focus on water-related investments in the region also meant it did not have diverse holdings at the local level outside its home market.[56]

Tucumán Province presented an even more challenging political environment for this new entrant than the previous two cases, Mendoza and Buenos Aires. At the time of contract award and immediately thereafter, the province experienced not only high levels of political competition, divided government, and executive turnover but also significant fragmentation within the governing Peronist party (Table 3.A.I, chapter appendix). Although Tucumán governor Ramón Ortega launched the privatization at the beginning of his term, the process bogged down as dissent increased, both within his own Peronist party and between the executive and the legislative branch more generally: whereas eleven of the twenty Peronist legislators had been "orteguistas" in September

[54] Générale des Eaux (later Vivendi and then Veolia) had also previously served as a junior partner in the 1993 Aguascalientes concession in Mexico. In addition, it became one of four consortia holding service contracts in Mexico City in 1994. (Data from PPIAF-World Bank, 2008). Shares were held by the following groups: Générale des Eaux (30% and the technical operator); Benito Roggio, a Córdoba-based conglomerate (22.5%); Grupo Dragados, a Spanish construction firm (22.5%); Supercemento, the construction arm of another Argentine conglomerate (14%); and the union (10%). Both of the Argentine investors pulled out in the first year.

[55] Générale des Eaux. 1994 *Annual Report*, p. 16; 1995 *Annual Report*, p. 3.

[56] Vivendi's efforts to diversify across sectors during the late 1990s focused primarily on telecommunications and entertainment in Europe and North America (Johnson and Orange 2003).

1991, his bloc was reduced to seven by May 1993.[57] In order to obtain legislative approval for the privatization program and model contract, it was necessary to change the contract significantly from the one originally proposed by the province's engineering consultants. The final version included very ambitious and front-loaded investment targets and retained a system of fixed-rate charges for consumers.[58] Meanwhile, the water system was in very bad shape, running an annual operating deficit of over AR$5 million and receiving AR$5–AR$10 million in subsidies per year; very little had been devoted to maintenance and investment following the devolution of services to the province because resources had been diverted from investment to personnel.[59]

The ambitious investment requirements, failure to provide a legal basis for the introduction of water metering, and poor state of the existing company – in addition to the numerous delays during the privatization process and the governor's decision to avoid raising consumer rates prior to privatization – reduced corporate interest in the concession. In the end, only one of the original five interested firms, a consortium led by Générale des Eaux, submitted a bid for the concession in August 1994. To satisfy the bidding requirements, the firm submitted a multiplier to the existing tariff formula; in preceding privatizations, this had generally resulted in a decrease in the average tariff.[60] To the government's dismay, the Générale des Eaux–led consortium proposed a multiplier of 1.941, which implied an almost doubling of the average tariff.[61] The provincial government pushed the company to lower this multiplier in ensuing negotiations. The Ortega administration and the junior partners in the concession, Spanish and Argentine construction companies, resisted lowering the investment requirements, which would have been necessary to lower the tariff further.[62] In the end, the two parties agreed on a 68 percent tariff hike by October 1994.[63] In pushing for a large, upfront rate increase, this foreign investor–led consortium chose a very different strategy than those pursued by domestic consortia under similar circumstances. In Salta Province, as Chapter 4 will show, a domestic investor interested in the

[57] Bloc membership figures from the provincial legislative archive and interviews with provincial legislators.

[58] The 1993 CETI Consulting study, "Análisis y evaluación de la estrategia de inversión," contains two investment scenarios. The government chose the accelerated investment option, which required the firm to reach universal water coverage in six years and universal sewerage coverage in eleven years. For more complete documentation, see Post (2008).

[59] CETI (1993: table 9.1).

[60] The structure of the bidding process was comparable to the Buenos Aires case.

[61] Diario de Sesiones, May 6 and 10, 1996, p. 1153.

[62] Charles-Louis de Maud'huy, vice chairman of Aguas de la Aconquija (interview, September 2006); not-for-attribution interviews in Tucumán.

[63] The final K coefficient (the multiplier) is specified in the final version of the concession contract (May 18, 1995), article 12.1. Including municipal and provincial taxes, the tariff increase would actually be higher. "Privatizaron los servicios de agua potable y cloacas." *La Gaceta*. May 19, 1995.

concession suggested that the government structure the bidding process on the basis of the largest proposed investment program rather than the lowest multiplier on the existing rate. They worried that a rate multiplier would not actually reduce existing consumer rates, given how low they were prior to privatization, and that a large increase at the beginning of the concession would sour public opinion.[64]

Because of the long negotiations between the government and firm before the contract was signed and subsequent delays attributable to other branches of government and the union, the takeover only occurred after the next gubernatorial election, three months before the new governor, Antonio Domingo Bussi of the Fuerza Republicana Party, assumed power.[65] The arrival of a new governor who had actually campaigned against the privatization, the consumer rate hikes almost immediately thereafter, and a subsequent severe water quality problem meant that the provincial administration and firm faced strong incentives to renegotiate the terms of the concession contract so that it would remain politically and financially viable. Following popular demonstrations in outlying cities and then in the capital, the Bussi administration and new legislature were forced to take notice of citizen discontent with the rate hikes.[66] Then, just a few months later in January 1996, manganese contamination in the state-managed reservoir supplying the water system caused the water delivered by the company to take on a brown cast. This "brown water" incident fueled the flames of controversy.[67] Public opinion swung firmly against the concessionaire, Aguas del Aconquija. In the midst of this crisis, the governor threatened to cancel the contract; meanwhile, legislators formed an investigative commission.[68] Water users began to organize a nonpayment campaign that drove payment rates down from 59 percent to 21 percent by December 1997.[69] This popular reaction led the governor to replace the board of directors of the regulatory agency and the provincial ombudsman to encourage the nonpayment of water bills.[70] On the

[64] Not-for-attribution interview, July 2006.

[65] The consortium Aguas de Aconquija finally assumed control of the system on July 22, 1995. "Aumentan las tarifas del agua." *La Gaceta*. July 23, 1995; "El contrato de concesión de DIPOS aún no se firmará." *La Gaceta*. May 5, 1995; "DIPOS, a manos privadas." *La Gaceta*. May 18, 1995; "Se suspendió la entrega de DIPOS." *La Gaceta*. June 1, 1995; "Violento desalojo de DIPOS para concreter su transpaso." *La Gaceta*. June 14, 1995; "La Cámara define si interpela a Dato." *La Gaceta*. June 16, 1995.

[66] Some protests occurred before the July 1995 elections but most were thereafter. Giarracca and Del Pozo (2005); "El gobierno preparaba la intimación al concesionario." *La Gaceta*. June 21, 1995; "Dictámenes en los armarios." *La Gaceta*. July 7, 1995.

[67] The contamination was a long-standing problem. The company apparently did not have an emergency plan in place to deal with the situation, though, when it started.

[68] "Protesta de dos países por un anuncio de Bussi." *La Nación*. Feb. 15, 1996; the commission report is published in the Diario de Sesiones, May 6 and 10, 1996.

[69] Rais et al., p. 26.

[70] Letters from the regulatory agency indicate the board of directors was replaced between January and May of 1996 (DIPOS file, Información Parliamentaria, Tucumán). The provincial ombudsman issued injunctions for refunds for the portion of the tariff meant to go toward a provincial tax (interview, Sergio Diaz-Ricci, former ombudsman, July 2006).

same scale used to rate government compliance in other cases in Table 3.1, the Tucumán government receives a 0/2, or 0 percent. The firm's investment program, meanwhile, never got off the ground – understandable since its relationship with the government started so badly.

The French firm's legal and formal efforts to pressure the new Bussi administration to negotiate a compromise did not bear fruit. (Its Argentine minority partners had pulled out by this time.)[71] Following Bussi's threat to cancel the contract, the firm threatened to seek protection under Argentina's bilateral investment treaty with France. This allowed Générale des Eaux to signal that it was not at fault in the dispute – important given that it was still vying for contracts in the region and anxious to retain World Bank support in other parts of the world. By May 1996, the national government – concerned about its ongoing privatization program – had agreed to facilitate a contract renegotiation.[72] The opposition-controlled legislature, however, did not approve the first revised agreement. The three parties began negotiations once again at the end of 1996, but this time the firm filed its formal complaint against the province with ICSID.[73] This process produced a new agreement that was ultimately accepted by both the governor and the company on April 8, 1997, with the support of the World Bank and the national government.[74] The legislature made seventy changes to the new contract, however, in its version of law 6826, including a 20 percent tariff reduction from that included in the original bill. The company then refused to sign the revised agreement.[75] Once the contract had become this politicized, there was no hope of returning to a constructive negotiating relationship. Even threatening international arbitration and support from international institutions and the national government was not sufficient pressure to get the provincial government to push through controversial measures. In August 1997, the company rescinded the contract, and in September 1997, Governor Bussi reciprocated, faulting the company for deficient service.[76]

Overall, the development of the Tucumán case conforms to theoretical expectations. When intense political hurdles arose, they placed the contractual arrangement under great strain. The main retaliatory measures at the firm's disposal – withholding investment or other items owed to the government, and filing for international arbitration – only tended to exacerbate conflict and made resolution less likely. The following section, which focuses on concessions controlled by domestic firms, will show that such escalation of tensions is not inevitable in the face of intense political hurdles: domestic firms with diverse

[71] The two Argentine conglomerates that participated in the bid found that they had overextended themselves financially and sold their stakes to the majority shareholders.

[72] Informe Tecnico del ENOHSA-Ref: Concesión DIPOS Tucumán, August 16, 1996.

[73] "Negociarán hoy con Aguas del Aconquija." *La Nación*. Jan. 2, 1997.

[74] Aguas de la Aconquija vice chairman de Maud'huy stressed how supportive the World Bank and national government were during negotiations (interview, September 2006).

[75] Artana et al. (1998: 28).

[76] "Bussi rescindió un contrato." *La Nación*. Sept. 19, 1997.

holdings have ways of dealing with such obstacles because of their intuitions regarding the political viability of particular policies, greater patience, and willingness to negotiate through informal channels.

Stepping back, it is clear that all three concessionaires controlled by foreign investors in provinces with moderate to high political hurdles encountered serious difficulties prior to the Argentine crisis, when MNCs possessed leverage because of their access to investment capital. The case narratives presented in the preceding pages highlight the common reasons that contractual relations became mired in conflict. In all three cases, concerns about short-term political survival and political fragmentation made governors either unwilling or unable to follow through with contentious revenue-raising measures included in the original contracts. This prevented concessionaires from improving their finances as originally envisioned. The primary investors in the concessions had few means of pressuring host governments to come to the negotiating table to work on revised contracts that would be both politically and commercially viable. Relatively impatient, willing to entertain only a limited set of outcomes, and with little political intuition regarding how their reactions would be perceived, they resorted to formal and often legalistic retaliatory measures. This tended to heighten tensions rather than move governments and investors toward mutually acceptable accords. Severe and unexpected episodes of water quality problems dealt a mortal blow to already shaky contractual relationships in the cases of Azurix and Tucumán. As a result, the concessions yielded little investment, and in the Azurix and Tucumán cases, simply imploded. The consistency between these "process observations" from each case and theoretical expectations is summarized in Table 3.A.II (chapter appendix).

Importantly, these common patterns emerged in both relatively prosperous provinces, such as Mendoza and Buenos Aires, and comparatively poor provinces, such as Tucumán. They appeared in provinces with high levels of state capacity and checks and balances in the local political system, such as Mendoza, as well as in more patrimonial political contexts, such as Tucumán. Similar tendencies arose when firms could formally appeal regulatory decisions, as in Tucumán, as well as when regulators enjoyed more formal independence because such appeals were prohibited, as in Buenos Aires and Mendoza.[77] Contracts held by consortia led by foreign firms also stumbled regardless of whether the foreign operators had domestic minority partners, as was the case in Mendoza and Tucumán. Variation among these cases correlates with the strength of the political hurdles in the provincial political environment; contractual relations soured more quickly and to a greater extent in Tucumán and Buenos Aires Provinces, as we would expect based on the argument presented in Chapter 1 regarding secondary sources of variation in negotiating outcomes.

Statist ideology also does not account for the failure of these three contracts. In Buenos Aires Province, problems between the concessionaire and the provincial

[77] Legal provisions for repeals from Azpiazu et al. (2008: 124).

government began while the governor who privatized was still in office. Moreover, the next governor also came from the Peronist Party and differed little in ideological disposition from his predecessor. In Tucumán, the Peronist Ortega, a Menem ally, was succeeded by a challenger from the political right; Bussi's actions against the company were driven more by a desire to differentiate himself from his predecessor and distance himself from a failed project than by statism. Finally, in Mendoza, problems surfaced as competitive elections drew closer and before power was turned over to the opposition Radical Party. Political turnover – one of the factors incorporated into the hurdle index used to code the different political environments – and alignment with President Menem exerted a much stronger effect than ideology.

DOMESTIC INVESTORS WITH AND WITHOUT LOCAL HOLDINGS IN HIGH-HURDLE ENVIRONMENTS: THE CORRIENTES CASE

This section compares the respective ability of two sets of investors to work in Corrientes Province, which – like the provinces discussed earlier in this chapter – witnessed tight elections and turnover to a nonaligned governor. The local political party system also broke down on two occasions, prompting federal interventions (Table 3.A.I, chapter appendix). The contract was originally awarded in 1991 to a consortium controlled by a group of Argentine firms without a significant local presence. The consortium managed the concession through 1995, a period of relatively high degrees contention and fragmentation; the provincial hurdle index was 2.42 (Figure 3.1), which ranks Corrientes above the Mendoza and Buenos Aires cases discussed in the previous section. In 1996, the consortium sold their stakes to a group of local investors in an even more challenging political environment; for the 1996–2001 period, the province receives a hurdle score of 3.00, still below Tucumán but well above all of the remaining cases. The section thus examines the performance of the two sets of domestic investors, which varied with respect to whether they possessed diverse local holdings.

Corrientes was the first Argentine province to privatize its water and sanitation services. The government of Ricardo Leconte of the Pacto Autonomista–Liberal, a coalition of provincial parties supporting free market policies, signed a concession contract in 1991 with a consortium of domestic companies, the vast majority based elsewhere in the country and looking for a foothold in the emerging market in privatized services, especially before the Buenos Aires metropolitan area contract was put out to tender.[78] The lead consortium members were domestic investors without significant operations

[78] Shareholders included: Sideco, 52%; Ingenieria Tauro, a Buenos Aires–based engineering and construction firm, 26%; Lockwood S.A., an engineering and equipment company, 6%; Emaco S.A. and Ginsa S.A., Corrientes firms, each with 6%; Thames Water, a British firm, brought on for technical expertise, 2%; union share, 2% (BID 1996: 95; "Fue privatizada O.S. Corrientes." *El Litoral*. April 4, 1991).

in the province. The arrangement proved fragile while these outside investors controlled the concession. The initial consortium, led by the Buenos Aires–based Sideco – a subsidiary of the Macri Group – managed from the outset to reinforce local perceptions regarding its "outsider" status. Employees resented a lack of respect for local customs, such as breaks to drink traditional mate tea, and efforts to make efficiency savings through layoffs only accentuated difficulties with the staff. The firm's relationship with the local water and sanitation union chapter grew so tense by 1995 that the union agitated to have the concessionaire's contract revoked.[79] Sideco also failed to develop strong relations with the political establishment, which prevented finding joint solutions to unexpected political and financial difficulties during the mid-1990s. Although the province granted some rate increases and did not block the firm from installing water meters as was stipulated in the contract,[80] the administration did not contain political reactions (including a judge's ruling) against the service cutoffs provided for under the concession contract as a means of achieving higher payment rates. It also failed to work with the firm to define a common response to higher than expected population growth within the concession area (22 percent between 1991 and 2001), which made it difficult for the firm to meet its coverage goals, and to unexpectedly high drops in consumption following the introduction of water meters required by the contract, which sparked a 24 percent drop in revenue.[81] Overall, government compliance with original contractual provisions can be scored at 62.5 percent (see Table 3.1), somewhat above the levels achieved by governments regulating foreign investors in other high-hurdle provinces.

Discouraged both by their inability to make headway regarding these unexpected problems and the award of a potentially lucrative Buenos Aires concession to a different group of investors, consortia members refused to contribute additional funds after the initial pool of capital constituted as part of the bidding process had been exhausted.[82] Members had assumed that investments would primarily be financed through retained earnings once efficiency savings had been introduced. They did not anticipate injecting large sums or taking on large, long-term loans to fund upfront investments, particularly given the difficulties that had arisen. Facing declining revenues and without a new infusion of capital, the concessionaire did not invest sufficiently during 1994 and 1995 to meet its contractual goals: investment as a fraction of revenues averaged a mere 4 percent during the 1992–1995

[79] Artana et al. (1999: 238).

[80] Artana et al. (1999) report that the regulator granted a 6.04% increase in July 1993 (the original request was for 16.84%) and another 2.65% in November 1993 in response to cost increases. By 1997, 84% percent of residential users were metered, an impressive achievement in comparative terms (ENOHSA-COFES 1999: 100).

[81] Artana et al. (1999: 237). Drop in revenue calculated from sales figures for 1991 and 1995 reported in Artana et al. (1999: 244).

[82] Not-for-attribution interview, 2006.

period.[83] As a result, although the company reportedly met its obligations in terms of coverage expansion for water, it lagged well behind its sewerage access and sewage treatment targets.[84] This investment cutback, of course, did little to help the Buenos Aires–based investors improve the company's relationship with the provincial government.

Between 1994 and 1996, the provincial political environment grew increasingly fractious because of factional struggles within the governing Pacto Autonomista–Liberal coalition (Artana et al. 1999: 236; Behrend 2011: 159). With few other investments at stake in Corrientes Province, Sideco and its partners chose to pull out of what increasingly appeared to be a business with few prospects. Tellingly, a Corrientes-based conglomerate that had joined the original consortium in 1991 with only 6 percent of the shares decided that it could manage the concession – particularly relations with the provincial government – more effectively than Sideco.[85] The Chamas brothers, owners of a local economic group that operated in diverse sectors such as agriculture, construction, real estate, and the media, bought up the shares of the Buenos Aires–based investors during 1995 and 1996.[86]

Between 1996 and 2001, the new owners forged a much more workable relationship with a succession of provincial administrations in an increasingly fractious political environment. As Figure 3.1 indicates, the aggregate level of political hurdles was higher during the 1996–2001 period than during the first half of the decade. This score reflects not only turnover in the governor's mansion but also a breakdown in the provincial political system in 1999: for a six-month period between June and December, the province was literally cut off from the rest of the country by protests against layoffs and poor administration that blockaded streets and bridges; many public services were suspended (Auyero 2005: 251). The province's political system grew so fractious that the federal government felt compelled to intervene, setting up an alternative administration in December 1999 that remained in place until December 2001.

Remarkably, the new local owners managed to work reasonably effectively with a variety of government partners during this challenging period. Patience, a strategy of informal negotiation, and openness to earning returns in related operations rather than in the concession itself convinced government officials to allow the concessionaire to implement important revenue-enhancing measures to cope with problems that had surfaced earlier in the decade. According to company officials, the firm deliberately eschewed a conflictive posture; long-standing social ties and regular interactions between the company's owners

83 Rate calculated as average investment as a fraction of net sales. Investment figures from Aguas de Corrientes and revenue figures from Carvalho (2003: 63).

84 BID (1996: 96).

85 Interview, Pablo Langus, commercial director, Aguas de Corrientes, June 2010.

86 ENOHSA-COFES (1999: 89).

and the political elite made such brinksmanship unappealing.[87] These efforts bore fruit. While the new governor inaugurated in 1997 did not allow the implementation of a discounted tariff for low-income consumers approved by the previous governor at the behest of the firm, the regulatory agency did not block Aguas de Corrientes's household census within the concession area in 1997 – an effort to improve their consumer database and collections efforts.[88] In effect, a system of mutual accommodation developed in which the government and firm were patient with each other: the company did not pay many of the fines levied by the regulatory agency, and the government often did not pay its water bills.[89] The local investor's nonpayment of fines must therefore be viewed in a different light than nonpayment by foreign investors, who were less forgiving of government nonpayment.[90] In addition, the new owners were better positioned than the previous ones to take advantage of synergies with their local operations in other sectors and thereby increase their earnings: projects funded by international loan programs needed to be tendered competitively, but the concessionaire could contract with the group's construction and service companies for projects funded out of tariff revenues. It routinely contracted with Ginsa, the group's construction arm, for infrastructure projects and with Urbatec, the group's services firm, for maintenance functions.[91] Table 3.1 shows compliance for Chamas's period of ownership of the Corrientes concession at 75 percent, a modest improvement over the early 1990s that is impressive given the increasingly challenging political climate within which they were working.

With revenues improving and a long-term commitment to the jurisdiction, the firm invested more heavily than its predecessor, devoting approximately 13 percent of revenues during the 1996–2000 period, compared with the 4 percent spent by the previous owners during the 1992–1995 period.[92] The concessionaire even chose to take out a small (US$6.7 million) long-term loan from the Inter-American Development Bank to finance system improvements. Between 1991 and 2001, coverage rates rose from 66 percent to 90 percent in water and 31 percent to 68 percent in sewerage, with the majority of this investment occurring under the new owners.[93] The company managed to stay in the black

[87] As one company representative stressed, there are limits to how far one can push when one's children attend school with major figures in the provincial administration (not-for-attribution interview, June 2010).

[88] ENOHSA-COFES (1999: 93–97).

[89] After 1995, the vast majority of fines were appealed and not paid (ASOC, the regulator). ENOHSA-COFES (1999: 98) reports that 44% of government users did not pay their bills within a year.

[90] For MNCs, nonpayment of fines was typically employed as a retaliatory strategy or tit-for-tat measure.

[91] Not-for-attribution interview with company representative, August 2006.

[92] Calculated by author from data from Aguas de Corrientes.

[93] Figures from ASOC, the regulator. Annual data is not available, although data from 1996 suggests that the concessionaire had only achieved 73% coverage in water and 42% coverage in sewerage before the ownership transfer (Artana et al. 1999: 244).

and retain the improved investment rates described earlier until the 2001–2002 economic crisis.[94] While the sector continued to be characterized by political contention, the situation never grew so volatile as to threaten either the public or the private sector's willingness to continue the arrangement, as had occurred with the previous consortia of Buenos Aires–based investors.

Overall, this comparison between the experiences of domestic investors with and without diverse holdings in the province illustrates their differential ability to conduct the sort of informal negotiations necessary to keep concession contracts viable in politically contentious environments – even during periods with high investor leverage. The close alignment between the experiences of the two Corrientes investors and theoretical expectations is summarized in Table 3.A.II (chapter appendix). We clearly cannot attribute the dramatic change in the concession's fate to factors other than ownership: the two groups of investors faced the same regulatory institutions, provincial demographics, and system infrastructure. In neither case did members of President Menem's party – who would be more disposed to support neoliberal reforms – control the provincial administration. Meanwhile, the political environment was, if anything, more difficult for the second set of investors. At the same time, it is important that the behavior of domestic investors in the Corrientes concession differed from that of foreign investors in other concessions discussed in this chapter: Sideco and its partners did not engage in legalistic negotiating tactics as did its peers in the provinces of Mendoza, Buenos Aires, and Tucumán.

CONCLUSION

This chapter has shown the striking differences in the contractual relationships held by different types of investors in challenging provincial political environments prior to the Argentine crisis. The overall patterns observed in these cases are summarized in Table 3.A.II (chapter appendix). All three foreign-held contracts faltered, and the two located in a more contentious political environment imploded and were cancelled within three years. The legalistic and formal bargaining tactics available to these firms proved ineffectual in pressuring local administrations to follow through with contractual commitments designed to improve concessionaire revenue streams, and the firms' lack of political intuition meant that they failed to anticipate politically consequential public reactions to their actions. Their subsequent reluctance to invest only worsened their relationship with host governments. This made it impossible to reach accords that would have made their contracts more politically and economically viable. A set of domestic investors with few local holdings in the similarly fractious province of Corrientes ran into similar, although not as extreme, difficulties. Unable to reach agreements with the provincial administration regarding unanticipated problems that surfaced during the concession's

[94] Company officials stressed that the concessionaire was able to maintain its financial equilibrium during this period.

first years, they decided to pull out. The local investors who took over managed to work much more effectively with the provincial administration, even as the local political environment grew more fractious. Their higher levels of patience and moderation, sensitivity to the political resonance of particular policies, and ability to accrue financial gains in other sectors of the local economy all contributed to their ability to keep their relationship with the changing heads of the local administration on track. As a result, service coverage improved dramatically and the concession actually managed to turn a profit. This striking variation in contract trajectories in contentious political environments appears not to stem from other factors. Ideology, institutional factors such as checks and balances and formal regulatory independence, and provincial state capacity do not explain differences between the cases.

CHAPTER APPENDIX

Political Hurdle Index

This additive index captures the presence (or absence) of six factors that shorten host government time horizons, contribute to transaction costs, or otherwise lead governments to be less supportive of private service providers at a given point in time:

1. Electoral competition
2. Provincial party system breakdown
3. Divided government
4. Number of times governor has changed
5. Privatizing governor has left power
6. Statist policy approach by governor

Scores are calculated at the provincial level for each year privatization contracts were in place between 1991 and 2009. Pre-crisis and post-crisis averages are calculated for each province in order to provide an overall characterization of the political context in which each contract unfolded.[95] Index components, as well as annual scores by province, are presented by year for high-hurdle provinces for the pre-crisis period in Table 3.A.I. The base data set used to construct this table and the index is included in the book's online appendix.

Details

The index incorporates two factors that tend to *shorten politician time horizons*: electoral competition and local party system breakdown. Electoral competition is operationalized as the margin of victory of the incumbent governor or

[95] One might worry about the possibility that conflicts over a contract give rise to higher levels of political competition, divided government, or other components of the political hurdle index. As the case studies illustrate, however, the causal chain tended not to work in this direction.

incumbent political party in either gubernatorial or legislative contests – whichever was more competitive. It is measured for years in which a gubernatorial or provincial legislative election occurred. For gubernatorial contests, the score is based on the margin of victory of the incumbent (or the incumbent's party). For legislative elections, the score is based on the margin of victory of the ruling party. Scores for the Aguas Argentinas contract are based on electoral margins for the presidency and, for legislators, for Buenos Aires's representation in the national congress; this reflects the fact that the concession was granted by the national government, but most of the households served lived in the province rather than the capital district. (Variable: MaxElecComp/3)

1. 0 if no election
2. 0.33 if incumbent party won by more than 10 percent
3. 0.66 if incumbent party won by 5 percent–10 percent
4. 1 if incumbent won by less than 5 percent (or lost)

Local party system breakdown can also shorten the time horizon of provincial administrations, as political uncertainty increases during such periods. For this reason, the index also includes a component capturing whether the federal government intervened in – that is, temporarily took control of – the provincial administration, an action that typically only occurs following a major breakdown in the party system and descent into political instability. (Variable: Fed_Intervention) (*Source*: towsa.com/andy/totalpais/)

The index also incorporates two indicators of the *level of transaction costs* in a given jurisdiction: a score indicating whether the provincial government was divided, and a score capturing the lingering effect of political turnover in the executive branch, which forces both parties to restart negotiations. The divided government component is a 0/1 indicator that reflects whether at least one chamber in the provincial legislature is controlled by the opposition. If the governor is from a different faction of the Partido Justicialista (PJ) than the majority in the legislature, the year is coded as *not* possessing divided government (0). I adopt this strategy because it is difficult to determine the degree of unity or division within PJ in a particular province in a particular year for each province (Variable: Divided_Gov). The transaction costs from turnover score take on a positive value each time a new governor comes to power and decrease at a flat rate over the following four years to reflect the necessity of restarting regulatory negotiations with each new occupant of the governor's mansion. Effects are largest during the first year of a new administration (1) and decline at a steady rate of 0.25 annually. (Scores therefore are 1, 0.75, 0.5, 0.25, or 0.) No costs are registered for governors who originally privatize (Variable: Effect_Turnover).

Finally, the index incorporates two additional political factors that affect governors' *reputational and ideological incentives to support privatized service providers*. Governors who did not privatize will have lower reputational incentives to support private providers. For this reason, the index codes instances in which power passes to a governor who did not privatize (Variable: Gov_Did_Not_Priv, 0/1, score of 1 when the administration turns over to a governor who did not privatize). This score remains present throughout the course of the new administration. Second, the index incorporates a component designed to capture whether governors have an incentive to implement statist policies. In Argentina, the best way to determine this is to examine patterns of political alignment with the national government. Provincial governors in Argentina tend not to assume strong ideological positions, as political competition at the local level tends not to be programmatic. Presidential administrations, however, have often espoused neoliberal or statist policies. Argentine presidents can greatly influence the policy decisions of governors who seek fiscal resources from the federal government or career advancement within the president's political party (Jones et al. 2000; Levitsky 2003). The Menem government, for instance, very clearly pursued a neoliberal policy platform promoting privatization. Allied governors felt strong political pressure to privatize and to provide supportive policy environments for privatized firms. Subsequent presidents, however, were more ambivalent regarding private sector service provision.[96] For this reason, the alignment component of the political hurdle index simply captures whether governors were aligned with Menem during the years he was in power. When the governor was a member of the PJ, score = 0. If the governor was from an opposition party, score = 1 – except if the governor privatized him- or herself. (In such cases, an opposition governor is unlikely to mobilize public opinion against a policy he or she instituted.) After the Menem period, the effect of alignment becomes much more ambiguous, so no score is coded for alignment after 1999 (*source for partisanship of governor*: towsa.com/andy/totalpais/) (Variable: Not_Aligned_Menem_NotPrivatizer).

Formula for index: (Max(Legislative, Gubernatorial Competition))/3 + Divided government + Governor did not privatize + Governor not allied with Menem and not privatizer (for 1999 and earlier) + Federal intervention + Effect of turnover score (1 – 0.25 * years since turnover)

These components are added to create an annual score for each contract. Period averages are then constructed for the pre-crisis period (through 2001) and the post-crisis period (2002–2009). When two sets of investors are in control during either the pre- or post-crisis period, averages for investor-specific intervals are calculated as well.

[96] Although the Kirchners froze consumer rates for services regulated at the national level and enacted a few prominent nationalizations, they have been much more hands-off regarding provincial level policies, often implicitly supporting private providers in provinces controlled by allies by transferring large sums that could be used for infrastructure projects that in effect subsidize private-service providers. Because of the Kirchners' ambivalence, alignment with the national government cannot be taken as a proxy for statist policies during their administration.

TABLE 3.A.1. *Political Hurdle Index Components for Pre-Crisis Period (High-Hurdle Provinces)*

Year	*Competition for governor*	*Competition for legislature*	*Divided government*	*Governor did not privatize*	*Governor not allied with Menem*	*Federal intervention*	*Hurdle index*
Mendoza							
1998	–	–	Divided				1
1999	High (3)	High (3)					1
2000	–	–		Not privatizer	Not applicable		2
2001	–	High (3)	Divided	Not privatizer	Not applicable		3.75
Buenos Aires Province (Azurix)							
1999	Medium (2)	Medium (2)					1.67
2000	–	–	Divided	Not privatizer	Not applicable		3
2001	–	Low (1)	Divided	Not privatizer	Not applicable		2.08
Corrientes 1991–1995							
1991	Medium (2)	Low (1)					0.67
1992	–	–		Not privatizer		Intervention	3
1993	Low (1)	Low (1)		Not privatizer			2.33
1994	–	–		Not privatizer	Unaligned		3
1995	–	Low (1)		Not privatizer	Unaligned		3.08
Corrientes 1996–2001							
1996	–	–		Not privatizer	Unaligned		2.5
1997	High (3)	High (3)		Not privatizer	Unaligned		3.25
1998	–	–		Not privatizer	Unaligned		3
1999	–	High (3)		Not privatizer		Intervention	4
2000	–	–		Not privatizer	Not applicable		2
2001	High (3)	Medium (2)		Not privatizer	Not applicable		2.75
Tucumán							
1995	High (3)	Medium (2)	Divided				2
1996	–	–	Divided	Not privatizer	Unaligned		4
1997	–	–	Divided	Not privatizer	Unaligned		3.75

Formula for index: Max(legislative, gubernatorial competition)/3 + Divided government + Governor did not privatize + Governor not allied with Menem and not privatizer (for 1999 and earlier) + Federal intervention + Effect of turnover score (1–0.25*years since turnover for 4 years following turnover)

TABLE 3.A.II. *Pre-Crisis Expectations and Findings in Provinces with High Political Hurdles*

	Investor portfolio structure					
	Foreign		***Domestic* without *diverse local holdings***		***Domestic* with *diverse local holdings***	
	Expect	***Observe***	***Expect***	***Observe***	***Expect***	***Observe***
Contractual outcomes						
Investor exit	High	Mendoza: No Azurix: Yes Tucumán: Yes	Medium	Corrientes I: Yes	Low	Corrientes II: No
Contract renegotiation (if warranted)	Low	Tucumán: No	Medium	Not applicable	High	Not applicable
Indicators of health of the negotiating process						
Government supports basic revenue-raising elements of contract	Low	Mendoza: Medium Azurix: Low Tucumán: Low	Medium	Corrientes I: Medium	High	Corrientes II: High
Concessionaire finances stabilize	Low	Mendoza: Medium Azurix: Low Tucumán: Low	Medium	Corrientes I: Low	High	Corrientes II: High
Firm employs legalistic retaliatory measures	High	Mendoza: Medium Azurix: High Tucumán: High	Medium	Corrientes I: Low	Low	Corrientes II: Low

TABLE 3.A.II. (*cont.*)

	Investor portfolio structure					
	Foreign		*Domestic* without *diverse local holdings*		*Domestic* with *diverse local holdings*	
	Expect	*Observe*	*Expect*	*Observe*	*Expect*	*Observe*
Investment as fraction of revenues	Medium (Low in long run)	Mendoza: Medium Azurix: Low Tucumán: Low	Low	Corrientes I: Low	Medium	Corrientes II: Medium
Improvement in service coverage and quality	Medium (Low in long run)	Mendoza: Medium Azurix: Low Tucumán: Low	Low	Corrientes I: Low-Medium	Medium	Corrientes II: Medium

4

Smoother Sailing for All Investors in Less Competitive Provinces

This chapter considers contracts located in provinces characterized by low or moderate levels of political hurdles during the pre-crisis period, comparing the respective ability of different types of investors to operate in these relatively propitious contexts. Given low levels of political competition and unified government, we would expect heads of governments to negotiate without major concerns about their immediate political survival. They had the political maneuvering room to allow firms to implement cost-recovery measures, which would in turn encourage concessionaires to invest. A demonstrated willingness to invest would in turn increase firm leverage during negotiations with host governments regarding common responses to unexpected difficulties.

Among this cluster of cases, then, we would expect all types of investors to have been able to maintain good working relationships with host governments that allowed for coordinated responses to unexpected problems, sustained rates of investment, and reasonable levels of profitability. This would have led to fewer instances of investor exit or contract cancellation because firms and host governments had the political leeway to negotiate regarding the few issues that did arise. These expectations regarding rates of investor exit in periods of high investor leverage and low to moderate political hurdles are summarized in Table 4.A.I (chapter appendix).

While we would expect all three types of investors to have been able to maintain smooth negotiating relationships with host governments when operating in low- to moderate-hurdle provinces, we would anticipate important differences in how negotiations unfolded. Investors' financing strategies, after all, affect their leverage with political authorities. As the analytic framework in Chapter 2 stresses, multinationals (MNCs) tend to be much more willing to take on long-term loans to finance upfront investment in infrastructure projects, especially in reassuring political contexts. This allows them to offer governments attractive projects and service improvements within a relatively short time frame.[1] Domestic investors from the developing world, however, are much more likely to finance investments out of retained earnings from their concessions and, as a result, to invest at lower rates at the outset. These differences in financing strategies give foreign investors additional leverage in the early years of a contract in low-hurdle political environments. As summarized in Table 4.A.I (chapter appendix), this leads us to expect host governments to be both particularly willing to comply with important commercial measures included in original contracts when regulating foreign companies and to be more likely to entertain firm requests for contract renegotiations. When states have strong incentives to comply with commercial measures, foreign investors will be far less likely to employ the sorts of legalistic retaliatory measures observed in Chapter 3; we should observe few such behaviors for all types of investors. Finally, we would expect to observe reasonable rates of investment for all types of firms in low- to moderate-hurdle environments. Foreign firms should exhibit particularly high rates during the first years of their contracts. The Tucumán, Buenos Aires (Azurix), and Mendoza cases described in Chapter 3, however, are a reminder that these advantages tend not to carry over to more contentious political settings.

Although domestic firms would be unwilling to invest as heavily up front in low- to moderate-hurdle political environments as MNCs, we would still expect them to maintain smooth relationships with host governments. We would, however, expect domestic investors with diverse local holdings to be somewhat more successful than domestic investors in securing governmental compliance with contractual provisions due to their ongoing relationships with elected officials across a number of policy areas, and as a result to invest more heavily.

FOREIGN-LED CONTRACTS IN PROVINCES WITH LOW TO MODERATE POLITICAL HURDLES

This section examines the evolution of the four concession contracts majority controlled by foreign investors that were located in less contentious political settings prior to the crisis: the Buenos Aires metropolitan area (regulated by a tripartite agency with directors from the national, province, and city governments) and the provinces of Santa Fe, Córdoba, and Misiones. As the contracts were regulated by different agencies – whose directors were appointed by

[1] Three factors contributed to this willingness to front-load investment. First, concession contracts in Argentina typically front-loaded investment obligations. Second, investing significantly up front in network expansion and improvement lets a concessionaire enlarge its customer base and improve operational efficiency earlier in the contract, thereby allowing it to enjoy a larger income stream and lower cost structure over a longer period. Third, foreign firms are generally more willing to assume exchange rate risk because of their ability to manage risk through cross-country diversification and complex financial instruments.

different governments – related political decisions should be viewed as more independent of one another than if the central government monitored all contracts. In contrast to the foreign-owned contracts discussed in Chapter 3, however, one investor controlled three of the four contracts. This section first considers French water and sanitation specialist Suez's investments, and then turns to the case of Misiones. These concessions, as we would expect, all evolved smoothly and yielded significant investments.

Foreign Investor Suez's Portfolio in Buenos Aires, Santa Fe, and Córdoba

The French firm Lyonnaise des Eaux (hereafter Suez, its name as of 1997) secured three water and sanitation concession contracts in Argentina during the 1990s: for the Buenos Aires metropolitan area (1993), Santa Fe Province (1995), and the city of Córdoba (1997). One of two main investors in the French water market for more than a century, the firm focused on water, communications, energy, and environmental services in Europe.[2] Its international expansion efforts focused on water and sanitation concession contracts, assuming they would bring stable returns from consumer fees and additional profits by granting construction and engineering contracts to its own specialist firms.[3] The Argentine market represented an opportunity to secure several high-profile contracts within what was seen as an expanding international market. The economic and political context was viewed as promising, anchored by Menem's reform program, an exchange rate peg to the U.S. dollar, and a new bilateral investment treaty between Argentina and France.[4]

Suez first secured a thirty-year concession contract for the Buenos Aires metropolitan area, which was still managed by Obras Sanitarias de la Nación (OSN), the national water utility.[5] Given the size and affluence of the concession area, competition for the contract was fierce; four consortia finally submitted bids.[6] Interested domestic firms joined consortia with foreign firms as junior partners because they were aware they would not be able to compete on the basis

[2] The firm began scaling back cyclical activities, such as construction, in the 1980s (Fridenson 2007: 73; Barjot 2011: 796). Lyonnaise des Eaux's CEO, Jerome Monod, articulated the rationale for his firm's international expansion efforts and their focus on water and waste in developing countries, in a lengthy interview with *The Wall Street Transcript*, published on June 19, 1995. Following its 1997 merger with Suez, the firm added electricity to its international expansion push.

[3] Lyonnaise des Eaux possessed a specialist water and sanitation construction firm, Dúmez, and its sanitation engineering consultancy, Degremont. These related companies did not already possess a strong presence at the time of market entry in Argentina. Contracting directly with related companies was only possible for projects financed from user rates rather than those financed by loans from international financial institutions, which required competitive tendering.

[4] Interview, Jean-Bernard Lemire, former general manager, Aguas Argentinas, May 2007. See also the *Wall Street Transcript* interview with Monod (note 2, this chapter).

[5] "Aguas Argentinas facturó rebajas del 14 al 25%." *La Nación*. May 31, 1993.

[6] At the time of contract award, the company delivered water to approximately 5.6 million people (see *Aguas Argentinas 1993–2004*, a compilation of Aguas Argentinas, annual report data, p. 2).

of their previous experience in the sector or asset base – factors stressed in the formal legal prequalification criteria for contract award.[7] Suez won the contract when it proposed the largest reduction to existing consumer rates. Although the city, province, and nation were each entitled to appoint directors to the board of the regulatory agency, Ente Tripartito de Obras y Servicios Sanitarios (ETOSS), the national government – as the grantor of the contract – exercised disproportionate influence over regulatory policy. The contract unfolded in a relatively calm political context during its first years that, for the most part, did not force elected officials to focus on short-run concerns about threats to their power. President Menem, who had spearheaded the country's privatization program, remained in power for most of the pre-crisis period and had strong reputational incentives to ensure that private sector service provision succeeded. (In fact, the political hurdle score for the post-crisis period was 1.08 [Figure 3.1], the lowest for all foreign-led contracts.)

Starting in late 1993, President Menem's hold on power was secure enough for his administration to allow the firm to follow through with revenue-enhancing measures included in the contract.[8] Aguas Argentinas, the concessionaire, conducted an aerial photography survey, which provided data for updating consumer databases and the property descriptions used as proxies for household income when calculating residential tariffs. This project generated approximately 70 percent of the revenue growth achieved during the first years.[9] The firm also moved forward with a program to gradually regularize clandestine connections without major incident. In addition, Aguas Argentinas recategorized most small offices and shops from domestic to commercial users, which could be charged rates 90 percent higher according to the contract. Reassured by the supportive policy environment, the firm invested heavily. It spent AR$217 million annually between 1994 and 1996 compared with $81.3 million invested by the former state company on

7 As the technical operator and lead investor, Suez took the lead in decision making regarding investment and regulatory compliance. This tendency increased over time, as Suez bought a greater portion of the concession shares. Argentine firms Sociedad Comercial del Plata S.A. and Meller S.A. held 20.7% and 10.8% of the concessionaire shares at the outset; these local partners sold their shares to Suez and Suez-owned Aguas de Barcelona in 1996 and 1997. By 1998, Suez owned 60% of the shares and by 2000, 64% of the shares (*Aguas Argentinas: 1993–2004*).

8 In November 1993, Menem concluded a pact with the opposition that ensured passage of a constitutional amendment allowing reelection to the presidency, thereby thwarting efforts by a Peronist rival, Governor Eduardo Duhalde of the province of Buenos Aires, to become the Peronist candidate in the 1995 elections. Jean-Bernard Lemire, former general manager, Aguas Argentinas, stressed that the firm was allowed to follow through with most revenue-enhancing measures (interview, May 2007). See also Aguas Argentinas annual reports to ETOSS.

9 Jean-Bernard Lemire, then-finance director of Aguas Argentinas, estimated that the AR$15–AR $20 million aerial survey and subsequent property database updates provided the main source of revenue growth during the first years of the concession (interview, May 2007). See also year-two annual report to ETOSS, cuerpo 1, pp. 43–45. For further documentation on commercialization policies implemented by Aguas Argentinas, see Post (2008).

average between 1981 and 1990.[10] To do this, the concessionaire relied on external loans, primarily from multilateral institutions such as the World Bank.[11]

The firm's willingness not only to fulfill existing investment obligations but also assume additional commitments allowed it to secure changes to the concession contract itself that were desirable for both parties. In 1994, Aguas Argentinas was granted a 13.5 percent rate increase in a set of decisions that also imposed new and accelerated investment commitments: the firm agreed to accelerate its program to remove nitrate-contaminated wells from circulation, move up improvements in one of the main water treatment plants so as to extend water service to an additional 300,000 residents during the first five years, and undertake a slum-upgrading program in the capital district.[12] This pattern continued even as the political environment became more contentious in the mid- to late 1990s. In 1997, the national minister for natural resources and sustainable development concluded contract renegotiations that replaced a controversial charge designed to finance network connections for new users with a flat-rate "infrastructure charge" for all users and assigned the firm additional investments in a downtown luxury development and a major new environmental program (Plan de Saneamiento Integral).[13] This deal made sense politically for Menem, whose Peronist Party depended more heavily on votes from lower-income residents on the urban fringe – those paying the infrastructure connection charge before its repeal – than on middle-class, central-city residents.

The national government not only complied with the vast majority of the revenue-raising measures provided for in the original contract but also collaborated with Suez to develop mutually acceptable solutions to new problems that arose, such as the controversy surrounding connection fees. In comparison with the governments regulating foreign-led contracts in high-hurdle environments described in the Chapter 3, the national government achieved an incredibly high level of compliance with its obligations; Table 4.1 shows a compliance rate of 93 percent, compared with the 0–50 percent rates achieved in Tucumán, Buenos Aires Province, and Mendoza.

[10] Figures for average investment levels for Aguas Argentinas are calculated from company balance sheets; amounts are in historic pesos. Figures for investments made by OSN, the former state operator, are from Ordoqui Urcelay (2006: 10), which reports data from the Sindicatura General de Empresas Públicas (SIGEN). Figures from SIGEN are quoted in 1993 pesos. Between 1992 and 2001, the peso was pegged to the U.S. dollar at a one-to-one exchange rate. Henceforth, the two currencies will be used interchangeably for this period, unless otherwise noted.

[11] The concession's debt grew from AR$59 million pesos in 1993 to AR$687 million in 2001. The size of the investment program over that period was AR$1.7 billion (current pesos). Of the AR $687 million debt held in 2001, 89% represented long-term loans with international institutions and banks (loan data from Aguas Argentinas annual reports).

[12] ETOSS resolution 81/94. For more detail, see Post (2008).

[13] Decree 149/97 opened the contract negotiation, and the new accord (Acta Acuerdo) was approved via decree 1167/97 in November 1997. For more detail, see Post (2008).

TABLE 4.1. *Government Contract Compliance for Pre-Crisis Period (Low- to Moderate-Hurdle Provinces)*

	Investor portfolio structure				
	Foreign investor			**Domestic investor without *diverse local holdings***	***Concession controlled by joint venture (domestic investors* with and without *diverse local holdings)***
	Aguas Argentinas* *(1993–2001)* *(2.8/3 = 93%)	***Santa Fe* *(1995–2001)* *(3/5 = 60%)***	***Misiones* *(1999–2001)* *(2.75/3 = 92%)***	***Formosa* *(1995–2001)* *(2/4 = 50%)***	***Salta (1998–2001)* *(2/4 = 50%)***
Allowing implementation of originally programmed tariff hikes, if scheduled	None scheduled	0.5 (Year 1 increase of 4% blocked, not instituted pre-crisis; year 2 increase finally instituted in 2000)	Not applicable (None scheduled)	Not applicable (None scheduled)	0 (Blocked 20% increase originally scheduled in contract for July, 1999 until 2002)
Allowing updates to consumer databases, regularization of clandestine connections as specified in contract	0.8 (Only exception is ETOSS refusal to recategorize offices smaller than 100 square meters)	1	1	1	1 (Consumer database updates, however, did not begin in earnest until 2001)

Not blocking efforts to enforce payment	1 (When collection of connection fees was controversial, 1997 contract renegotiation replaced them with the surcharge for all customers)	0.5 (Service cutoffs, first instituted in October 1997, blocked following judicial order in November 1997)	1	1 (Exception is the 2000–2002 period, during which a law preventing service cutoffs was in effect)	0.5 (Province and firm both agreed to terminate the collection of historic debt)
Paying promised subsidies or contributions specified in contract, if applicable	None required	1	0.75 (Some delays on part of national government due to turnover)	0 (Investment contributions delayed)	0.5 (Subsidies paid, although government pushed company to assume small towns on accelerated schedule)
Following through with inflation adjustments included in contract	1 (Tariff increases in 1994, 1997, 2001, outpacing inflation. Changes tied to new investment obligations.)[a]	0 (Second contract renegotiation was approved by governor but was never ratified)	Not applicable	0 (Requests refused)	Not applicable (No requests before crisis other than for original 20% increase)

[a] Lentini (2004) tracks the relationship between tariff increases and changes in the consumer price index between 1993 and 2003.

The government's willingness during the first years of the concession to allow implementation of key revenue-enhancing measures included in the contract allowed Aguas Argentinas to gradually improve its finances. Returns on sales increased from –15 percent in the first year of the concession, ranging between 9 and 17 percent for the remainder of the pre-crisis period.[14] Returns on equity started at –24 percent and then ranged between 13 and 29 percent. The firm, in other words, was earning a very generous rate of return, especially given that these figures do not include the management fees for which Suez billed the concession or any potential gains from contracts with related companies, such as Suez's specialist sanitary engineering consultancy firms.[15] It must be stressed, however, that most earnings were retained rather than paid out as dividends to shareholders, which helped the concessionaire accumulate sufficient capital to borrow in order to fund investment. Enjoying such a supportive relationship with the state, Suez felt it unnecessary to use legalistic measures employed by international firms working in the more contentious political environment described in Chapter 3. While the foreign investors in Mendoza, Tucumán, and Buenos Aires Province all employed legalistic retaliation strategies frequently (Table 3.A.I, chapter appendix), Aguas Argentinas did not.

This supportive political environment encouraged Aguas Argentinas to channel retained earnings toward investment rather than dividends: it invested sums amounting to 59 percent of revenues during the 1993–1997 period and 31 percent of revenues during the 1998–2001 period, a high rate in comparative context.[16] Between 1993 and 2001, the concessionaire invested \$1.7 billion pesos and increased water coverage from 5.6 to 7.8 million residents and sewerage coverage from 4.5 to 5.9 million residents.[17] Meanwhile, water production and treatment capacity increased substantially, and water quality improved dramatically.[18] According to regulatory agency estimates, for the 1993–1998 period, this amounted to meeting approximately 58 percent of the firm's original contractual obligations.[19] In other words, Aguas Argentinas invested significantly, although not in line with its original contract or the revised commitments adopted under the 1994 and 1997 negotiations.

[14] See *Aguas Argentinas 1993–2004*.

[15] The percentage of Aguas Argentinas investment executed by related companies before the crisis ranged between 6.5% in 2001 and 43.1% in 1995 (see *Aguas Argentinas 1993–2004*, p. 26).

[16] The average annual investment in the first period was AR\$203 million. Calculations by author from balance sheets of Aguas Argentinas.

[17] Data from Aguas Argentinas annual reports 1993–2004.

[18] Water production reportedly increased by 66% between 1994 and 2001, and the percentage of quality samples exhibiting turbidity declined from 65% to 4%, the percentage with abnormal PH levels from 96% to 3%, and the percentage with inadmissible levels of chlorine from 28% to 1%. (Data from *Aguas Argentinas 1993–2004*, pp. 44–45). Less progress was made in improving leakage from the system, unaccounted water accounting for 36% of the flow in 1993 and 32% in 2001; also, very little progress was made on improving levels of sewage treatment.

[19] ETOSS. 2003. *Informe Sobre El Grado de Cumplimiento Alcanzado por el Contrato de Concesión de Aguas Argentinas S.A.* Nota UNIREN No. 73.

Suez's positive experience with Aguas Argentinas led it to bid for, and invest heavily in, two additional concessions in the relatively affluent provinces of Santa Fe (1995) and Córdoba (1997).[20] Of its three concessions, Aguas Argentinas was by far the largest and most lucrative.[21] In both Santa Fe and Córdoba, the privatizing governor left office quickly after Suez assumed control. There were far fewer political hurdles however, than in the provinces treated in the previous chapter.[22]

The Santa Fe contract was the more difficult of the two. Suez had bid aggressively, proposing a 4 percent rate reduction at the time of entry, which competitors argued was disingenuous.[23] Suez found it difficult to stabilize the concessionaire's finances when Governor Carlos Reutemann was succeeded by Jorge Obeid in December 1995, immediately after the privatization. Under the new governor, the regulator denied the firm a 4 percent tariff increase scheduled in the contract as an award for meeting its first-year obligations, thereby going back on an unofficial agreement between the firm and the previous administration to substitute emergency investments for those specified in the contract for year one.[24] Although the regulator did not block consumer database or property valuation updates and the governor concluded a contract renegotiation replacing high connection fees for new users with a 13.85 percent rate increase for all users, a judge blocked service cutoffs for nonpayment provided for under the contract.[25] The legislature also failed to ratify a second renegotiation agreement.[26] Using the comparative scheme to code levels of government compliance with its contractual commitments, the government achieved a 60 percent rate of compliance with its original and assumed commitments, far worse than that achieved in Buenos Aires (Table 4.1). This contributed to significant annual losses, which persisted until 2001.[27]

[20] Three consortia of international and domestic investors bid for the Santa Fe contract (Roitman and Ferro 2003). In 1992, the provincial GDP per capita was $5,912 in Córdoba and $6,367 in Santa Fe (in historic pesos).

[21] Billing figures from ENOHSA-COFES (1999).

[22] Referring back to Figure 3.1, we see that Santa Fe received an average pre-crisis political hurdle score of 1.70, whereas Córdoba received a score of 1.52. Table 4.A.II (appendix) displays the components of the measure.

[23] A consortium led by Saur filed a legal complaint regarding the Suez bid, arguing that it would be impossible to operate the service with such a tariff, given the cyclical nature of the Argentine economy. "Dipos: Mosset Iturraspe dio detalles de la impugnación." *El Litoral*. July 21, 1995.

[24] Bidding conditions (Pliego de Bases y Condiciones, appendix IX) and "Cómo evolucionarán las tarifas de aguas." *El Litoral*. April 1, 1999; not-for-attribution interviews, July 2006.

[25] ENOHSA-COFES (1999: 144). Roitman and Ferro (2003) describe technical aspects of the renegotiation, which is similar to the first renegotiation of the Aguas Argentinas contract.

[26] Roitman and Ferro (2003: 23).

[27] Return on sales was −124% in 1996, −65% in 1997, −12% in 1998, −26% in 1999, and −15% in 2000. Ratios calculated by author using data from Aguas Provinciales de Santa Fe.

Concerned about maintaining its reputation for service quality and a good relationship with the national government – which held the Aguas Argentinas contract – the concessionaire invested heavily despite these difficulties.[28] Investments as a portion of revenues averaged 70 percent between 1996 and 1999.[29] The original bid estimated the total cost of the thirty-year investment program to be roughly AR$40 million a year if distributed equally,[30] but the concessionaire invested AR$42.5 million a year (on average) between 1996 and 2001. This was funded via long-term, dollar-denominated loans with multilateral banks, implying that Suez and other shareholders were planning to stay in the market.[31] Meanwhile, the concessionaire refrained from utilizing the sorts of legalistic retaliatory strategies employed by foreign firms operating in somewhat more contentious political environments, such as Mendoza, Tucumán, and Buenos Aires Province, instead focusing on contract negotiations with the executive branch.

Suez's concession in the province of Córdoba, secured in 1997, presented fewer problems.[32] Power turned over to a new governor soon after privatization as well, but the newcomer, Peronist José Manuel de la Sota, was aligned with outgoing President Carlos Menem, and hence predisposed to support privatization policies. Encouraged by the supportive local political environment and concerned about maintaining the health of its overall investment portfolio in the country, Suez devoted significant funds to investment in the Córdoba concession before the crisis: AR$35 million during its first year, a sum that exceeded the amount proposed in its bid for the concession and that represented 71.5 percent of revenues.[33] During the pre-crisis period, it invested the equivalent

[28] Alberto Gregorini, former general manager of Aguas Provinciales de Santa Fe, spoke of the concern to maintain a level of service that would live up to Suez's market reputation (interview, May 2007).

[29] Balance sheet data from Aguas Provinciales de Santa Fe.

[30] The consortium's investment estimate from its bid was reported in the following article: "Gayá niega trabas para la licitación de la Dipos." *El Litoral.* July 12, 1995. Admittedly, the firm and government expected to invest at a greater rate upfront than during later years of the contract.

[31] The debt of the concession totaled AR$359 million in December 2001. The concessionaire contracted several major loans with international institutions. In addition to assuming the province's World Bank (PRONAPAC) loan at the time of the concession award (AR$29.4 million), it contracted a loan from the Inter-American Development Bank (IDB) of AR$30 million and received IDB syndication worth AR$55 million in 1996. In 2001, the year before the crisis, it contracted an additional AR$20 million loan from the International Finance Corporation (loan data from PPIAF-World Bank (2006) and the concession contract. The peso was pegged to the U.S. dollar at this time).

[32] "Los Franceses, con el agua de Córdoba." *La Nación.* March 19, 1997. Suez and Aguas de Barcelona, part owned by Suez, owned 53% of the shares. The remaining shares were held by Argentine construction and services firms, one of which was based in Córdoba (Empresa Constructora Delta with only 15% participation). See Nickson (2001). The contract encompassed only water services in the city of Córdoba.

[33] Ratio calculated from investment figure reported in "Aguas Cordobesas: bajo análisis." *La Nación.* March 14, 1998, and revenue levels reported in ENOHSA-COFES (1999). Note that this is a comparatively large ratio, second only to Santa Fe among the cases examined here.

of approximately 35 percent of net sales.[34] It also assumed a long-term, US$40 million loan with the European Investment Bank in 1998 to help fund these investments.[35] This allowed the concessionaire to improve water service coverage from 84 to 90 percent of the population.[36]

The Suez cases conform to theoretical expectations in general terms. Faced with far fewer political hurdles than in provinces described in Chapter 3, political incumbents could allow concessionaires to follow through with most cost-recovery measures included in their contracts. This, in turn, encouraged the Suez concessionaires to invest heavily. Although Suez grew dissatisfied with roadblocks and losses in its Santa Fe concession, concerns about its other two contracts in the country prompted it to keep investing and refrain from lodging legal complaints against the Santa Fe government. Suez worried that failing to perform well in Santa Fe would jeopardize its most important holding, the Aguas Argentinas contract, which had been granted by the national government. In this sense – because of the anomalous coexistence of a national-level contract and subnational regulatory agencies in a single country – Suez possessed a concern for assets outside of the concession more commonly observed among domestic investors with diverse local holdings in Argentina. This being said, its interests were concentrated in the water and sanitation sector – which ultimately made it more vulnerable when political conditions changed following the Argentine crisis, as later chapters in this book show.

The Aguas Argentinas case also shows how a willingness to invest gives MNCs leverage during negotiations in calm political environments: firms have something concrete and of value to offer politicians. MNCs' reluctance to invest in more contentious political environments, described in Chapter 3, suggests that investors lose this main source of leverage in high-hurdle political environments.

A Smooth Start for the Foreign-Held Contract in Misiones Province

With its proposal for a 30 percent reduction in consumer rates, the Spanish construction giant Grupo Dragados won a fierce contest for the Misiones Province concession contract against six competitors in 1999.[37] Located in the poor northeast, the contract attracted significant interest because the federal government and World Bank had committed to providing financial support for the concessionaire's investment program. For Dragados, it was an opportunity to obtain a foothold in the Latin American water market, although admittedly as

34 Investment ratio calculated with data from Aguas Cordobesas.

35 Loan data from PPIAF-World Bank (2006).

36 Coverage data from Aguas Cordobesas.

37 Six consortia, including a mix of foreign and domestic investors, submitted bids. "Puerta dejará el gobierno con una cadena de obras públicas en marcha." *El Territorio*. July 15, 1999; "La concesión de Apos saldrá antes que finalice el primer semestre." *El Territorio*. Jan. 20, 1999; "Apos: cambios pedidos por el BM." *El Territorio*. July 15, 1999; "Los españoles tomaron el control de los servicios sanitarios de Posadas." *El Territorio*. July 31, 1999. The tariff decrease is reported in the concessionaire's first year report, *Servicios de Aguas de Misiones S.A.* 2000, p. 2.

a latecomer. Dragados had already become a large player in the Argentine construction sector through its purchase of the Argentine firm Dycasa and aimed to increase its holdings in infrastructure services through acquiring water and highway concession contracts – consistent with the thrust of the firm's international expansion strategy more generally.[38] At the time of contract award, Dragados had no major projects in Misiones.[39]

The Misiones political environment presented similar political hurdles to those in Santa Fe and Córdoba Provinces: the governor faced reasonably tight elections immediately following the concession award, and power soon turned over to a new governor (Table 4.A.II, chapter appendix).[40] Carlos Rovira came to power only four months after the privatization, but he did not openly assert independence from his political patron – former governor Ramón Puerta – until a few years into his administration. In fact, during the first few years of the concession, Rovira retained a large number of Puerta's ministers, including the regulatory agency director.[41] Within this comparatively calm context, the governor and regulatory officials allowed the firm to implement customer database updates and regularize clandestine connections.[42] When significant problems cropped up during the first month of operations and several months later during the summer, politicians did not take the firm to task as they had in high-hurdle provinces such as Tucumán and Buenos Aires (discussed in Chapter 3). Rather, newspaper articles sympathetically described the firm's efforts to tackle the serious infrastructure deficits inherited from the state company.[43] In comparative terms, the government complied with most of its obligations (92 percent compliance rate in Table 4.1). This restraint on the provincial administration's part speaks to the fact that the governor felt no immediate political threats and that significant World Bank and national government financial support for the concessionaire's investment program – granted on the condition that the province privatize services – was to be transferred in installments, with receipt contingent on satisfactory progress.[44]

[38] See comments by Santiago Foncillas, president of Dragados, in "El grupo quiere aumentar el beneficio un 35% en dos años Dragados busca su 'Vivendi.'" *Actualidad Económica*. May 17, 1999.

[39] The firm possessed several highway concessions in other parts of Argentina, however.

[40] The hurdle index score for the pre-crisis period is 1.7, equivalent with that for Santa Fe (Figure 3.1).

[41] Rovira assumed power in December 1999, but much of the government remained under Puerta's control for the first three years of his administration.

[42] Not-for-attribution interviews, Posadas, June 2007.

[43] See press coverage in *El Territorio* following the handover in August of 1999. For example: "Samsa, cada vez con más problemas." Aug. 25, 1999; "Si falla una bomba, barrios de Posadas se quedarán sin agua." Aug. 26, 1999. The provincial paper depended heavily on state advertising and so should not be seen as independent politically.

[44] See Post (2008) regarding improvements funded under the World Bank program, financed by BIRF loan 4484-AR.

This carrot was attractive because it was to fund 26,000 household connections at the end of the program.

Although it had yet to earn positive returns, the concessionaire, Servicio de Aguas de Misiones S.A. (SAMSA), moved forward with its investment program as promised, reassured by the favorable regulatory climate and aiming to make its new venture work. According to its first year report, it invested AR$5.04 million, more than 100 percent of its revenues in that same year – although less than one-fifth of the AR$37 million the company promised to spend in the first five years according to its original bid.[45] Once the national government approved the loan agreement with the World Bank, the firm finalized its loan agreement with the European Investment Bank for AR$18 million meant to fund its 40 percent of the project.[46] It is a sign of the firm's optimism regarding the concession that it chose to finalize this loan – large in relation to the size of the concession – in 2001 in the context of a worsening economic climate.[47] This behavior contrasts starkly with decisions made by French investor Saur in Mendoza Province, who did not take on a major external loan during the same time period because regulatory policy in this higher-hurdle province had proven to be less favorable (Chapter 3).

This set of four cases suggests that foreign investors can maintain productive negotiating relationships with host governments when at least two conditions obtain: (1) contracts are located in relatively calm political environments that present few short-term threats to incumbent power, and (2) investors possess significant leverage due to their ability and willingness to mobilize funds for investment in the short run. In the Buenos Aires metropolitan area, Santa Fe, Córdoba, and Misiones cases, governments not only allowed concessionaires to follow through the majority of revenue-raising provisions contained in their contracts but also addressed investor concerns after contract award through contract renegotiations. With relatively high levels of government support, foreign investors did not resort to legalistic retaliatory strategies of the sort observed in provinces characterized by significant hurdles. Moreover, they invested at substantial rates during the pre-crisis period. Although investments often failed to meet the targets originally included in concession agreements and bidding documents, they nonetheless yielded impressive improvements in the

45 Proposed investment figure from "Los Españoles tomaron el control de los servicios sanitarios de Posadas." *El Territorio*. July 31, 1999. Data on realized investments from SAMSA. 2000. *Servicio de Aguas de Misiones S.A.* pp. 9–10. To put this figure in context, Aguas Argentinas invested the equivalent of 68.1% of its revenues during its first year of operation.

46 The loan agreement was signed on December 12, 2000, and announced via a bank press release on January 17, 2001 (reference #2001-003-EN). This loan had been arranged prior to the bid for the concession but had not been confirmed.

47 Similarly sized concessions managed by domestic investors in other provinces only amassed loans of AR$4–AR$6 million. This loan is large in comparison with the debt burden assumed by the Mendoza concession, which began one year earlier. While more than six times the size in terms of revenues, the Mendoza concession's total debt was AR$64 million during this period (see Chapter 3).

reach and quality of services. These outcomes are summarized in Table 4.A.II (chapter appendix). While we would have expected investment rates in provinces with moderate (rather than low) levels of political hurdles to be somewhat lower, this did not occur for idiosyncratic reasons: in Santa Fe, Suez's concerns regarding its other holdings prompted it to invest heavily despite local setbacks, and in Misiones, federal government and World Bank involvement helped convince the provincial administration to follow through with its obligations.

The ability of foreign investors to maintain constructive negotiating relationships with host governments during periods of relative political calm held under a variety of conditions that alternative approaches to regulatory politics stress are important. Concessionaires maintained smooth relationships with the political establishment when regulated by agencies with greater formal independence, as in Córdoba Province, as well as by agencies whose activities were more circumscribed, as in the Buenos Aires metropolitan area, Santa Fe, and Misiones.[48] In Misiones, the foreign investor managed to keep its relationship with the provincial government on track even in the absence of domestic partners. Moreover, although levels of checks and balances and state capacity were comparably high in the cases of the Buenos Aires metropolitan area, Santa Fe, and Córdoba, Misiones is one of the poorer and more patrimonial provinces in the country.

DOMESTIC INVESTORS PRESIDE OVER RESILIENT CONTRACTS IN PROVINCES WITH LOW AND MODERATE POLITICAL HURDLES

This section examines the evolution of the four concession contracts where local and domestic investors held majority controlling shares that were also located in less contentious political settings prior to the crisis: the low-income and relatively patrimonial provinces of Salta, La Rioja, Santiago del Estero, and Formosa. Governors in these provinces faced low levels of electoral competition and enjoyed unified governments (Table 4.A.II, chapter appendix). Only in Formosa did power pass to a governor not associated with privatization during the pre-crisis period. As the first section of this chapter stresses, we would expect all of these contracts to have proceeded smoothly during that period because politicians were not tempted to block cost-recovery measures and faced few difficulties passing legislation approving contractual amendments – despite the fact they were in poorer locales. This being said, we would expect the firm operating in Formosa – a domestic investor with few local holdings – to have encountered more difficulties than contemporaries operating in provinces without gubernatorial turnover. In addition, we would expect

48 In Córdoba, regulatory decisions could not be appealed to the executive branch, whereas in Santa Fe, Buenos Aires, and Misiones, enabling legislation for the regulatory agencies allowed such appeals (Azpiazu et al. 2008: 124).

aggregate levels of investment to have been lower than those achieved by foreign firms operating in similar environments.

Smooth Sailing for Domestic Investors in the Low-Hurdle Provinces of Salta, La Rioja, and Santiago

The Salta provincial government awarded its water and sanitation concession in February 1998 on the basis of the largest proposed investment program within the parameters of a government-defined rate schedule for consumers. Necon S.A. (later JCR), a diversified domestic conglomerate working in construction, electricity generation, petroleum, hotels, and other sectors, beat out two other consortia.[49] Although the owners of this firm were based in the province of Corrientes, they had important local operations, including highway contracts and a petroleum extraction facility in Aguaragüe.[50] Given Governor Juan Carlos Romero's political popularity and commitment to privatization – demonstrated by his previous privatizations of the provincial electricity distributor and bank – the concession was viewed as a promising opportunity to gain a foothold in the new utilities management industry. Necon's directors expected it would offer cash flow at different points in the economic cycle than did their construction, petroleum, and real estate holdings.[51] They also realized that the concession would likely not produce strong returns during the first years, when it would be necessary to invest more heavily in order to increase efficiency and widen the customer base.[52] In 1999, the owner of Necon transferred half of the concession shares and technical oversight to Latinaguas, a specialized water company that was a subsidiary of another Corrientes-based multisector group (Saltiel 2003).

The investor's intention to hold on to the concession over the long run and its conciliatory orientation – along with the reasonable levels of gubernatorial support to be expected in a low-hurdle environment – ensured that the concession evolved smoothly between 1998 and the 2001 crisis. The regulatory agency did not block firm efforts to update its customer directory and enforce payment. The agency postponed implementation of a contractual provision for a 20 percent tariff increase one year into the contract when Romero was maneuvering to thwart rivals within his own party jockeying to succeed him in the May 1999 gubernatorial elections,[53] but it also postponed the firm's investment obligations

[49] "El Excel group quiere ahora Aguas de Salta". *La Nación*. Feb. 11, 1998. Necon was ranked no. 23 in the construction sector in Argentina (*Prensa Económica*. October 1999: 98).

[50] "Necon se quedó con las aguas de Salta." *La Nacion*. Feb. 12, 1998. J.C. Relats is the owner of Necon, now J.C.R.; "Rutas en abandono tras el fuerte recorte." *La Nación*. May 14, 1999.

[51] Not-for-attribution interview, firm director, June 2007.

[52] Ibid.

[53] To this end, loyalists in the legislature passed an amendment to the provincial constitution (6991/98) that made it impossible for alternative Peronist Party candidates to run against him in the general election and allowed Romero to run for reelection (law 6691/98).

and levied very few fines.[54] The firm accepted a reformulation of its investment program that the administration considered more politically opportune: investments in a sewerage treatment plant were to be postponed and substituted with water distribution pipes to facilitate immediate expansion to new users.[55] The firm acceded to provincial requests to assume control of deficit-running services in municipalities that had previously operated their own systems, a move that did not promise to be profitable; the original concession contract required Aguas de Salta to take on the municipal systems, but only following case-by-case negotiations.[56] Overall, the government could be rated as complying with its original obligations 50 percent of the time – a rate lower than that obtained by foreign firms operating in similar political environments (Table 4.1) but softened by the fact that firm obligations were adjusted to compensate for the government's failure to increase tariffs.

Necon's continuing interest in maintaining a diversified presence in the province led it to channel its rising revenues into investment rather than paying its parent company dividends. In the short term, Necon was bidding for other projects and therefore had a strong interest in staying in the good graces of the provincial government. For instance, at the time of the water concession award, Necon was simultaneously proposing a toll highway to the provincial government of Salta that would connect the provincial capital with that of neighboring Jujuy Province.[57] The province subsequently conducted a bidding process and awarded the project to a consortium led by Necon in May 1999, almost a year into the water concession.[58] In the medium run, the province could offer additional opportunities in areas where the firm already did substantial business: energy extraction, tourism, and construction. Moreover, the concession itself could provide construction contracts and a steady source of income in periods when the state had less money to spend on infrastructure.[59]

Buoyed by these broader interests, the new concessionaire invested 66 percent of what it had originally proposed, despite the worsening economic climate and the fact that the original investment requirements had been legally suspended.[60] The ratio of investment to net sales was 27 percent in 1998 (at a time when the

[54] In a period of virtually zero inflation, net sales rose from AR$27 million in 1999 to AR$33 million in 2001. The regulatory agency only levied AR$10,000 in fines prior to the crisis. Data from Aguas de Salta S.A. and En.Re.S.P.

[55] En.Re.S.P. resolution 168/99. For more detail, see Post (2008).

[56] "Es precaria la provisión de agua en varias localidades." *El Tribuno*. July 11, 2002.

[57] "Con su privatización, el agua costará en Salta un 20% más." *La Nación*. May 15, 1998.

[58] "Qué pasa." *La Nación*. May 31, 1999.

[59] At the beginning of the concession period, Necon and Latinaguas, the operator, jointly formed a new construction company that specialized in water and sanitation infrastructure and services, Urbanoa. The idea was that this firm could be contracted for projects related to the concession. Because Aguas de Salta did not rely on loans from international financial institutions, it had opportunities for direct contracting.

[60] Concessionaire investment obligations were specified in the concession contract, appendix III; figures for realized investment from Aguas de Salta.

contract had not yet officially gone into effect), 40 percent in 1999, and 35 percent in 2000.[61] These ratios compare favorably with investment rates by other domestic operators and with rates by international firms working in more contentious political environments. The firm financed investments primarily via short-term debt.[62] At the behest of the governor, most investment during the first years was devoted to network expansion; coverage rose from 76 to 95 percent of the population for water and stayed constant for sewerage between July 1998 and July 2002.[63] As a result of this emphasis on investment, earnings were lower than they might otherwise have been: return on sales stayed between 4 and 5 percent for the pre-crisis period, and returns on equity hovered between 2.4 and 3.3 percent, far below the cost of capital.[64]

Overall, the arrangement in Salta was workable because each party was willing to sit down on a yearly basis and revisit priorities with respect to investment and other goals; as political and economic circumstances changed, contractual goals would be amended or postponed. Negotiations proceeded amicably, and like other investors working in political environments with low or moderate political hurdles, the firm did not utilize the sort of legalistic retaliatory strategies employed by foreign firms in more contentious political environments (Table 3.A.I, chapter appendix). In spite of delays in promised rate increases, the concessionaire invested comparatively large fractions of its revenues during the initial years of the contract, spurred at least in part by its commitment to diversification and its broader interests in the provincial economy.

In contrast to the Salta case, the domestic investor that secured the Santiago del Estero concession did not possess important local holdings in the province. Sagua S.A., the subsidiary of the Buenos Aires–based Sielecki Group, secured the concession.[65] The Sielecki Group worked in sectors as diverse as petrochemicals, pharmaceuticals, viticulture, and banking. Its contract also unfolded in a province with low levels of political competition. Although the governorship formally changed hands several times before the Argentine crisis, Carlos Juarez and his wife – who originally oversaw the privatization – maintained informal control through proxies. Facing no real political competition and possessing a

[61] Calculations by author based on data from Aguas de Salta.

[62] Loan data from Aguas de Salta.

[63] Ratios from Aguas de Salta, cited in Saltiel (2003: 21). Note that the area against which percentages are calculated changed dramatically as new municipalities were incorporated. The number of accounts (i.e., the number of households and industrial or institutional users) increased 27% between 1998 and 2002 (account data from Aguas de Salta).

[64] Data from Aguas de Salta and En.Re.S.P., the regulatory agency.

[65] Sagua assembled a consortium that included the most important political and economic figures in the province: (1) Victor Curi, Juárez's longtime favorite state contractor (15%); b) Juárez's more recent business ally, Nestor Ick, who assumed solitary control of many other privatized state companies, such as the provincial bank and cable station (15%); and c) the Castiglione family, the owners of the main provincial newspaper, Editorial El Liberal (15%). Share percentages from ENOHSA-COFES (1999). The union received the remaining 10% of the shares. Ick was reportedly the "testaferro," or proxy owner, for Governor Juárez.

unified government, the Juarezes had no immediate political incentive to block cost-recovery measures included within the concession contract. Supportive provincial policy allowed Aguas de Santiago to make the transition to cost recovery quite smoothly. Collection rates increased from 20 percent to 57 percent during the first year of service.[66] Meanwhile, the state granted the company an AR$500,000 monthly subsidy to cover payments for the poorest category of users.[67] Water metering was the main area in which political difficulties prevented the firm from moving ahead with measures outlined in the contract; protests delayed implementation of the metering plan until 2000 (Tenti 2005: 165). Solid political support, in other words, helped the firm withstand the backlash against more systematic billing that occurred in other provinces. This being said, the firm had weaker incentives to invest heavily than its counterpart in Salta, which possessed important holdings in other sectors that could suffer should it fail to stay in the good graces of the government. The concessionaire only made modest progress toward expanding system capacity and access, concentrating on system maintenance and investments in commercial operations. The main accomplishment was completing 75 percent of a basic sewerage infrastructure project in the capital.[68] Census data indicates that between the 1997 contract award and 2001, however, the concessionaire did not take advantage of this increase in system capacity to expand sewerage coverage.[69]

The La Rioja contract – another one controlled by a domestic investor with few local operations – also unfolded in a province in which the governor who privatized stayed in power throughout the pre-crisis period and faced unified government and little electoral competition (Table 4.A.II, chapter appendix; Figure 3.1).[70] In 1999, Governor Ángel Maza awarded a management contract to Latinaguas, the Corrientes-based firm that served as the technical operator of the Salta concession, following a failed privatization attempt in 1996.[71] The firm did not possess other

[66] ENOHSA-COFES (1999), report on Aguas de Santiago. Percentage reflects collections as a portion of billing for November 1997–August 1998.

[67] Tenti (2005: 164). According to Petrecolla and Ferro (2003: 11), these subsidies covered up to 70% of the tariff for users falling below a certain income level.

[68] World Bank. 2001. *Implementation Completion Report on a Loan in the amount of US$100 Million to the Republic of Argentina for a Water Supply and Sewerage Project.* Report No: 21403.

[69] Census data from INDEC, the Argentine statistics agency, for 1991 and 2001 yields the same percentage coverage figure (19.8%) for sewerage access in the Santiago-La Banda metropolitan area, where the new mains were being constructed. The contractual goal for 2001 for Santiago was 28% and for La Banda 32% (Pliego de Bases y Condiciones: appendix V). The concessionaire's failure to increase the percent of the population covered could be attributed at least in part to population growth, which meant it had to expand access even to maintain coverage at existing levels. Nevertheless, the concessionaire still came nowhere near the contractual goal for 2001.

[70] As in Salta, factionalism within the Peronist Party constrained the actions of the governor to a certain extent (Leiras 2007: 224–227), even though Peronists controlled both the executive and legislative branches.

[71] Management contracts delegate management and maintenance responsibilities to a private firm, whereas concession contracts delegate investment responsibilities as well.

significant holdings in the province. Facing no credible threats to his hold on power, Governor Maza allowed Aguas de la Rioja S.A. to follow through with vital revenue-raising provisions in the contract. This enabled the concessionaire to improve its financial situation dramatically: payment rates climbed from 27 percent to 89 percent and revenues rose from AR$7.5 million to AR$15.9 million between 2000 and 2003.[72] Securing such improvements in payment rates is inevitably highly political and would have been difficult for the governor to support in a more contentious environment, given the small percentage of the population who had been accustomed to paying their bills at the start of the contract. The financial health of the utility put it in a good position to invest following the Argentine crisis, when the contract was converted into the standard concession format that required the operator to assume investment as well as management responsibilities.

These three contracts – all of which unfolded in political environments with low levels of political hurdles – suggest that domestic with (Salta) and without (La Rioja, Santiago del Estero) diverse local holdings can work effectively with host governments in relatively calm political settings. Political authorities face fewer political incentives to renege on revenue-enhancing measures contained in the original contracts than in more contentious environments, which in turn allows firms to improve utility revenue streams and, the Salta case suggests, regularly devote funds to investment. Admittedly, the Salta concessionaire possessed the strongest incentives to invest, given the lead investor's holdings in other sectors in the province. These findings, consistent with expectations, are summarized in Table 4.A.I (chapter appendix).

Formosa's Domestic Operator Presides over a More Brittle Contract

In August 1995, Formosa governor Vicente Joga awarded a concession contract for the province's water and sanitation system to Sagua S.A., the subsidiary of the Buenos Aires–based Sielecki Group (described earlier for the case of Santiago del Estero). The group originally formed Sagua in order to bid for the Formosa concession and thereby gain a foothold in the new concession market.[73] The group's management considered water concessions attractive additions to their diverse portfolio because they were regulated monopoly assets – presumably a stable source of returns because they were not vulnerable to competition from other players.[74] The concession was its only major holding in the province. In fact, the governor's appointees to the privatization commission chose to award the contract to Sagua rather than a competitor, IATE, which already held the

72 Figures from Aguas de la Rioja S.A. A good portion of this rise, we can assume, occurred before the 2001–2002 economic crisis. The revenues collected before the devaluation would have been equivalent to the same sum in dollars.

73 "La privatización de AGOSF: IATE no bajará los brazos." *La Mañana*. July 13, 1995. The firm held a technical assistance contract with Northumbrian Water, a British firm, for the first six years to satisfy legal requirements. Sagua S.A. took over the technical operator role thereafter.

74 Not-for-attribution interview, August 2006.

provincial electricity distribution concession, out of a desire to keep IATE from amassing too much power within the local economy.[75]

Whereas the governors who privatized presided over the contracts held by domestic investors in Salta, La Rioja, and Santiago, power in Formosa turned over to Gildo Insfrán, a new governor, just a few months after the concession award.[76] Largely because of this immediate change in the governor's mansion, the province is coded as experiencing moderate political hurdles during the pre-crisis period with a score of 1.40 (Figure 3.1). On assuming office, Insfrán did not feel constrained by commitments made by his predecessor regarding provincial support for the concessionaire's investment program. To ensure that the concession would be attractive despite its location in one of the country's poorest provinces, Governor Joga had decided to include a substantial government contribution to the investment program, a common approach in low-income provinces.[77] Insfrán not only refused to deliver the promised infrastructure but also prevented the firm from assessing consumers directly to cover the cost of the project and building it on its own – a fallback option outlined in the contract.[78] Governor Insfrán and the firm did not reach an agreement regarding funding of the outstanding infrastructure projects until March 1998. The province eventually carried out the investment program, although with a considerable delay.[79] This drawn-out process got the contract off to a bad start, failing to deliver service improvements at the outset that might have improved the provider's public image.

Although Insfrán's administration delayed the investment program, facing little electoral competition, it had little reason to block firm efforts to update consumer databases or improve payment rates via a program of service cutoffs targeting middle- and upper-class consumers who had not paid their bills.[80] This

[75] For more detail on the award process, see Post (2008).

[76] The contract was adjudicated to Sagua on August 2, 1995. The contract was finally signed on November 16, after the gubernatorial elections, which took place on October 1, 1995. The company assumed control of the system on December 4, and Insfrán took office on December 11, 1995. See "Adjudican la AGOSF a Aguas de Formosa." *La Mañana*. Aug. 3, 1995; "Se firmó el convenio de traspaso de la AGOSF." *La Mañana*. Nov. 17, 1995; Aguas de Formosa advertisement, *La Mañana*. Dec. 4, 1995, p. 3.

[77] While the per capita income in Argentina was approximately AR6,703 pesos in 1992, the per capita income was $1,881 in Formosa and $3,477 in Salta (1992 estimates from the ministry of the interior, Argentina.) The agreement provided for US$4.5 million in water main investments and treatment in the capital. See PRONAPAC documentation for BIRF-3281 and World Bank *Implementation Completion Report* No. 21403.

[78] Auditoría General de la Nación (AGN), Argentina. 1999. "Informe de Auditoría de Gestión sobre los Contratos de Préstamos No. 3821/AR-BIRF, No. 621-OC/AR y 855-SF/AR – BID," p. 17. See also article 19 of the concession contract.

[79] According to national government auditors, the provincial project was 77% complete in August 1999 (AGN 1999: 18).

[80] The company divided its customer base into categories by income and focused on improving payment rates among the top three out of five categories. This strategy was described by the director of Sagua (and president of Aguas de Formosa) Federico Qüerio and the legal and commercial director of Aguas de Formosa Karina Pavon (interviews, August 2006), as well as

allowed the company to improve its collection rate from 35 percent at the time of handover to 62 percent in 1997.[81] The firm was also allowed to bill without granting subsidies to various user groups the provincial company had previously applied;[82] in other words, the company was not prevented from following through with the new billing scheme as occurred in some other provincial cases.[83] Finally, the province subsidized, at a rate of 50 percent, bills for residents living in areas that only received service for half of each day because of delays in the infrastructure projects the province had promised to deliver starting in 1998. This also represents a marked difference from the Azurix and Tucumán cases discussed in Chapter 3, where the governments sanctioned nonpayment campaigns when service quality suffered. The provincial administration also did not block the firm's efforts to institute a voluntary retirement program that more than halved the size of the employee union.[84] On a comparative scale (Table 4.1), governmental compliance is rated at 50 percent.

What emerged between the Buenos Aires–based investor and the provincial administration was a pattern of mutual accommodation that involved low investment levels and fairly low politicization levels. The government reined in the regulatory agency and ignored criticisms by opposition politicians, did not block firm efforts to maintain better collection rates than the previous public sector company had achieved, and did not interfere significantly with the firm's efforts to curb the employee union's power. The two parties were able to engage in dialogue and devise revised agreements at various points in time. Examples include the already cited reprogramming of the loan agreement in 1998 and a subsequent agreement announced in October 1999 that obliged the province to construct 4,000 sewerage connections, forgave fines levied by the regulator, and required the firm to forgive AR$6–AR$7 million in accumulated debts owed by users.[85] Also, firm management was careful about which battles it chose to fight; managers knew, for instance, that enforcing payment among poor users would be politically disastrous and futile. Within this context, the firm was gradually able to improve its financial situation. Although sales stayed relatively flat, collections increased as a larger portion of the customers paid their

ENOHSA-COFES (1999: 105). The firm initiated judicial proceedings against 1,500 users in 1997 and 6,500 users in 1998, against a customer base of 35,197.

81 Revenue as a percentage of billing was 63% in 1997, while the percentage of users that paid their bills was 61% (ENOHSA-COFES 1999: 111). Original collection rate figures are from interviews with Karina Pavon (Aguas de Formosa) and Marcelino Ybars (water manager at the regulatory agency), August 2006. BID (1996: 37) published a figure for the percentage of revenue collected in 1993 as 44%.

82 ENOHSA-COFES (1999: 108).

83 See, for instance, the cases of Mendoza and Buenos Aires (Azurix) in Chapter 3.

84 Of Aguas de Formosa's 268 original unionized workers, only 41 remain (out of 141 employees). Employees were encouraged to retire via voluntary retirement programs (interview, Dionisio Sanchez, head of the Water and Sanitation Union, Formosa, August 2006).

85 See "Condonaron la 'deuda histórica' de 12 mil usuarios de Aguas de Formosa." *La Mañana*. Oct. 6, 1999.

bills.[86] The firm was also able to reduce its operating costs. This allowed returns on sales to improve from −4.5 percent in 1996 to 15.1 percent in 2001 and returns on equity to move from −4.2 percent to 14.2 percent over the same period. The firm began paying significant dividends to its shareholders in 2000.

However, the province's substantial delay in providing the basic infrastructure intended to help the concessionaire meet its obligations detracted significantly from the concession's development. Faced with the province's unwillingness to invest and without a strong stake in the provincial economy outside of the concession, the firm only met a portion of its obligations as well. Investment after the first year leveled off and stayed low. The firm chose to divert funds that might have gone to investment into dividends, as expectations for long-run payoffs were relatively low: investment represented 11 percent of revenues on average before the Argentine crisis, compared with 32 percent for the Salta concessionaire.[87] It chose not to contract large loans with the multilateral banks to fund major pieces of infrastructure: less than 20 percent of the firm's debt was in dollars between 1997 and 2001.[88]

Considering the four contracts held by domestic investors with and without diverse local holdings in provinces with low to moderate levels of political hurdles, a number of patterns are evident. First, host governments in political environments with minimal levels of political competition and turnover – such as in Salta, La Rioja, and Santiago del Estero – were more willing to permit the introduction of cost-recovery measures and search for mutually agreeable solutions to problems than were provincial governments where the privatizing governor had left power, as occurred in Formosa. Second, the one case in which a domestic investor with significant local holdings controlled the contract, Salta, witnessed substantial investment – even following governmental decisions to delay consumer rate increases. (Chapter 3 describes a similar tendency under more difficult political circumstances in Corrientes once the Chamas Group took control.) The consistency of these findings with expectations is summarized in Table 4.A.II (chapter appendix).

The observed commonalities and differences between these cases of domestic investors with and without diverse local holdings do not appear to be driven by factors emphasized by alternative approaches to regulation in weak institutional environments. Among the Argentine provinces, Salta, La Rioja, Formosa, and Santiago del Estero fall at the lower end of the income distribution. The provinces were controlled by Peronist governors; all had fallen in line with President Menem's economic program. Admittedly, Salta, where the concessionaire invested more heavily, possessed stronger sets of checks and balances within its political environment.[89] Its regulatory agency also enjoyed more formal

[86] Collections increased from AR$5.3 million in 1996 to AR$8.4 million in 2000 during a period of almost zero inflation. Data from Aguas de Formosa S.A. and EROSP, the regulatory agency.

[87] Investment as a fraction of net sales, calculated from data from Aguas de Formosa and Aguas de Salta.

[88] Data from Aguas de Formosa S.A. and EROSP, the regulatory agency.

[89] This distinction is based on Giraudy's provincial "dispersion of authority" scores for the 1983–2006 period (Giraudy 2010).

political independence than agencies in the other three provinces.[90] As the case discussion highlights, however, the reason investment proceeded in Salta is that high-level ministers and firm owners could negotiate directly about adjustments to the original contract, thereby adapting it to changing political and economic circumstances. Factors contributing to generally higher levels of policy stability in the province, in other words, were not responsible for the concessionaire's comparative success during the pre-crisis period. In fact, contracts evolved smoothly precisely because of the flexibility shown by both host governments and firms.

CONCLUSION

This chapter compares the respective ability of different types of investors to maintain productive bargaining relationships with host governments in low- to moderate-hurdle provinces during the pre-crisis period. As we would expect based on the theoretical framework presented in this book, the trajectories of contracts controlled by different types of investors did not vary as dramatically as the cases did in the more contentious political environments described in Chapter 3. Concessions controlled by foreign, or domestic investors with and without diverse local holdings, all proceeded relatively smoothly. Because political incumbents faced few immediate threats to their political survival, they were more willing to follow through with the majority of contractual provisions. Levels of open political conflict remained low, and firms and host governments managed to negotiate means of adapting their agreements to changed circumstances in most cases. No investors chose to exit the market, and no host governments felt compelled to cancel concessionaires' contracts.

Variation does exist among the contracts held by different types of investors in provinces experiencing low to moderate levels of political hurdles during the pre-crisis period, but it is of a more subtle type. Investors varied systematically in their willingness to invest large sums during the initial years of their contract within these relatively propitious political contexts. MNCs tended to contract external debt to finance upfront investments, which in turn gave them a great deal of leverage in the regulatory environment. Their demonstrated willingness to invest and promises of future investment gave politicians strong incentives to allow implementation of cost-recovery measures included in the concession contracts, as well as to negotiate regarding contractual amendments that adapted original contracts to changed political and economic circumstances. As the contract renegotiations described for the Buenos Aires metropolitan area (Aguas Argentinas) case suggest, although negotiation outcomes offered concrete benefits for both parties, firms could emerge with particularly good deals. Domestic investors,

[90] Whereas the enabling legislation for the Santiago, Formosa, and La Rioja regulatory agencies allowed for appeals to the executive branch, the Salta agency was not required to allow such appeals (Azpiazu et al. 2008: 124).

however, preferred to finance investments in infrastructure out of retained earnings. This gave them less leverage during the initial years of concession contracts, while they were working to move concessions toward cost recovery – which required the government to allow them to follow through with potentially controversial contractual measures such as consumer database updates and water meter installation. Because these domestic investors were unwilling to offer large amounts of investment up front, incumbent administrations had fewer reasons to follow through on all of their contractual commitments. Domestic investors with diverse local assets could partly overcome these difficulties, despite a reluctance to borrow large sums, because their long-term interest in the jurisdiction encouraged them to invest at greater rates even in the face of government failure to allow implementation of important revenue-raising measures.

These differences in financing strategies and consequent differences in firm leverage were clearly evident in the contracts examined in this chapter. Of the contracts granted prior to the crisis, only foreign investors contracted for *major*, long-term, and dollar-denominated loans from multilateral institutions. Aguas Argentinas, Aguas Cordobesas, Aguas Provinciales de Santa Fe, and SAMSA in Misiones Province assumed new direct loans with the World Bank, Inter-American Development Bank, and European Investment Bank during the pre-crisis period.[91] Note that in the Misiones case, the concessionaire assumed these loans for projects in a relatively low-income province. Balance sheet data also suggests debt levels were higher for foreign investor–controlled concessionaires. Whereas Aguas de Salta's ratio of debt to annual net sales stayed between 0.4 and 0.5 for the first four years of the concession (the pre-crisis period), the ratio for Aguas Argentinas grew from 0.36 to 1.02 during the first four years (1993–1996). Moreover, whereas Aguas de Salta's debt was held in the form of short-term loans and debts with suppliers, the vast majority of Aguas Argentinas's debt was dollar denominated and held by international institutions: by 1996, 90 percent was held by the International Finance Corporation and the Inter-American Development Bank.[92] These differences in financing strategies influence investment levels directly, particularly during the initial years of the contracts, before new owners have had a chance to grow revenue streams enough to fund investment out of tariff revenue. Table 4.2 compares investment rates for a subset of the contracts discussed in this

[91] Loan data from PPIAF-World Bank (2006). The PRONAPAC loans mentioned in this chapter also were with the World Bank and IDB, yet in all but one case (Corrientes), these were requested by and granted in advance of privatization to provincial governments rather than assumed directly by concessionaires. They also tended to be much smaller (on the order of AR$20 million rather than AR$20200 million). PRONAPAC loans were also guaranteed by the national government.

[92] Ratios calculated from data for Aguas Argentinas and Aguas de Salta. In this comparison, the ratio of debt to net sales provides a better sense of the size of the debt with respect to the size of the business than do debt-equity ratios. This is because the concessions controlled by domestic conglomerates tended not to put as much capital into the concession at the outset, thereby inflating their debt-equity ratios.

TABLE 4.2. *Investment Rates[a] for Pre-Crisis Period: International and Domestic Operators in Provinces with Low to Moderate Political Hurdles*

		Investment rates								
	Case	*1993*	*1994*	*1995*	*1996*	*1997*	*1998*	*1999*	*2000*	*2001*
International	Aguas Argentinas	68%	45%	70%	59%	56%	33%	36%	34%	22%
	Aguas Provinciales de Santa Fe				117%	68%	47%	56%	26%	15%
Domestic	Aguas de Salta (50% *with* diverse local holdings)						27%	40%	35%	22%
	Aguas de Formosa (*without* diverse local holdings)				19%	9%	6%	8%	14%	−1%

Source: Percentages calculated by the author drawing on company data.
Note: Contracts included particularly ambitious goals for the first years, meaning that greater investment was required during this time. For this reason, in comparing investment rates, it is important to keep the year of the contract in mind as well as the calendar year.
[a] Investment rate refers to the ratio of investment to net sales in a given year* 100.

chapter; those controlled by MNCs clearly outstrip the domestic firms operating under similar circumstances.

Although foreign-controlled contracts clearly witnessed higher levels of investment in provinces with low to moderate political hurdles, their advantages were limited to these settings. As Chapter 3 shows, contracts held by international investors either stumbled seriously or imploded in more contentious and fragmented political environments during the pre-crisis period. Moreover, as Chapters 5 and 6 show, foreign investor advantages eroded in the post-crisis period, particularly when the state regained access to capital for infrastructure investment. The superior ability of domestic investors with diverse local holdings to negotiate effectively with host governments in the face of changing political and economic circumstances also comes across much more clearly. Local investors in the province of Corrientes, as Chapter 3 shows, outperformed domestic investors in an extremely difficult political environment. The superior ability of domestic investors with diverse local assets to secure revised agreements becomes even more clear in the following chapters, which compare the respective ability of different types of investors to secure revised contractual agreements viewed as satisfactory by both firms and host governments following the Argentine crisis.

CHAPTER APPENDIX

TABLE 4.A.1. *Pre-Crisis Expectations and Findings in Provinces with Low to Moderate Political Hurdles*

	Investor portfolio structure					
	Foreign		***Domestic* without *diverse local holdings***		***Domestic* with *diverse local holdings***	
	Expect	***Observe***	***Expect***	***Observe***	***Expect***	***Observe***
Contractual outcomes						
Investor exit	Low	Aguas Argentinas: No Santa Fe: No Córdoba: No Misiones: No	Low	Formosa: No La Rioja: No Santiago: No	Low	Salta: No
Contract renegotiation (if warranted)	High	Aguas Argentinas: Yes Santa Fe: Yes	Medium	Formosa: Not applicable La Rioja: Not applicable Santiago: Not applicable	High	Salta: Not applicable
Indicators of health of the negotiating process						
Government supports basic revenue-raising elements of contract	High	Aguas Argentinas: High Santa Fe: Medium Córdoba: High Misiones: High	Medium–High	Formosa: Medium La Rioja: High[a] Santiago: Medium[a]	High	Salta: Medium

Concessionaire finances stabilize	High	Aguas Argentinas: High Santa Fe: Low Córdoba: High Misiones: Medium[b]	Medium–High	Formosa: High La Rioja: High[a] Santiago: High	High	
Firm employs legalistic retaliatory measures	Low	Aguas Argentinas: Low Santa Fe: Low[a] Córdoba: Low[a] Misiones: Low[a]	Low	Formosa: Low	Low	Salta: Low
Reliance on long-term, external loans to fund investment	High	Aguas Argentinas: High Santa Fe: High Córdoba: High Misiones: High	Low	Formosa: Low La Rioja: Not applicable[c] Santiago: Low	Low	Salta: Low
Firm invests significant fraction of revenues	High (at least in short run)	Aguas Argentinas: High Santa Fe: High Córdoba: Medium Misiones: High	Low–Medium (low for moderate hurdle environment)	Formosa: Low La Rioja: Not applicable[c] Santiago: Not available	Medium	Salta: Medium

[a] Case coding is based on less information than cases for which separate charts exist in this chapter and should therefore be viewed as less precise. The case narratives in this chapter contain the empirical details on which coding is based.

[b] The Misiones concession only started in 1999. Given that concessions rarely achieve profitability in the first year or so, we would not expect it to achieve profitability by the time of the crisis.

[c] La Rioja was a management contract between 1999 and 2002 and therefore did not impose investment commitments.

TABLE 4.A.II. *Political Hurdle Index Components for Pre-Crisis Period (Low- to Moderate-Hurdle Provinces)*

Year	*Competition for governor*	*Competition for legislature*	*Divided government*	*Governor did not privatize*	*Governor not allied with Menem*	*Federal intervention*	*Hurdle index*
Santa Fe							
1995	High (3)	Medium (2)					1
1996	–	–		Not privatizer			2
1997	–	–		Not privatizer			1.75
1998	–	–		Not privatizer			1.50
1999	Low (1)	Medium (2)		Not privatizer			1.92
2000	–	–		Not privatizer	Not applicable		2
2001	–	–		Not privatizer	Not applicable		1.75
Misiones							
1999	Medium (2)	Medium (2)					0.66
2000	–	–		Not privatizer	Not applicable		2
2001	–	Medium (2)		Not privatizer	Not applicable		2.42
Córdoba							
1998	High (3)	–			Not aligned		1
1999	–	High (3)			Not aligned		1
2000	–	–		Not privatizer	Not applicable		2
2001	–	Low (1)		Not privatizer	Not applicable		2.08
Formosa							
1995	Low (1)	Low (1)					0.33
1996	–	–		Not privatizer			2
1997	–	Low (1)		Not privatizer			2.08
1998	–	–		Not privatizer			1.5
1999	Low (1)	Low (1)		Not privatizer			1.58
2000	–	–		Not privatizer	Not applicable		1
2001	–	Low (1)		Not privatizer	Not applicable		1.33

Buenos Aires metropolitan area (scores for national government)						
1993	–	Low (1)				0.33
1994	–	Low (1)				0.33
1995	Low (1)	Low (1)				0.33
1996	–	–				0
1997	–	High (3)				1
1998	–	–	Divided			1
1999	High (3)	Medium (2)	Divided			2
2000	–	–		Not privatizer	Not applicable	2
2001	–	High (3)		Not privatizer	Not applicable	2.75
Santiago del Estero						
1997	–	Low (1)				0.33
1998	–	–				0
1999	Low (1)	Low (1)		[a]		1.33
2000	–	–		[a]	Not applicable	1
2001	–	Low (1)		[a]	Not applicable	1.08
La Rioja						
1999	Low (1)	Low (1)				0.33
2000	–	–			Not applicable	0
2001	–	Low (1)			Not applicable	0.33
Salta						
1998	–	–				0
1999	Low (1)	Low (1)				0.33
2000	–	–			Not applicable	0
2001	–	Low (1)			Not applicable	0.33

Formula for index: Max(legislative, gubernatorial competition)/3 + Divided government + Governor did not privatize + Governor not allied with Menem and not privatizer (for 1999 and earlier) + Federal intervention + Effect of turnover score (1–0.25*years since turnover for 4 years following turnover)

[a] Although power turned over in Santiago del Estero, Carlos Juarez and his wife essentially maintained control through proxies until 2004. For the purposes of the hurdle index, therefore, turnover is not registered.

5

Home Court Advantages Magnify after the Crisis

Chapters 5 and 6 analyze investor-government relations following the 2001–2002 Argentine crisis. Examining the varying ability of different types of investors to work effectively following crises is critical, as long-term infrastructure contracts in developing countries will almost inevitably encounter them given the high levels of economic and political volatility observed in weak institutional environments. The analytic framework presented here suggests that although investors possessed strong leverage before the Argentine crisis, the tables turned afterward. In the short run, the crisis would force politicians to focus on the needs of an electorate reeling from a dramatic income shock and sour public opinion regarding anything associated with neoliberal reform efforts of the 1990s, including privatized utilities. In the medium run, increasing state access to revenues during the economic recovery and the subsequent commodity boom would put provincial governments in a strong bargaining position relative to concessionaires.

These chapters examine the respective ability of foreign investors, domestic investors *without* diverse local holdings, and domestic investors *with* diverse local holdings to negotiate workable post-crisis settlements with host governments, and investor decisions regarding whether to subsequently exit the market, within post-crisis Argentina. Chapter 5 examines the divergent contractual trajectories of these different types of investors in provinces characterized by high levels of political competition, turnover, and fragmentation during the post-crisis period. Chapter 6 compares the respective ability of these different types of investors to reach workable settlements in provinces with low to moderate levels of political hurdles.

The first section of this chapter compares the intensity of political hurdles for the jurisdictions in which concessionaires operated during the post-crisis period. It then outlines expectations for concession contracts operated by each type of investor within political environments characterized by high levels of political hurdles. The second section examines post-crisis negotiations between host governments and foreign-controlled concessionaires in the high-hurdle provinces, all of which failed to produce workable long-term agreements and culminated in market exit. The final section analyzes the contrasting experiences of domestic investors with and without diverse local holdings operating in similarly contentious environments, highlighting the more workable and mutually beneficial settlements obtained by investors with diverse assets in their contract jurisdiction.

THEORETICAL EXPECTATIONS FOR HIGH-HURDLE ENVIRONMENTS

The Argentine financial and political crisis (2001–2002) generated major challenges for concessions held by both international and domestic investors. The same public emergency law (25,561) that ended the exchange rate peg to the U.S. dollar also stipulated that all concession contracts would be renegotiated and that consumer rates could no longer be pegged to the dollar. Provincial governments quickly issued laws and decrees confirming their adherence to the national law.

It is hard to imagine another course of action that the national and provincial governments might have pursued, given the magnitude of the income shock and dramatically reduced public support for privatized utilities. This being said, the combination of the economic crisis and the suspension of original contractual provisions presented major challenges for private concessionaires in the water and sanitation sector. High levels of unemployment and reduced earnings for employed individuals meant the percentage of customers paying their water bills dropped significantly. In addition, when the national government removed the exchange rate peg for the peso, its value dropped threefold. As a result, the costs of imported inputs used by concessionaires, such as chemicals, rose considerably. A severe bout of inflation in 2002 (41 percent) raised the cost of important domestic inputs, especially those related to construction, while consumer rates remained frozen at pre-crisis levels.[1] Finally, governments were less predictable partners in the immediate aftermath of the crisis because of shocks to their own income stream; promised subsidies for poor households and investment contributions were less likely to be delivered, and provincial government employees might be paid late or in provincial bonds rather than standard currency, which made it more difficult for them to pay their water bills. International investors in concessions faced additional challenges. Repatriated profits fell to one-third of their previous

[1] Admittedly, electricity and manpower comprised approximately 60% of concessionaires' operational costs. The extent to which wage increases could be delayed or electricity rate increases avoided, however, depended upon the local political context.

value following the devaluation of January 2002. Interest payments grew threefold for concessionaires that had contracted debt outside the country.[2]

Within this new post-crisis environment, investors sought contract renegotiations with host governments to provide a higher level of legal certainty and to adapt their contracts to current economic realities. Reaching an accord that lessened their investment commitments, raised tariff levels, and/or provided for subsidies, after all, represented a major improvement to the status quo. Provincial governments also had incentives to conclude negotiations; addressing investors' concerns would provide a framework for some renewed private sector investment in provincial water and sanitation systems, albeit usually at lower than pre-crisis levels. They were, however, constrained by negative reactions from consumer groups, ombudsmen, and local and federal judges to the prospect of raising consumer rates.[3] A 2003 survey, for instance, found that 68 percent of Argentine households opposed raising residential utility rates as a means of compensating companies for dramatic shifts in their cost structure because of the 2002 devaluation (OPSM 2003: 13). As time went on, the federal government's increasing stream of revenues from commodities such as soy allowed provinces to execute infrastructure projects on their own, turning to federal infrastructure programs or transfer payments rather than private providers to fund projects. This gave governments the upper hand in negotiations.

Based on the analytic framework presented in Chapter 1, we would expect the ability of different types of investors to negotiate workable post-crisis settlements and subsequent patterns of investor exit to vary dramatically in jurisdictions with significant political hurdles. High levels of political competition and instability would tend to reduce leaders' time horizons, making them less interested in concluding post-crisis contract renegotiations with firms, while high levels of fragmentation would make it difficult for governments to present a united front and secure legislative approval of contractual revisions once they were agreed on. As a result, domestic investors with diverse local operations – which have incentives to be more patient with host governments, are open to a broader range of negotiating outcomes because of concerns for other assets, and employ a more informal set of bargaining tactics – would be best placed to reach accords. Foreign investors would exhibit less patience, have a more restricted and legalistic set of negotiating strategies, and as a result be far less likely to conclude mutually beneficial contractual agreements that would provide sufficient incentives to stay in the market. Domestic firms with few local assets would occupy a middle ground: while less disposed to resort to legalistic negotiating strategies, they would be less patient and have less flexibility in negotiations than

[2] While the Argentine government "pesified" debts denominated in dollars that had been contracted inside the country, it did not "pesify" debts contracted outside the country in foreign currency.

[3] "Economía apela el fallo que frena el aumento en las tarifas." *La Nación*. Dec. 16, 2002; "Controversias en las inversiones de las empresas de servicios públicos." *La Nación*. Dec. 8, 2002.

would domestic investors with a significant local presence. As a result, rates of contract renegotiation should be highest and rates of exit lowest for domestic investors with diverse local holdings We should observe the opposite result among foreign investors, while domestic investors with few local holdings should represent an intermediate case. Chapter 3 outlines similar expectations for the pre-crisis period; these differences among investors should be more pronounced in the post-crisis period, when investors – and foreign investors in particular – no longer had superior access to capital.

Beyond these broad correlations between investor organizational structures and rates of contract renegotiation and exit, we should expect the character of renegotiation processes to vary with investor portfolio structure. These expectations are summarized in Table 5.A.I (chapter appendix). We should first of all observe a *difference in the responsiveness of host governments to concessionaire concerns*. Provincial governments all formally suspended the original concession contracts following the crisis, thereby freezing rates and suspending firms' investment commitments. They differed, however, in the extent to which they blocked firms from implementing or continuing to employ basic commercial measures such as updating consumer databases and regularizing clandestine connections. They also differed in whether they withheld promised contributions for subsidized rates for poor households or investment programs. Government adherence to such commitments during a period when contracts had been formally suspended was particularly important for concessions that had started late in the pre-crisis period because investors had had less of an opportunity to implement the basic measures designed to put system finances on more stable footing. And in high-hurdle environments, such measures were politically risky for host governments. We would expect them to be more likely to follow through with revenue-enhancing measures or institute compensatory measures – such as partial agreements addressing a subset of investor and government concerns – when working with domestic investors with diverse local holdings in high-hurdle environments.

Greater governmental willingness to support original contractual terms or alternative, compensatory measures designed to enable concessionaires to improve their revenue streams would in turn allow local investors to cope financially with post-crisis economic realities. (Foreign investors' finances would be, somewhat ironically, further handicapped by their willingness to obtain international financing for large, upfront investments during the pre-crisis period.) As a result, we would expect the *financial health* of concessions held by domestic investors with diverse local holdings – particularly if we count operations in related sectors – to be far better than those of domestic investors with few local assets and particularly foreign investors that invested heavily before the crisis.

A third indicator of the character of firm-government negotiation processes following the crisis is the extent to which investors turned to *legalistic pressure tactics* to bring host governments to the bargaining table. During the post-crisis period, foreign investors – without access to informal means of pressuring host governments – could draw on a legalistic pressure tactic unavailable to domestic firms: threats to take governments into international arbitration. We would therefore expect to observe foreign investors using such tactics more frequently than their domestic counterparts.

Finally, we should expect to observe differences in the *investment rates* achieved by foreign, domestic, and local firms in high-hurdle environments in the post-crisis period. With few other operations in their contract jurisdiction, foreign investors discouraged by a lack of progress with contract renegotiations had limited means – other than decreasing investment – of pressuring host governments. Such efforts to curtail investment, however, were likely to be less effective during the post-crisis period because of governments' increasing ability to finance such investments on their own. Given the more restricted set of pressure tactics at their disposal, we would expect domestic investors with few local operations and especially foreign investors to decrease rates of investment more than domestic investors with significant local holdings. Differences between investment rates following the crisis would be accentuated by the greater ability of domestic investors with diverse local holdings to conclude contract renegotiations yielding new, government-financed contributions to concessionaire investment programs.

CATEGORIZING POLITICAL ENVIRONMENTS FOR THE POST-CRISIS PERIOD

Provincial political environments during the post-crisis period can be scored using the political hurdle index introduced in Chapter 3. To recapitulate, this additive index captures the presence (or absence) of six factors that tend to shorten government time horizons, contribute to transaction costs, or otherwise lead governments to be less supportive of private service providers at a given point in time: (1) electoral competition, (2) provincial party system breakdown, (3) divided government, (4) number of times governor has changed, (5) privatizing governor has left power, and (6) statist policy approach by the governor. Figure 5.1 presents the post-crisis average for each province. The figure suggests that – as in the pre-crisis period – provinces varied considerably in terms of degrees of competition, turnover, fragmentation, and other factors that would detract from the political feasibility and attractiveness of supporting potentially controversial policy changes, such as rate increases, desired by concessionaires.

Chapters 5 and 6 take 1.90 as a cutoff point between high and moderate to low scores along the index spectrum. This allows us to compare the performance of different types of investors within more similar political environments during the post-crisis period. This chapter examines the high-hurdle cases: (1) foreign investor-controlled concessions in Buenos Aires Province (Aguas de Buenos Aires), Greater Buenos Aires (Aguas Argentinas), and Mendoza (Obras Sanitarias de Mendoza (OSM)); and (2) domestic investors with diverse local

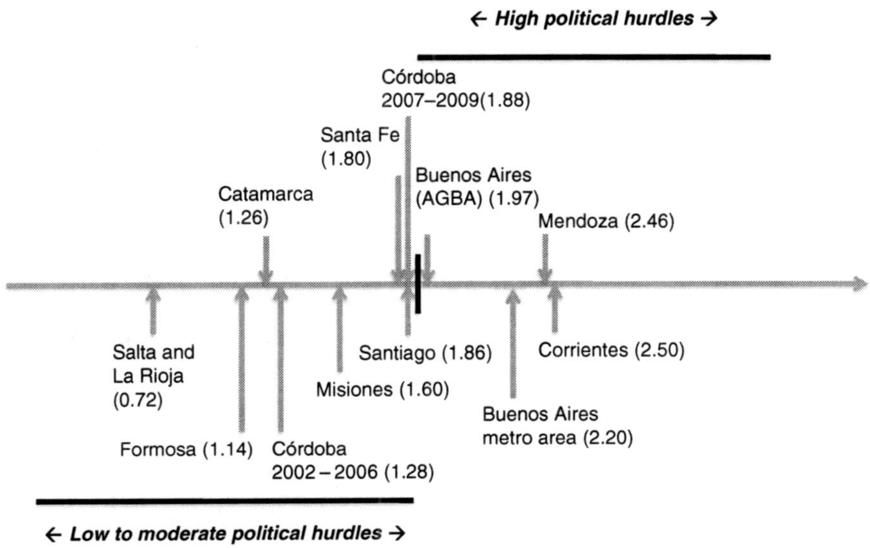

FIGURE 5.1. Provincial Political Hurdle Scores: Averages for Post-Crisis Period

holdings in the province of Corrientes (Aguas de Corrientes). The case study discussions will acknowledge, however, that contracts in Corrientes, Mendoza, and Greater Buenos Aires faced greater challenges than those near the political hurdle index cutoff. Annual scores for each province are reported in Table 5.A.II (chapter appendix).

THE IMPLOSION OF FOREIGN-LED CONTRACTS IN JURISDICTIONS WITH HIGH POLITICAL HURDLES

This section examines the evolution of the three concession contracts majority controlled by foreign investors that were located in politically contentious provinces after the crisis: Aguas de Gran Buenos Aires (Buenos Aires Province), Aguas Argentinas (Buenos Aires metropolitan area), and Obras Sanitarias de Mendoza (Mendoza Province). We would expect the lead investors in each of these concessions to reach impasses in their efforts to negotiate workable post-crisis settlements with host governments, eventually growing so frustrated that they seek to exit their contracts.

Negotiations Break Down in Metropolitan Buenos Aires and the Province of Buenos Aires

As shown in Chapter 4, the Aguas Argentinas concession for the Buenos Aires metropolitan area was successful in comparative terms before the crisis. The concessionaire invested heavily in basic infrastructure and water network expansion, incorporating approximately 2.2 million residents into the water network and 1.5 million into the sewerage network.[4] Although an intergovernmental agency regulated the contract, the national government – the signatory of the contract – stepped in at various points in time to renegotiate terms with Suez, the lead investor. The Menem administration and the firm were able to develop mutually satisfactory solutions to unforeseen problems, such as a political backlash against charges for new connections provided for in the original contract. This amicable relationship between the national government and the French multinational (MNC) Suez is explained by the firm's willingness to invest large sums up front before the crisis. At that time, low levels of political competition and the president's strong identification with a privatization he conducted gave officials few reasons to block the implementation of revenue-enhancing measures included in the original contract or refrain from negotiating new agreements to address mutual concerns.

The concession's trajectory, however, changed dramatically following the Argentine crisis. While 1997 amendments to the concession contract provided that the firm could continue charging customers in dollars if the country removed the exchange rate peg, the national government invalidated such provisions, dramatically reducing the firm's revenues in real terms.[5] Meanwhile, the concessionaire's reliance on foreign debt meant that the devaluation triggered a threefold increase in the cost of its interest payments. Aguas Argentinas's debt-equity ratio, which had grown from 0.6 to as high as 2.1 in 1998, jumped to 17.1 in 2002, before falling again to 8 in 2003.[6] The value of dividends and management fees that could be repatriated fell in value by two-thirds as well. To make matters worse, the consumer price index rose 41 percent in 2002 alone. As a result, Aguas Argentinas's reported losses in 2002 were greater than its total retained earnings from the pre-crisis period.[7]

The crisis, and the national government's subsequent decision to suspend existing concession contracts and exchange rate guarantees, prompted Suez to view its Argentine water contracts with shorter time horizons. Share prices for the company dropped precipitously because of exaggerated concerns about its exposure to the Argentine market.[8] One year after the crisis, in fact, Suez

[4] Data from Aguas Argentinas annual reports 1993–2004.

[5] On the introduction of the exchange rate guarantee in the contract, see the discussion of decree 1167/97 in the preceding chapter. The economic emergency law, law 25,561, outlawed tariff indexation to the dollar and authorized the executive branch to negotiate new tariffs.

[6] Suez paid off some of the concession's debts in 2002 in an effort to placate the markets.

[7] Aguas Argentinas's losses in 2002 totaled AR$833 million pesos, whereas accumulated earnings were AR$445 million. (Numbers have not been adjusted for inflation; 2002 was the only year with significant inflation (42%). Data from *Aguas Argentinas 1993–2004*, published by Aguas Argentinas (a compilation of annual report data).

[8] Suez's share price fell 24% between January and June of 2002, even though Argentine activities accounted for just 2.5% of revenues in 2001. "Argentina-Suez Sets Aside 500m Euro to Cover Exposure." *WMRC Daily Analysis*. June 28, 2002.

announced it would reduce its holdings – even more focused on utilities management than during the 1990s – in emerging markets.[9] Given this shift in strategy, there was no need to hold on to its Argentine contracts because of reputation concerns. This led Suez managers to focus on ensuring that its water concessions returned to profitability in the short run. Company directors understood that a threefold hike in consumer rates was politically impossible following the crisis but felt strongly that a significant consumer rate adjustment or contract revision was in order. Without an agreement for each contract that addressed their concerns, it was not worth staying in the market.

Suez's negotiations with the national government over the Aguas Argentinas contract unfolded in a much more difficult political context than negotiations during the pre-crisis era. Similar to other cases discussed in this chapter, negotiations not only followed an income shock that made any increase in consumer utilities rates politically unpalatable but also were handled by heads of government who did not originally privatize services – and in the context of electoral uncertainty.[10] In spite of this, Suez pursued strong-arm tactics to force the government to address its concerns – first with interim president Eduardo Duhalde and later with President Néstor Kirchner. In February 2002, Aguas Argentinas threatened to suspend certain services and all of its construction plans if the central bank did not guarantee the company an exchange rate of one-to-one for its external debt. Receiving no response, the concessionaire suspended payments on its US$706 million debt in April 2002 and initiated its restructuring.[11] That June, the firm threatened to take the government into international arbitration if it did not begin negotiations.[12] Suez paired legal pressures with a curtailing of investments: the concessionaire invested AR$87 million, an amount equivalent to 14 percent of its revenue stream, during 2002 – less than half of what it was investing before the crisis.[13] It also stopped paying fines levied by the regulatory agency.[14] In the face of pressure from Aguas Argentinas and other firms, the Ministry of the Economy finally launched a

[9] In 2000, Suez sold Dumez, its water and sanitation construction arm. On its shift away from emerging markets, see "Suez Introduces Its 2003–2004 Action Plan." Suez press release. January 9, 2003.

[10] The Buenos Aires metropolitan area contract, effectively regulated by the national government, unfolded in a political environment receiving a political hurdle score of 2.38 for the post-crisis period (Figure 5.1), whereas it received a score of 1.08 for the pre-crisis period.

[11] Aguas Argentinas was one of many foreign-owned companies to default following the devaluation. See "Aguas de Barcelona Will Continue Operating." *El Cronista*. April 12, 2002; "Transener and Ciesa in Default." *El Cronista*. April 24, 2002.

[12] "Suez recurre tratado bilateral." *Agencia EFE-Servicio Económico*. June 28, 2002.

[13] Calculations in Argentine pesos for 2002–2005, the last year of the concession, using data from *Aguas Argentinas 1993–2004* and the 2005 *Aguas Argentinas Annual Report* and 2005 balance sheet data.

[14] "Informe sobre el grado de cumplimiento alcanzado por el contrato de concesión de Aguas Argentinas S.A." (Nota UNIREN No. 73, August 15, 2003).

renegotiation process with privatized service providers in August 2002, but these stalled in anticipation of upcoming presidential elections in April 2003.[15]

Néstor Kirchner became president on May 25, 2003, without a clear mandate, having only secured 22 percent of the popular vote. Because he was concerned about consolidating power before the 2005 congressional elections and finalizing negotiations with creditors, discussions with privatized utilities dragged on. This led Suez to file a formal case with the International Centre for the Settlement of Investment Disputes (ICSID) in July 2003 regarding the effects of the devaluation on its three concessions in Argentina. It also enlisted the help of the French ambassador. Enticed by the possibility of French support in its negotiations with the IMF, the national government signed a transitory agreement with Suez in May 2004, in which Suez agreed to temporarily suspend its ICSID claim, while tariffs remained frozen in the short run; in return, the government temporarily suspended AR$150 million in fines.[16] Announcing the agreement to the public, Kirchner described the company as a "model" and thereby set a precedent for upcoming negotiations with other foreign-owned private utilities.[17]

Further negotiations foundered, however. Suez followed up on the transitory agreement in September with a proposal reflecting the conditions under which the firm was willing to keep the Aguas Argentinas concession: a 60 percent increase in concessionaire income financed by a combination of tariff hikes, tax reductions, and other measures, and an equal division of financial responsibility for investments between the state and company.[18] This proposal resembled agreements ultimately achieved by domestic investors – such as the Chamas Group in Corrientes – for other contracts, except in one important respect: it asked for everything at once, rather than for bits over time. However, Suez's main means of exercising pressure – French diplomatic intervention, threats of international arbitration, and withholding investment – were not enough to convince the Kirchner administration to agree to these terms. All in all, Suez's legalistic approach to bargaining – typical among concessionaires led by international investors – did not yield state policies as supportive as those secured by domestic investors with diverse local holdings (Table 5.1).

By this point, Suez realized that it probably would not be able to reach a workable agreement with the Kirchner administration. After several months of preparation, it announced plans to withdraw on September 21, 2005.[19] At the government's behest, Suez entered discussions regarding a possible sale to a

[15] See, for example, "Más noticias de aguas y residuos en LatAm." *Business News Americas*. Aug. 26, 2002.

[16] "Gobierno firma acuerdo transitorio con empresa Aguas Argentinas." *La Nación*. May 12, 2004.

[17] Ibid.; "Kirchner le rescindió el contrato a Aguas Argentinas." *La Nación*. March 22, 2006.

[18] "Argentina: Suez Renegotiates Concession Contracts with Argentina." *El Cronista*. Dec. 15, 2004.

[19] "Finalizó traumáticamente una de las concesiones más cuestionadas." *La Nación*. March 22, 2006.

TABLE 5.1. *Government Responsiveness Post-Crisis, 2002–2008 (High-Hurdle Provinces)*[a]

	Investor portfolio structure		
	Foreign investor	***Joint foreign-domestic investor** (with **diverse local holdings**)*	***Domestic investor** with **diverse local holdings***
	***Aguas Argentinas** (1/2) 50%*	***Mendoza** (1.75/4) 44%*	***Corrientes** (1.5/2) 75%*
Allowing implementation of originally programmed tariff hikes, if scheduled	None scheduled	None scheduled	1
Allowing updates to consumer databases, regularization of clandestine connections as specified in contract	Not applicable (Already accomplished)	0 (Introduction of database updates blocked (continuation of block from pre-crisis period))	Not applicable (Already accomplished)
Not blocking efforts to enforce payment	1 (No major episodes highlighted by press)	1 (No major episodes)	Not applicable (Already accomplished)
Paying promised subsidies or contributions specified in contract, if applicable	Not applicable (No subsidies in contract)	0.5 - State withheld payment of subsidies, and firm withheld canon payment in retaliation - Two parties reached an agreement about mutual debt forgiveness in 2005	Not applicable (Subsidies only introduced following contract renegotiations)

TABLE 5.1. (*cont.*)

	Investor portfolio structure		
	Foreign investor	*Joint foreign-domestic investor* (with *diverse local holdings*)	*Domestic investor* with *diverse local holdings*
	Aguas Argentinas (1/2) 50%	*Mendoza* (1.75/4) 44%	*Corrientes* (1.5/2) 75%
Following through with inflation adjustments included in contract	0 (Agreement on tariff hike and/or change in investment commitments never reached following invalidation of contract)	0.25 - Discussion of rate hikes delayed until after preliminary accord reached in 2005 - Modest 19.5% increase finally approved in 2008 (prior to state intervention)	0.5 - Contract negotiation finally reached in 2005; provincial investment contributions substituted for major rate hike - Overall tariff increase of 195% by 2010 (against 200% inflation)

[a] Score for Aguas Argentinas for 2002–2006, years in which the contract was still in effect.

number of Argentine conglomerates.[20] In the end, Suez could not find an investor that would both assume the concessionaire's debt, one of its main conditions for desisting with its ICSID claim, and forgo a tariff hike, the government's condition for a new investor.[21] On March 21, 2006, six months after Suez announced its intention to withdraw from the concession, the Argentine government unilaterally canceled the contract and created a media spectacle designed to shift all blame for the failed negotiations onto the French firm. Arguing that the concessionaire had failed to meet its obligations, the government physically ejected French administrators from the company facilities. In subsequent weeks, the outline of the government's new management scheme emerged: services would be provided by a company incorporated as a private firm, with shares owned by the government and the union, thereby avoiding public sector contracting rules.[22] The central government agreed to fund the entirety of the company's investment program, and investments would focus on water coverage expansion in the metropolitan area's most important electoral district, La Matanza, and other municipalities in the southern section of the conurbation.[23]

Similar fates befell the concessions held by foreign investors under the jurisdiction of Buenos Aires Province following the crisis, where the original privatizer had also left office, and elections were very competitive (Table 5.A.II, chapter appendix).[24] The province had divided its territory into three sections when privatizing its water and sanitation services prior to the crisis. One portion was included in the Buenos Aires metropolitan area contract granted to Aguas Argentinas. A second section, which included the provincial capital, La Plata, and Bahía Blanca, was granted to Azurix, the Enron subsidiary discussed in Chapter 3. The Azurix concession had effectively ended before the crisis, with Azurix filing a claim with ICSID in September 2001.[25] A final and less lucrative contract encompassing most of the remaining territory was granted in 2000 to the Aguas del Gran Buenos Aires (AGBA) consortium led by the Italian construction firm Impregilo.[26] The area included 1.8 million inhabitants, most of whom did not yet have access to networked services: only 35 percent enjoyed connections to the water network and 20 percent to the sewerage network.[27] At

[20] "El Gobierno rescindió el contrato con Aguas Argentinas." *La Nación.* March 21, 2006; "Kirchner le rescindió el contrato a Aguas Argentinas." *La Nación.* March 22, 2006.

[21] "Hay que invertir 500 milliones y los debe poner el estado." *El Clarín.* March 23, 2006; "Argentina: Banco Galicia Holding onto Private Ideal for Water Concessions." *El Cronista.* Feb. 1, 2006.

[22] Executive decrees 303 and 304 of 2006.

[23] "Kirchner lanzará inversiones en la nueva empresa de aguas." *El Clarín.* March 29, 2006.

[24] The province received a political hurdle score of 1.97 for the post-crisis period.

[25] Azurix finally returned management of the system to the state in February 2002. "El debate por los servicios públicos: el caso bonaerense." *La Nación.* Oct. 24, 2003.

[26] "Solá también avanza con la reestatización de otra empresa de aguas." *La Nación.* March 23, 2006.

[27] "Rescindirá el contrato con una empresa ítalo-española." *La Nación.* March 22, 2006.

the time of its bid, Impregilo – the leading construction firm in Italy – was attempting to shift its focus to infrastructure services, emulating the business model of French multi-utility firms such as Vivendi.[28] Although many of its new concessions were located in Argentina, the AGBA concession was its only asset regulated by the province of Buenos Aires.[29]

In most provinces, concessionaires had been in place long enough to at least have had the opportunity to improve payment rates and update consumer databases prior to the crisis. Such efforts were far more difficult for AGBA because the crisis hit during the first years of the contract, when revenue-enhancing measures are typically first implemented, and therefore prevented the firm from moving the concession onto stable economic footing. Major investments were, unsurprisingly, unappealing in this context. Given that Impregilo did not have other assets in the province, it had little to lose by aggravating provincial officials by withholding investment. The firm called for an adjustment to its investment commitments and pressed the provincial government to renegotiate its contract after the crisis. Following the 2002 cancellation of the Azurix contract and the formation of a new state-owned company to take over services, the government saw little reason to accede to the firm's requests.[30] The receipt of a AR$170 million loan from the World Bank to fund sewerage infrastructure, which gave the province more financial leeway to address infrastructure deficits on its own, also weakened AGBA's bargaining position.[31] Negotiations reached an impasse. When the national government cancelled the Aguas Argentinas contract in March 2006, the governor of Buenos Aires Province took the opportunity to cancel the AGBA contract.[32] A year later, the main partners began international arbitration proceedings against Argentina, alleging that the government had expropriated their investments.[33]

28 See statements by company managing director Giorgio Romiti and major shareholder Alfio Marchini in "Marchini Aims to Create Utilities Conglomerate on French Vivendi Model." *Il Sole 24 Ore*. July 1, 1999; "Impregilo Expects Good Revenue Figures to 2001, Targets Water, Airports." *Il Sole 24 Ore*. Feb. 23, 2000.

29 In 2000, 53% of its concession revenues came from Argentina, where it possessed a number of highway and other infrastructure concessions. See Intermonte Securities. "Impregilo." May 8, 2001: 11; Crédit Agricole Indosuez Cheuvreux. "Impregilo Construction: 2001 Results." April 2002: 13.

30 The ICSID award for Impregilo documents the firm's reluctance to invest after the crisis, its appeals for contract renegotiations, and the provincial government's decision to grant tariff increases to the province's state-owned provider, Aguas Bonaerenses, but not to AGBA.

31 Regarding the loan, see "Rescindirá el contrato con una empresa ítalo-española." *La Nación*. March 22, 2006.

32 "Solá también avanza con la reestatización de otra empresa de aguas." *La Nación*. March 23, 2006.

33 "Constructora italiana Impregilo denuncia a Argentina ante CIADI." *Agencia EFE-Servicio Económico*. Aug. 3, 2007; "Aguas de Bilbao y Urbaser llevan a Argentina a los tribunales." *Expansión*. Oct. 27, 2007.

Overall, these cases demonstrate the difficulties faced by concessions led by foreign investors in high-hurdle political environments following the Argentine crisis. Aguas Argentinas managed to work well with the national government prior to the crisis, but its managers could not broker a workable agreement afterward – even after enlisting the French ambassador and threatening to take the country into international arbitration. Somewhat ironically, the fact that Aguas Argentinas presided over a significant debt-financed investment program during the 1990s made it difficult to find buyers for Suez's stake in the concession. As a result, the state finally stepped in and took over the service, justifying its actions with strong allegations of contract noncompliance. As of mid-2013, the case was still in international arbitration. Foreign investors presiding over the AGBA concession in Buenos Aires Province fared even worse, not having had an opportunity to get their utility on firm financial footing before the crisis.

A Foreign-Domestic Joint Venture Reaches a Similar Stalemate in Mendoza

Even before the Argentine crisis, the Mendoza concession was not faring well. Relations between the provincial government and the concession's lead investors, the French MNC Saur and the American MNC Azurix, had become acrimonious and ensnared in legal conflicts. The crisis presented major challenges for the Mendoza concession – although not to the extent experienced by concessions located in what had been low-hurdle political environments prior to the crisis, which had tended to oversee higher rates of investment. Because the company had not taken on a large amount of dollar-denominated debt to fund major investments as had many other international operators, its debt-equity ratio only jumped from 0.41 to 0.99 following the devaluation.[34] Interest payments and operating costs had still risen substantially enough, however, for the company's modest returns on sales to go negative: in 2002, the company reported that its return on sales was −103 percent, which improved to −14 percent by 2003.[35]

Like other provinces, Mendoza adhered to the national government's economic emergency law, which forbade indexation of tariffs to the U.S. dollar and opened up all concession contracts for renegotiation. Wanting to ensure that its primary asset in the country would return to profitability, lead investor Saur filed for a tariff revision almost immediately, citing changes in its cost structure.[36] The

34 Ratios calculated from OSM income statements, supplied by the sector regulator, EPAS.

35 Calculated from the company balance sheets and regulatory agency data. Returns on equity are not quite as dire, ranging from −42% in 2002 to −2% in 2005.

36 Chapter 3 describes Saur's holdings in Argentina, which the OSM concession anchored. On its application for a rate increase, see "OSM quiere un aumento de tarifas." *Los Andes*. April 5, 2002.

firm then applied additional pressure by cutting its investment rate from 26 percent of revenues (the pre-crisis average) to 14 percent, a low rate that would still ensure infrastructure quality did not deteriorate significantly.[37] Unhappy with the progress on contract renegotiations attained by mid-2002, Saur filed a case in August with the World Bank arbitration court.[38] These highly public pressure tactics served mainly to turn regulators and provincial legislators more firmly against the private concessionaire, especially given high levels of electoral competition and divided government (Table 5.A.II, chapter appendix). The provincial regulatory agency advised the executive branch not to grant a tariff increase under the renegotiation, given the firm's failure to meet investment obligations prior to the crisis.[39] Governor Roberto Iglesias did not want to take such a strong line, because the government had also failed to meet some of its contractual obligations – which meant it could lose millions if the case went into international arbitration – but negotiations remained stalled.

The tenor of the negotiations shifted in early 2004 with the arrival of a new governor and the sale of Azurix's stake in the concession to an Argentine conglomerate with local operations. Julio Cobos, also of the Radical Party, succeeded Iglesias as governor in December 2003. Just a few weeks later, Sagua S.A. – the Argentine firm that already led the concessions in Formosa and Santiago del Estero – purchased Azurix's 32 percent stake in the concession. The Sielecki family, the owners of Sagua S.A., had been working in the province of Mendoza for decades in sectors as diverse as pharmaceuticals, petrochemicals, and wineries.[40]

Saur and its new domestic partner were able to reach a partial renegotiation agreement that provided for the cancellation of mutual debts. Governor Cobos only managed to secure legislative approval for the agreement in the opposition-controlled legislature at the end of 2005.[41] Although the agreement represented a concrete step forward, it only partly addressed the financial problems facing the concessionaire, which reportedly continued to lose money: returns were negative in 2005, resulting in a –4 percent return on sales and –2 percent return on equity.[42]

Following this accord, negotiations moved on to a second set of more controversial topics, including a tariff revision. Saur agreed to temporarily suspend

[37] Average ratio of investment to revenue, calculated for 2002–2005 period from OSM income statements.

[38] Decree 487/02 opened contract renegotiations. "French Saur Suspends Legal Claim vs. Argentina with World Bank Court." *Latin American News Digest*. April 17, 2006.

[39] For more detail, see Post (2008).

[40] It was public knowledge that Azurix would withdraw from the concession by the end of 2001. "La crisis de Enron preanuncia cambios en accionista de OSM." *Los Andes*. Dec. 1, 2001; "South Water compró acciones de OSM." *Diario UNO*. Jan. 8, 2004; "South Water formaliza su interés por las acciones de Saur en OSM." *Los Andes*. April 17, 2007.

[41] The agreement, which dates to October 2005, was finally ratified via law 7491.

[42] Ratios calculated using data from EPAS and OSM.

its ICSID claims during this renegotiation process and decided to take the lead in negotiations with the provincial government. After roughly a year, however, Saur lost patience and announced it was giving up. It would permanently withdraw its ICSID claim if the province would let it sell its shares and transfer its status as the technical operator of the concession to another firm.[43] The administration reached an agreement with the French operator in April 2007 that allowed it to sell its shares under a number of conditions – including that the incoming firm would receive only a 19.7 percent tariff increase and would commit to invest AR$11 million per year, and Saur would retract its ICSID claim – but negotiations continued to drag because of electoral concerns. Governor Cobos left office to become the vice president with the concession in limbo and Saur's international arbitration claim still in place. His successor as governor, Peronist Celso Jacque, finally took control of the company when it became clear that no domestic firm would invest heavily under these conditions. (Saur's local partner, Sagua, continued to pressure for an additional tariff increase.)[44] The province announced the cancellation of the concession contract and its takeover of the company in July 2010 after a one-year "intervention" in the company's administration.[45]

In summary, foreign investors in the comparatively contentious province of Mendoza failed to negotiate a workable post-crisis settlement with a series of different provincial administrations, and finally pulled out of the country. Although Saur secured a new joint venture partner with a significant local presence in 2004, this was not enough to rescue the concession. Sagua adopted a more conciliatory approach with the government, but the two firms often worked at cross-purposes. Saur's very public pressure tactics ultimately yielded little fruit: the government's responsiveness to the concessionaire's concerns can be rated at 44 percent, somewhat lower than in metropolitan Buenos Aires and far lower than in Corrientes, where a local investor managed a concession under even more difficult political circumstances (Figure 5.1).

This analysis of the post-crisis trajectories of contracts in Buenos Aires Province, Greater Buenos Aires, and Mendoza suggests that MNCs controlling concessions in high-hurdle environments face major difficulties in negotiating with host governments. Government authorities in these relatively contentious and fragmented political environments were constrained by concerns about reelection and often had difficulty obtaining approval for revised contractual agreements because an opposition party or faction controlled the legislature. This made contractual amendments allowing for rate increases and other potentially unpopular measures very difficult for authorities to support. Foreign investors' tendency to pressure governments through highly public measures

[43] "Se van los accionistas franceses de OSM." *Los Andes*. April 8, 2007.

[44] "Por su déficit, OSM busca otro aumento, pero de 40%." *Los Andes*. March 29, 2008.

[45] "Jacque reestatizó Obras Sanitarias tras revocar el contrato al concesionario." *Infobae*. July 12, 2010.

such as threats to initiate international arbitration proceedings only raised the visibility and contentiousness of contract renegotiations. Frustrated by their lack of progress, investors decided to exit, and contracts were canceled.

INVESTORS WITH DIVERSE LOCAL HOLDINGS SECURE BETTER DEALS

A domestic investor with diverse local holdings in the Corrientes concession managed to secure a comprehensive contract renegotiation addressing pressing financial concerns, while operating in the most challenging political environment of any concessionaire. Figure 5.1 shows that the province's average political hurdle score for the post-crisis period, 2.5, was higher than that of any other jurisdiction.

During the pre-crisis period, two sets of owners controlled the Corrientes concession. A group of Buenos Aires–based investors had first secured the concession but found it difficult to negotiate responses with provincial authorities to problems that surfaced, particularly as the political environment grew more factionalized in the mid-1990s. They sold their operations in 1996 to the Corrientes-based Chamas Group, which had local operations in agriculture, construction, engineering, media, and real estate. The new owners managed to improve the concessionaire's relationship with the political establishment and invest at three times the rate of their predecessors prior to the crisis.

The Argentine economic and political crisis of 2001–2002 ushered in major challenges for the Corrientes concession. As in other provinces, the devaluation brought about a tripling in the cost of imported inputs and substantially eroded consumers' ability and willingness to pay for services, while significant inflation affected important input costs. Corrientes's political environment was particularly unstable during and after the crisis. Following the implosion of the provincial political party system in 1999 and as the country careened into the 2001–2002 crisis, the federal government appointed administrators to run the province; the federal intervention continued through December 2001. A new administration from the Radical Party came to power that month (the nadir of the crisis) and was working to establish political authority under very difficult circumstances, including tight fiscal conditions.[46]

The concessionaire cautiously yet continuously pushed for contract renegotiations following the crisis. With other investments and social relationships at stake in the province, the owners of Aguas de Corrientes refrained from legal appeals and public threats to exit the concession (Table 5.A.I, chapter appendix). The company president stressed that the group's local ties offered them access to local officials but

[46] Provincial government expenditures (accounting for inflation) did not approach pre-crisis levels until 2004 (data from Ministry of the Interior, Argentina).

also forced them to moderate their requests.[47] Concerned about maintaining good relations with the administration, the firm kept investing as negotiations proceeded. Between 2002 and 2006 it invested on average 9 percent of revenues, its 2005 and 2006 investments far exceeding amounts in previous years.[48] The firm also needed patience because each time a new governor arrived, it had to revisit many aspects of negotiations that had already been conducted with the previous administration (Table 5.A.II, chapter appendix).

Over time, negotiations yielded a reconfigured set of contractual responsibilities that helped the concession return to profitability while also avoiding raising consumer rates to the extent that would be required to fully address the devaluation and inflation. The firm received rate increases of roughly 10 percent annually, an amount that compensated for inflation of the post-crisis period.[49] The firm and governor also agreed that the state would fund half of the concession's investment program and subsidize services for low-income consumers in 2005.[50] This effectively led to a doubling of the rate of investment. Government-funded tariff subsidies for low-income consumers were introduced to raise collections for the firm, as nonpayment is more common within this group. The lead investor's diverse holdings in the province offered the government opportunities to allow it to earn returns outside of the concession itself, partly compensating for the concession's economic fragility: the province-financed investment fund established in 2005 does not prevent the concessionaire from contracting with related companies, and the province actively involved the firm in other state contracts. For example, the provincial government awarded the Chamas group a contract to improve the management of the provincial electricity service in December 2007.[51] Comparing the responsiveness

47 Interview with Pablo Chamas, president of Aguas de Corrientes, June 2010.

48 According to company records, the concessionaire invested AR$1.2 million in 2002, AR$1.1 million in 2003, AR$1.5 million in 2004, AR$2.5 million in 2005, and AR$3.7 million in 2006. This amounts to approximately 5.8%, 5.2%, 7.3%, 12%, and 22% of revenues for each year. The state has funded approximately AR$2.5 million per year on top of this after the 2005 agreement, which doubled the amount invested.

49 ASOC resolutions 042/03, 028/04, 144/04, 80/05, 078/07, 083/08, 189/08, 232/08, 032/09, and 038/10 and gubernatorial decree 2533/08. The total increase is of approximately 195%, whereas inflation has been approximately 200%.

50 Provincial decree number 2940, which ratifies the 2005 contract agreement, was issued on December 7, 2005.

51 The group was first granted a consulting contract, which was converted into a management contract, that gave them 30% of the returns earned by the provincial electricity company. See "Una empresa del Grupo Aguas brindará asesoramiento a la Dirección de Energía." www.el-litoral.com.ar. Dec. 23, 2006; "Urbatec asoma por la ventanilla de la Dpec." www.el-litoral.com.ar. Dec. 27, 2006; "Cuando el sistema democrático se convierte en un buen negocio." www.corrientesaldia.com.ar. Feb. 11, 2008. While this case illustrates the opportunities afforded to investors by including construction firms in their local portfolios, other combinations also offer opportunities: any sector in which government policy influences the terms in which an investor does business (hotels, real estate, minerals and oil extraction, etc.) would offer opportunities for trade-offs.

of the political authorities with that observed in metropolitan Buenos Aires and Mendoza shows that this local economic group achieved far better results: the level of government responsiveness score is 75 percent, compared with 50 percent and 44 percent for the other two concessions, which were controlled by foreign investors (Table 5.1).

The long-run evolution of the Corrientes concession, it should now be clear, matches theoretical expectations: even in the context of a volatile political and economic environment, the government and a local investor negotiated adaptations to the concession contract, reconfiguring the investment program and tariff structure. These contractual adaptations brought about changes in the split between private and public sector responsibility over time. The investor's diverse portfolio of local holdings also allowed it to benefit from revised contractual agreements unavailable to firms without other local operations, such as provisions allowing for contracting with related enterprises. The fluid relationship in this case was not a model of transparency and did not bring about the sort of massive jump in investment levels often undertaken by large MNCs in the first years of their contracts, but it was politically resilient under difficult circumstances and yielded a steady rate of investment over time.[52] As inflation levels rose at the end of the decade and the provincial government received fewer financial transfers from the central government than expected, the concession became quite fragile. Investment levels dropped. However, at the end of 2012, the Chamas Group continued to operate the concession, and the province proposed to extend the concession's remit to additional municipalities in the province.[53]

CONCLUSION

This chapter examines the post-crisis trajectories of concession contracts located in provinces with significant political hurdles. After the crisis, investors and host governments needed to agree on revised contractual terms following the national government's 2002 passage of an economic emergency law that opened all concession contracts for renegotiation. Until contracts were renegotiated, the concessions hovered in a legal limbo and were unprofitable. Investors possessed less leverage during these negotiations than they had during ongoing discussions regarding contract compliance and formal revisions to existing contracts during the pre-crisis period. In the first years following the crisis, this lower leverage stemmed from a reduced willingness to invest given legal and political uncertainties, as well as politicians' concerns about consumer sentiment. As the Argentine economy improved and the state obtained important new sources of revenue, such as taxes on agricultural commodities,

[52] Investment levels by domestic investors with diverse holdings working in provinces with more stable political environments were higher both before and after the Argentine crisis. In Salta, the concessionaire invested the equivalent of 31% of revenues before the crisis and 22% after the crisis (ratios calculated with data from Aguas de Salta).

[53] "Nuevo rechazo al traspaso del servicio de agua potable." www.el-litoral.com.ar. July 4, 2012.

it was able to fund infrastructure investment on its own, gaining another important source of leverage.

The respective abilities of foreign investors, domestic investors without local operations, and domestic investors with diverse local assets, to secure workable post-crisis agreements and subsequent decisions regarding market exit emerge clearly in the cases examined. Foreign investors failed universally to secure renegotiation agreements that provided rate increases that partly addressed inflation during the post-crisis period or shifted the responsibility for investment programs. Instead, their legalistic and public negotiating tactics tended to make their relationships with host governments tenser. Frustrated by their lack of progress, the foreign investors controlling the concessions in metropolitan Buenos Aires, Buenos Aires Province, and Mendoza decided to exit the market. Unable to find suitable domestic investors to take their places, governments assumed control of the systems. In contrast, a domestic investor with a diverse local portfolio in the province of Corrientes fared far better in post-crisis negotiations under more difficult political circumstances: the Chamas Group's high levels of patience, sensitivity to the political resonance of particular policies, and ability to accrue financial gains through other operations the local economy all contributed to its ability to keep its relationship with the changing heads of the local administration on track. Following the successful conclusion of an agreement in 2005 that provided a framework for tariff increases and shifted some investment responsibilities to the state, operations returned to profitability. The firms' situation continued to improve with subsequent negotiations. These findings are summarized in Table 5.A.I (chapter appendix).

This correlation between the type of investor and the ability of host governments and concessionaires to negotiate workable post-crisis settlements does not, the evidence suggests, stem from alternative factors. It would be difficult to attribute the observed variation to differences in regulatory institution design. First of all, as the case studies highlight, negotiations occurred directly between high-level government ministers and lead investors; regulatory agencies tended to be sidelined, regardless of their formal powers. In addition, variation in formal independence does not correlate with patterns of contract cancellation or investor exit.[54] The Kirchner administration would not have spent months searching for an appropriate private sector replacement for Suez in metropolitan Buenos Aires before announcing the government would assume control over services if it were ideologically disposed to support public sector provision. The cases do suggest a growing conviction on the part of the Kirchner administration that it was easier to work with domestic investors than foreign investors; however, this preference does not account for variation in the post-crisis experience of domestic investors, which will become clear in Chapter 6.

[54] While all agencies were formally independent, investors possessed a right of administrative appeal in the cases of Corrientes and metropolitan Buenos Aires. Appeals were not allowed in Mendoza and Buenos Aires Province (Azpiazu et al. 2008: 124.).

CHAPTER APPENDIX

TABLE 5.A.1. *Post-Crisis Expectations and Findings for Provinces with High Political Hurdles*

	Investor portfolio structure					
	Foreign		*Domestic* without *diverse local holdings*		*Domestic* with *diverse local holdings*	
	Expect	*Observe*	*Expect*	*Observe*	*Expect*	*Observe*
Contractual outcomes						
Investor exit	High	Aguas Argentinas: Yes Buenos Aires Province (ABGA): Yes Mendoza:[a] Yes	Medium	No cases	Low	Corrientes: No
Contract renegotiation (if warranted)	Low	Aguas Argentinas: No accord Buenos Aires Province (ABGA): No accord Mendoza: Partial accord	Medium	No cases	High	Corrientes: Full, formal accord
Indicators of health of the negotiating process						
Government addresses concessionaire financial concerns	Low	Aguas Argentinas: Medium Buenos Aires Province (ABGA): No data Mendoza: Medium	Medium	No cases	High	Corrientes: High
Concessionaire finances Stabilize	Low	Aguas Argentinas: Low Buenos Aires Province (ABGA): Low Mendoza: Low	Medium	No cases	High	Corrientes: High

Firm employs legalistic retaliatory measures	High	Aguas Argentinas: High Buenos Aires Province (ABGA): High Mendoza: High	Low	No cases	Low	Corrientes: Low
Firm invests significant fraction of revenues	Low	Aguas Argentinas: Medium Buenos Aires Province (ABGA): No data Mendoza: Medium	Low	No cases	Medium	Corrientes: Medium

[a] Case coding is based on less information than cases for which separate charts exist in this chapter and should therefore be viewed as less precise. Consult the case narratives in this chapter for the empirical details on which coding is based. Note that starting in 2004, half of the private shares in the Mendoza concession were controlled by a domestic investor with significant local holdings.

TABLE 5.A.II. *Political Hurdle Index Components for Post-Crisis Period (High-Hurdle Provinces)*

Year	*Competition for governor*	*Competition for legislature*	*Divided government*	*Governor did not privatize*	*Federal intervention*	*Hurdle index*
Buenos Aires Province						
2002	–	–				0
2003	Low	Low		Not privatizer		2.33
2004	–	–		Not privatizer		1.75
2005	–	High	Divided	Not privatizer		3.5
2006	–	–	Divided	Not privatizer		2.25
Buenos Aires metropolitan area (scores for national government)						
2002	–	–		Not privatizer		2
2003	High	Low		Not privatizer		2.75
2004	–	–		Not privatizer		2
2005	–	High		Not privatizer		2.75
2006	–	–		Not privatizer		1.5
Mendoza						
2002	–	–	Divided	Not privatizer		2.5
2003	Medium	Medium	Divided	Not privatizer		2.92
2004	–	–	Divided	Not privatizer		3
2005	–	High		Not privatizer		2.75
2006	–	–		Not privatizer		1.5
2007	High	High		Not privatizer		2.25
2008	–	–		Not privatizer		2
2009	–	High		Not privatizer		2.75

Corrientes					
2002	–	–	Divided	Not privatizer	3
2003	–	High		Not privatizer	2.75
2004	–	–		Not privatizer	1.5
2005	Low	Low		Not privatizer	1.58
2006	–	–		Not privatizer	2
2007	–	Medium	Divided	Not privatizer	3.42
2008	–	–	Divided	Not privatizer	2.5
2009	Low	High	Divided	Not privatizer	3.25

Formula for index: Max(legislative, gubernatorial competition)/3 + Divided government + Governor did not privatize + Governor not allied with Menem and not privatizer (for 1999 and earlier) + Federal intervention + Effect of turnover score (1–0.25*years since turnover for 4 years following turnover)

6

Diverse Local Holdings Also Prevail in Calm Political Contexts

While Chapter 5 compares the performance of different types of investors in contracts located in relatively contentious political environments during the post-crisis period, this chapter considers contracts located in provinces characterized by low or moderate levels of political hurdles in the wake of the Argentine crisis. In other words, it compares the respective ability of different types of investors to operate in what this book's theoretical framework suggests are more manageable contexts, but at a time when all types possessed little leverage because of their reduced willingness to invest.

We would expect investor organizational structure to also be a strong predictor of the longevity and constructiveness of firm-government negotiations in environments with fewer political hurdles during the post-crisis period. Foreign investors should, in most cases, face tremendous difficulties securing agreements, grow impatient in the process, and exit the market. Domestic investors *without* local holdings should stand a somewhat better chance of concluding contract renegotiations and persist longer in their contracts but still fail the majority of the time. Domestic investors *with* local holdings, in contrast, should be able to negotiate more effectively than their foreign or domestic counterparts, securing better post-crisis agreements that provide incentives to persist in their contracts. We would also expect that indicators of the health of ongoing negotiations between host governments and firms would vary with investor portfolios, as observed in the contentious political environments in Chapter 5. This being said, all types of investors should find it easier to negotiate with host governments in low- to moderate-hurdle environments than in the high-hurdle environments examined in Chapter 5. Heads of government in low- to moderate-hurdle environments will be less concerned about the short-run political consequences of granting policy concessions, such as tariff increases, to firms. These expectations, as well as scoring for the cases examined in this chapter, are summarized in Table 6.A.I (chapter appendix).

THE FAILURE OF FOREIGN-LED CONTRACTS IN PROVINCES WITH LOW TO MODERATE POLITICAL HURDLES

This section examines the post-crisis evolution of four contracts, majority-controlled by foreign investors, that were located in provinces with low- to moderate-political hurdles following the 2001–2002 crisis: Aguas Cordobesas (Córdoba Province), Aguas Provinciales de Santa Fe (Santa Fe Province), Aguas del Valle (Catamarca Province), and SAMSA (Misiones Province). In each province, original privatizers had left office and their successors faced moderate to low levels of political competition (Table 6.A.II, chapter appendix).

We would expect to observe contentious and fraught negotiations between provincial governments and lead investors in all four cases, with the foreign investors controlling the concessions placing large and highly public demands on political authorities, which would prove difficult to accommodate even in less contentious political settings. As the ensuing discussion shows, this indeed occurred: only in Misiones Province did a foreign investor secure an agreement sufficiently attractive to make it worthwhile to stay in the market.

Foreign Investors Exit Contracts in Santa Fe, Córdoba, and Catamarca

The foreign investors holding controlling stakes in the Santa Fe, Córdoba, and Catamarca concessions failed to secure workable post-crisis settlements providing a viable financial basis for continuing to operate in the country. The Santa Fe and Córdoba concessions were led by Suez, the French utilities giant that also controlled the Aguas Argentinas concession for the Buenos Aires metropolitan area, discussed in Chapter 5. Suez responded to the Argentine crisis by questioning its expansion efforts in the utilities sectors in emerging markets. This led it to enter renegotiations willing to accept only accords that returned individual concessions to profitability. Otherwise, it made no sense to hold on to contracts, given that Suez no longer needed to demonstrate its ability to work in emerging markets.

Prior to the crisis, the Santa Fe concessionaire invested significant sums in the provincial water and sanitation system. As Chapter 4 shows, Suez undertook such investment out of concern for its larger contract for the Buenos Aires metropolitan system, as the Santa Fe provincial administration was only moderately supportive. Conditions grew far more difficult for the concessionaire, however, following the crisis. The costs of foreign inputs rose considerably, contributing – alongside a 41 percent rise in the consumer price index in 2002 – to difficulties meeting operational costs.[1] In addition, interest payments

[1] According to company records, the cost of chemical inputs rose 106%, and the cost of electricity and other types of fuel rose 44% between 2001 and 2002.

on debt grew substantially because a high proportion of its debt had been contracted overseas: the concession's debt-equity ratio increased from 2.2 in 2001 to 6.56 in 2002.[2] The concessionaire suspended its debt payments in an effort to cope with the situation, and Suez transferred a total of US$545 million to its Argentina subsidiaries to pay down their collective losses.[3]

Following the passage of the national government's economic emergency law, Governor Carlos Reutemann – the governor who had originally privatized services – issued a decree in March 2002 suspending investment goals included in the original concession contract and initiating contract renegotiations.[4] A second gubernatorial decree rejected a separate firm request for a tariff increase to compensate for inflation, stating that the contract renegotiation needed to be completed before such requests could be considered.[5] Suez applied pressure on the government to move forward with negotiations by cutting back on investment dramatically, investing only the equivalent of 8% of revenues in 2002 and 12% in 2003, compared with pre-crisis levels of 60%.[6] Suez also initiated international arbitration proceedings regarding its three Argentine concessions in June 2002.[7] Almost a year later, the firm announced that if negotiations did not yield a workable agreement, it would advance with international arbitration proceedings.[8]

These pressure tactics yielded no results during Reutemann's tenure, and ultimately backfired during the administration of his successor, Jorge Obeid (2004–2008).[9] By halting investments and filing for international arbitration, the firm opened itself up to political attacks. Obeid, following Kirchner's example at the national level, maintained that Suez should invest significantly before receiving any sort of compensation for the devaluation. He also made public statements indicating that he would be happy if the firm left.[10] In response to governmental pressure, Suez submitted an investment plan for 2004–2005 but argued that, without a rate increase, it could not finance even a modest investment program designed to maintain existing infrastructure.[11] The firm, in other words, pursued an all-or-nothing strategy, pushing for a

[2] Calculated with data from Aguas Provinciales de Santa Fe.

[3] "Aguas Argentinas Suspends Repayment of $700 Million Debt over Devaluation." *El País*. April 11, 2002; "Suez Claims Compensations." *El Clarín*. March 3, 2003.

[4] Decree 221/02.

[5] Decree 391/02. Cited in Roitman and Ferro (2003, 24).

[6] Investment as a portion of net sales, calculated from Aguas Provinciales de Santa Fe balance sheets.

[7] "Suez recurre tratado bilateral exigir indemnizaciones Argentina." *Agencia EFE-Servicio Económico*. June 28, 2002.

[8] "Suez Claims Compensations." *El Clarín*. March 3, 2003.

[9] Reutemann was governor from 1992–1995 and 2000–2003, while Obeid was governor from 1996–1999 and 2004–2008.

[10] The governor was quoted as saying: "I hope that they leave.... They provide a bad service and on top of it they act as if they have been wronged." Translation by author. "Acuerdo en Córdoba, Guerra en Santa Fe." *La Nación*. Aug. 19, 2004.

[11] "Sanitaria presenta alternativas de inversión." *Business News Americas*. Sept. 23, 2004.

single large tariff increase and revised investment program as a condition for withdrawing its arbitration claim and staying in the market. The governor lashed out publicly in response, and entertained the idea of holding a binding public referendum on the future of the concession.[12] Several days later, he issued a decree invalidating all resolutions passed after 2000 regarding negotiations with the concessionaire. The Santa Fe government's level of responsiveness to firm concerns following the crisis can only be seen as low in comparative perspective (Table 6.1).

By early 2005, Suez saw no way forward in Santa Fe and began looking for domestic investors to take over the concession, even as it continued operating the water systems for the Buenos Aires metropolitan area and Córdoba. The provincial government also began to search for replacement firms. Ultimately, however, they were unable to find alternate investors willing to both operate the system without a tariff increase and assume the concessionaire's debt.[13] The province took over services and immediately announced a tariff increase.[14] This case, then, conforms to theoretical expectations: Suez had shorter time horizons and was partial to brinksmanship-like negotiating strategies and so had little chance to make the concession work in the post-crisis period.

The political and economic context for negotiations was more favorable for Suez in Córdoba Province. Although the value of the concessionaire's debt in local currency more than tripled and the concessionaire reported losses in 2002 almost as large as its annual revenue stream, its debt as a fraction of revenues was lower than in Santa Fe.[15] This meant that in Córdoba the concessionaire needed a less generous settlement to be able to address its financial difficulties. Perhaps more importantly, the governor of Córdoba province, José Manual De la Sota, was a longtime ally of former president Menem and supportive of neoliberal policies. In addition, the October 2003 elections delivered his Peronist Party a majority in the provincial legislature (Table 6.A.II, chapter appendix).

Suez's short time horizons and emphasis on legalistic negotiating tactics also presented problems in Córdoba, however. As noted previously, Suez lost no time in registering its claim with the International Centre for Settlement of Investment Disputes (ICSID) regarding the impact of the devaluation on all three of its Argentine concession contracts; it did so six months after the devaluation, in July 2002. It also scaled back investments and withheld its annual canon payment to the province as additional means of bringing the province to the

12 "Llamarán a un plebiscito en Santa Fe." *El Cronista*. Sept. 29, 2004.

13 A number of domestic business groups expressed interest. See Post (2008).

14 "Aguas Santafesinas aumentará las tarifas." *La Nación*. Jan. 24, 2006.

15 The firm's reported liabilities grew from AR$65 million in 2001 to AR$192 million in 2002. The concession reported a net loss of AR$71 million in 2002 against an income of AR$77 million. (Calculated from data from Aguas Cordobesas.) See Post (2008) for more detail.

TABLE 6.1. *Government Responsiveness Post-Crisis, 2002–2008 (Low- to Moderate-Hurdle Provinces)*[a]

	Investor portfolio structure					
	Foreign investor			*Domestic investor* without *local holdings*	*Domestic investor* with *local holdings*	
	Santa Fe (0.5/3) 17%	*Córdoba* (2002–2005) (0.75/3) 25%	*Misiones* (3.5/5) 70%	*Formosa* (1.5/5) 37.5%	*Salta (Joint venture: domestic* with *and* without *local holdings)* (5.5/6) 92%	*Córdoba* (2006–2011) (4.75/5) 95%
Allowing implementation of originally programmed tariff hikes, if scheduled	Not applicable (Contract suspended for renegotiation when crisis hit)	Not applicable (Contract suspended for renegotiation when crisis hit)	1	Not applicable	1 (Originally programmed 20% hike finally implemented in 2002)	1 (Rate hikes, provided for under new contract, implemented)
Allowing updates to consumer databases, regularization of clandestine connections as specified in contract	Not applicable (Already accomplished)	Not applicable (Already accomplished)	Not applicable (Already accomplished)	Not applicable (Already accomplished)	1 - Aerial photography for consumer database updates begin in earnest in 2001; implementation not blocked - State supported introduction of metering (up to 15% in 2007)	Not applicable (Already accomplished)
Not blocking efforts to enforce payment	Not applicable (Already accomplished)	Not applicable (Already accomplished)[b]	1	0.5: - Blocked service cutoffs for 2002–2003 - Required firm to accept provincial bonds for bills following crisis	1 (No major episodes)	1 (No major episodes, state actually supports firm efforts to install water meters)

Paying promised subsidies or contributions specified in contract, if applicable	0.5 (Government institutions not paying bills)	0.5 (Not all government institutions paying bills (accord for forgiveness of mutual debts in 2004)	0.5 (Not all government institutions paying bills)	0.75 (Introduced new subsidy for the poor but always several months late with payment)	0.75 - State has lagged a bit behind with infrastructure it has committed to providing but has mostly met commitments - Governor secured federal grant for AR$58 million aqueduct	0.75 (State has sometimes lagged with promised contributions to investment program but is generally supportive)
Progress toward contract renegotiation	0 (No accord)	0.25 - Transitory accord reached 8/04 - Contract negotiations finally concluded 12/05, but withdrawn	0.5 (Partial accord)	0 (No accord)	1 (Full accord)	1 (Full accord)
Tariff adjustments beyond contract renegotiation	0 (Inflation adjustments postponed until after contract renegotiations)	0 (Inflation adjustments postponed until after contract renegotiation)	0.5 (Inflation adjustments made after comprehensive contract renegotiation)	0.25 (Tariff unchanged until 2008, but subsidy added)	0.75 - Tariff adjustments granted late, but have happened - Tariff hikes not repealed	1 (Rate adjustments of 80% for residential consumers and 124% for commercial users Dec. 2007–March 2010)

[a] Scores reflect years in which contracts still in effect.

[b] The concessionaire was still allowed to disconnect customers for nonpayment following the crisis, but a provincial judge ruled that the firm needed to increase the amount of lifeline water supply it delivered to households whose service had been cut off. "Aumentan el cupo de agua para indigentes." *La Nación*. April 15, 2002.

bargaining table.[16] Whereas Suez made no progress toward contract renegotiation in Santa Fe, it reached a provisional accord in Córdoba in 2004 that provided for the forgiveness of mutual debts. Aguas Cordobesas then pushed for a comprehensive renegotiation that included a tariff increase that would increase its revenue stream by 50 percent.[17] In December 2005, Suez finally did manage to reach such an agreement with the governor.[18] Under these conditions, Suez would be willing to stay on, even though it had already announced that it would be pulling out of its other two contracts in the country.[19]

The firm's insistence on a single and very significant tariff increase – rather than the sorts of staged, more moderate tariff increases requested by concessionaires controlled by domestic investors – ultimately proved to be the concession's downfall.[20] The weight of the one-time rate increase was to fall on middle- and upper-class consumers, who would experience tariff increases of 25–100 percent. There was a public outcry in February 2006, when households received the first bills that included the rate increases.[21] The newspapers carried stories alleging errors in how the company had applied the new tariff formula, and De la Sota's main political opponent in the province, the mayor of the capital city of Córdoba, seized the opportunity to mobilize against the governor.[22] De la Sota backed down in the face of pressure from his opponent, the public, and the national government, first suspending the application of the new rates for ninety days and then unilaterally reducing them to increases of 15 percent for the middle class and 18 percent for higher income brackets.[23] In the face of this turnaround, Suez announced that it would pull out of the Aguas Cordobesas concession.[24] Its ICSID claim would progress unless the province was able to help it transfer its shares and debt to another company. Over the next few months, the province and firm worked out an arrangement under which one of Suez's minority partners – which had previously held only 16 percent of the concession's shares – would be willing to assume control. The fact that the

16 Whereas Suez had invested the rough equivalent of 35% of net sales before the crisis, it scaled back investments to 11% of net sales following the crisis. (Calculated from Aguas Cordobesas data.) On the firm's decision to stop paying the canon, see Ducci (2007: 89).

17 "Acuerdo en Córdoba, Guerra en Santa Fe." *La Nación*. Aug. 19, 2004; "Subirá el agua hasta un 50% en Córdoba." *La Nación*. Dec. 23, 2005; "Aguas debe invertir $55 millones hasta 2008." *La Voz del Interior*. March 23, 2006.

18 Ratified by the legislature by law 9,279. "Subirá el agua hasta un 50% en Córdoba." *La Nación*. Dec. 23, 2005; "Aguas debe invertir $55 millones hasta 2008." *La Voz del Interior*. March 23, 2006.

19 Suez and Agbar announced their intentions to exit the Santa Fe and Aguas Argentinas contracts earlier in 2005.

20 The provincial legislature ratified by accord on December 28, 2005, via law 9,279.

21 "Ola de protestas por la suba del agua en Córdoba." *La Nación*. Feb. 19, 2006.

22 "El temor por el malhumor social." *La Voz del Interior*. March 24, 2006.

23 "Frenan alzas en Córdoba." *La Nación*. Feb. 24, 2006; "De la Sota rectificó el aumento del agua: será de 15% promedio." *La Voz del Interior*. March 20, 2006.

24 "La Provincia no proyecta reestatizar el agua." *La Voz del Interior*. April 2, 2006.

concessionaire had contracted comparatively little debt prior to the crisis made it possible to find a buyer willing to assume the project and its debt.

Foreign investors' post-crisis efforts to renegotiate their concession contract in Catamarca Province, another jurisdiction characterized by moderate levels of political hurdles (Figure 5.1; Table 6.A.II, chapter appendix), suggest that they encountered similar difficulties in more remote and less affluent provinces. Proactiva, a joint venture between Fomento de Construcción y Contratas (FCC) – a leading Spanish construction firm – and the French sanitation giant Vivendi, assumed responsibility for the Catamarca system in September 2000.[25] For both companies, the concession represented another step toward establishing an important presence in the Latin American water and sanitation market, which was viewed as a growth area.[26] Proactiva had already acquired of a number of water and sanitation concessions in other countries in the region – including Brazil, Colombia, and Venezuela – in the late 1990s. Proactiva operated other local government services in Argentina, such as waste collection, but it had no other operations in Catamarca.[27]

The Argentine crisis prompted both partners to consider the long-run viability of the Catamarca concession as well as their Latin American operations more generally. When the crisis hit, Aguas del Valle had barely begun operations. While this meant that it had not yet had a chance to accumulate large debts outside the country, it also meant that the concessionaire had not had the opportunity to implement basic revenue-raising procedures included in its contract. This left the firms trying to introduce politically salient cost-recovery measures typically introduced at the beginning of a concession *during* and immediately following the crisis, encountering political resistance as a result. During 2001 and 2002, the firm could make no headway in improving payment rates given the economic context and its effects on the population of this poor province. Although the provincial government instituted subsidized tariffs for one-quarter of the population, payment rates stayed extremely low: in August of 2004, the firm complained that only 20 percent of the population paid its bills, an incredibly low rate in comparative terms.[28] Given these difficulties, it should

[25] "FCC obtiene un contrato en Argentina por 60.000 millones." *El Mundo*. April 28, 2000.

[26] Both firms also had a relatively focused profile, especially in the region. When Vivendi Universal began to sell off its stake in Vivendi Environnement – its water and environmental services arm – in 2000, Vivendi's overall profile also became more specialized. (The firm's name was changed to Veolia following the disposal so as to further differentiate between the water services firm and the more diverse French conglomerate.) FCC's 1990s expansion in Latin America was centered on urban services, with the aim of counterbalancing cycles in the Spanish construction market. See "Marcelino Oreja, el hombre para internacionalizar FCC." *Gaceta de los Negocios*. Dec. 9, 1999.

[27] Proactiva held contracts for garbage collection and street cleaning in various residential districts in Buenos Aires. "Catamarca: A partir de abril, el servicio del agua será responsabilidad del Estado." *Noticias de Argentina*. Feb. 22, 2008.

[28] "Aguas del Valle se queja de la morosidad de los usuarios, supera el 80% por ciento." www.catamarcaaldia.com.ar. Aug. 17, 2004.

come as no surprise that the concessionaire ran losses.[29] This led two foreign investors to view a contract renegotiation addressing their economic difficulties to be important for continuing in the market, especially as they did not possess other holdings in the province that could counterbalance their losses.

Like other foreign investors in the Argentine water sector, Vivendi and FCC were prompted by the Argentine crisis to reevaluate their expansion efforts in Latin America. Vivendi resolved to concentrate future expansion in developed countries, whereas FCC decided to continue expanding in the region despite shareholder concerns.[30] Because of FCC's long-term outlook, the consortium did not file an international arbitration claim immediately and simply pushed for contract renegotiations. As in Córdoba Province, the governor was reasonably responsive – in part because he did not have to worry about high levels of political competition and worked with a unified government (Table 6.A.II, chapter appendix). The governor and firm reached an accord in 2004 that increased tariffs by 20 percent and allowed the firm to stop paying its canon (lump sum) payment and devote this money instead to investment.[31] As in Córdoba, however, the agreement proved unpopular, and the government retracted it following political pressure.[32] Without a comprehensive renegotiation, the contract was uneconomical for Vivendi and FCC, and they decided to negotiate terms of exit. The company and governor agreed to cancel the contract and reached an agreement under which the firm continued to manage services temporarily while the province searched for a replacement operator.[33] The consortium managed the system at a loss, finally convincing the government to let it withdraw in April of 2008, despite the fact that the government had not found another firm to take its place.[34]

The failed negotiation experiences in Santa Fe, Córdoba, and Catamarca, each of which unfolded in a much less competitive and fragmented political environment than the foreign investor-led contracts analyzed in the previous chapter, provide a number of insights. In none of these cases did post-crisis negotiations yield financially and politically viable settlements providing a basis for investor continuation in the market. Foreign investors' impatience and reliance on formal and public pressure tactics worked against the

[29] The president of the firm reported that the firm was not collecting enough to cover daily operating costs in 2003. "La mitad de los usuarios no paga el agua." *La Unión*. June 13, 2003.

[30] "Grupos españoles revisan su estrategia en Argentina." *El Cronista*. June 20, 2002; "Expansion: FCC Wins Waste Collection Contract in Argentina." *Expansión*. Sept. 15, 2004; "Q4 2004 Veolia Environnement SA Earnings Conference Call – Final." *FD (FAIR DISCLOSURE) WIRE*. Aug. 20, 2005.

[31] "Habrá un incremento del 20% en la tarifa del agua." www.catamarcaaldia.com.ar. Oct. 3, 2004.

[32] "Marcha atrás del Frente Cívico con el tarifazo del agua." www.catamarcaaldia.com.ar. Dec. 8, 2004.

[33] "Rescinden el contrato a la empresa de agua de Catamarca." *El Clarín*. Dec. 23, 2004.

[34] "Se fue Aguas del Valle: lo que deja y lo que lleva." *Catamarca es noticia*. April 1, 2008; "Qué pasa: servicios estatales." *La Nación*. March 31, 2008.

achievement of renegotiation agreements acceptable to firms and politically viable in the post-crisis environment. Negotiating efforts even failed in the relatively propitious context of Córdoba, where comparatively low debt levels tempered Suez's demands and an ideologically receptive administration wished to conclude an agreement. Suez's demand for a single large rate increase rather than staged increases as a condition for staying in the market ultimately proved unworkable politically. A similar effort foundered in Catamarca as well.

Outside Support Crucial for the Foreign-Led Misiones Contract

Only one of the foreign investors holding a provincial water contract remained in Argentina the entire decade following the crisis: the Spanish construction firm Dragados, which was absorbed by Spanish construction group Actividades de Construcción y Servicios (ACS) in 2003. As Chapter 4 stresses, this contract was unique in the Argentine context in terms of the unusually large national government commitment to improving the province's water and sanitation infrastructure and the close involvement of the World Bank and the national government in designing and funding the investment program.[35] This outside support encouraged ACS to hold out longer in the concession, despite the fact that it was still losing money in late 2010.

The Argentine crisis also brought the Misiones concession to a standstill. In addition to the usual crisis effects – increasing the cost of imported inputs, inflationary pressures on wages, and ballooning interest payments – the national government's significant contribution to the concession's investment program was halted temporarily. Following President Fernando de la Rua's resignation in 2001, the incoming Duhalde administration took almost a year to recertify the US$20 million World Bank loan meant to fund the national government's 60 percent share of the concession's initial investment program.[36] (The concessionaire was responsible for the remaining 40 percent.) As in other provinces, the concessionaire requested contract renegotiations following the crisis.

A number of factors led the lead investor – ACS, after its 2003 purchase of Dragados – to be more patient in negotiations with the Misiones provincial governments than other foreign investors in the Argentine water sector. ACS's international expansion had focused more on Latin America than those of the French utility firms holding concessions in the country. Although ACS's expansion in Argentina was on hold, it planned to remain in the region in the long run.[37] Given its long-term outlook, ACS desisted from lodging

[35] The scale of national government assistance in this case was far larger than other instances discussed in this chapter.

[36] Funds were finally released in November 2002.

[37] For public statements by the firm's management on its post-crisis view of prospects in Latin America and Argentina, see "ENTREVISTA-Española Dragados va por fusión con ACS, no este año." *Reuters–Noticias Latinoamericanas*. July 9, 2002; "En los acuerdos que selló Argentina con el FMI el pasado día 20, ..." *El País*. Sept. 28, 2003.

international arbitration claims, because the Argentine national government had made it clear that it did not look favorably on firms that lodged complaints with ICSID.[38] ACS also enjoyed an unusual degree of leverage with its main creditor, the European Investment Bank, because it held a very large number of loans with the institution; the bank let it postpone interest payments on its US$18 million loan in the wake of the crisis, thus lowering the concession's carrying costs considerably.[39]

In addition, the World Bank and national government's unusually high level of involvement in the concession's investment program ensured that the provincial government had ongoing incentives to honor its contractual commitments and that the concession witnessed major system upgrades. The World Bank loan that the national government had secured to finance its 60 percent contribution to a sewerage system upgrade was only disbursed in stages, following the successful completion of each phase.[40] Investments in treatment plant capacity and network expansion completed through this program allowed the concessionaire to increase water production by 70 percent, the number of household water connections by 67 percent, and the number of household sewerage connections by 168 percent, which in turn greatly increased revenues.[41] Until these investments materialized, the governor – Carlos Rovira, who had not presided over the privatization program – had an interest in allowing the concessionaire to implement revenue-raising measures included in the contract in order to ensure that the investments were made. The firm was granted a 15 percent tariff hike in January 2002, which addressed some of its immediate cash flow problems arising from the crisis. The governor also did not block firm efforts to install water meters for the vast majority of its users in the years following the crisis, despite negative public reactions.[42] Finally, the provincial government refrained from blocking firm campaigns to significantly improve rates of bill payment.[43] Admittedly, low levels of political competition in the province made it easier for Rovira to withstand political controversy surrounding such efforts than it was for governors in more competitive provinces, as described in Chapter 5 (Table 6.A.II, chapter appendix). These considerations encouraged the Misiones government to be more responsive to firm concerns than in other cases of foreign management (Tables 5.1, 6.1), which in turn eased the concessionaire's financial situation to a certain extent and contributed to ACS's willingness to hang on to the asset.

38 "Las firmas españolas piden un rumbo claro." *El Cronista Comercial*. Aug. 4, 2003.

39 Interview, Christian Hilbert, former commercial director, SAMSA, June 12, 2007.

40 See Chapter 4 and Post (2008) for more detail.

41 "Duplican cantidad de agua potable en Posadas." *El Territorio*. Aug. 3, 2010; "Cloacas: financiarán instalaciones domiciliarias a través de una línea de créditos 'muy blanda.'" www.noticiasdel6.com. Sept. 30, 2010.

42 The percentage of customers with water meters increased from 15% to 85% between 1999 and 2007 (data from SAMSA).

43 Whereas fewer than 15% of customers paid in 1999, 80% paid in 2007 (data from SAMSA).

Contract renegotiations, however, remained stalled, despite World Bank pressure.[44]

The Misiones contract's peculiar structure, ACS's leverage with its creditors, and the firm's continuing interest in business in Argentina thus encouraged the company to delay turning to pressure tactics commonly used by foreign investors to bring provincial governments to the negotiating table. Only in March 2005 did ACS threaten to stop investing in the concession if the administration did not renegotiate its contract.[45] In June 2006, ACS finally threatened to pull out and filed the preliminary paperwork to take the province into international arbitration, as counterparts in other provinces had done in 2002.[46] Governor Rovira's posture regarding contract renegotiation changed after he lost a high-profile referendum that would have repealed gubernatorial term limits and thereby allowed him to run for reelection. During the referendum campaign, he had threatened to take over the water service.[47] After the election, Rovira did an about-face under pressure from the water and sanitation union to keep the firm private and grant tariff increases that would allow for salary increases.[48] He gave the regulatory agency the go-ahead to negotiate an accord and approve a set of staged tariff increases totaling 49 percent, much of which was to be devoted to salary increases.[49] Although far more generous than any accord reached by other foreign investors, however, the benefits obtained did not approach those received by domestic investors with significant holdings in their contract jurisdiction for contracts in the provinces of Corrientes, Córdoba, and Salta.

After Rovira transferred power to his successor, Maurice Closs, and the nationally financed investment program was concluded, the province and concessionaire began to adopt an approach observed in cases of domestic investor management: the province assumed most investment responsibilities, while the concessionaire focused on billing and system maintenance. Both parties failed to comply with provisions of their contracts: government offices often did not pay their water bills, and the firm – with the informal consent of the government – did not pay some local taxes.[50] The province would then lobby the national administration for funds for specific infrastructure projects. In other respects, however, the concession differed from cases of management by domestic

44 As late as 2004, the World Bank was delaying the bidding process for projects it had agreed to fund until a revised contract had been negotiated. "Posadas water plant tender pending Samsa renegotiation." *Business News Americas*. May 31, 2004.

45 "Samsa no quiere invertir si no se renegocia el contrato." *El Territorio*. March 10, 2005.

46 "Samsa reclama a nivel nacional una renegociación del contrato." www.territoriodigital.com.ar. June 16, 2006.

47 "Rovira amenazó con reestatizar Samsa." www.territoriodigital.com.ar. Sept. 20, 2006.

48 The union's numerous strikes, opposition to state takeover, and wage requests are chronicled in *El Territorio* between September 2006 and January 2007.

49 "Samsa se queda y no se tocará la tarifa de pequeños usuarios." www.misionesonline.net. Jan. 9, 2007.

50 Not-for-attribution interview, June 2010.

investors, particularly those with diverse local holdings. Because ACS did not possess operations in other sectors, its earnings in the province depended solely on the concession. Even after the rate increases of 2007 – most of which were devoted to salary increases – the concession continued to lose money. And the province chose not to award significant, related construction contracts to ACS – a common problem for companies that had not historically occupied a role in the local market.[51] As of 2012, ACS continued to manage the concession, viewing the costs of exit to be higher than carrying costs.

Overall, this set of four cases suggests that while foreign investors can maintain productive negotiating relationships with host governments in provinces with few political hurdles when they are able and willing to provide funds for infrastructure investment (as shown in Chapter 4), they fare less well when they lose this important source of leverage. Because of their reluctance to invest, their relatively low levels of patience, and their tendency to turn to legalistic and public pressure tactics to bring host governments to the negotiating table, foreign investors in Santa Fe, Córdoba, and Catamarca failed to secure amended contractual terms that were both politically and financially viable. In Misiones, the concessionaire secured better results because a massive federal assistance program and World Bank oversight ensured significant and largely government-funded investment following the crisis, improving the utility's finances. Except in this latter case, foreign investors abandoned their Argentine holdings, leaving host governments to locate alternative private operators or, as a last resort, assume system management themselves.

Alternative theories suggest contractual difficulties would stem from factors other than investor portfolio structure: contracts would be less likely to fail in provinces with strong state capacity, robust checks and balances, or regulatory independence. Foreign investors' demonstrated inability to maintain constructive negotiating relationships with host governments during the post-crisis period in these low- to moderate-hurdle provinces, however, occurred under a variety of these conditions. Similar tendencies became visible in more affluent provinces with comparatively strong state capacity and systems of checks and balances, such as Santa Fe and Córdoba, and in the less affluent and more patrimonial province of Catamarca. They emerged even though concessionaires expressed demands of varying ambitiousness stemming from variation in the gravity of their financial situation. Foreign investors were also unable to secure mutually beneficial post-crisis agreements when regulators enjoyed relatively high levels of formal independence, as in Córdoba, and when formal regulatory independence was far more limited, as in Santa Fe and Catamarca.[52] Formal

[51] In not-for-attribution interviews, numerous investors – foreign and domestic – stressed the political difficulties of securing construction contracts, or awarding construction contracts to related companies, in provinces where they had not been active historically.

[52] Enabling legislation for regulatory agencies in Santa Fe, Catamarca, and Misiones allowed firms to appeal regulators' decisions through administrative channels, whereas formal appeals were prohibited in the case of Córdoba (Azpiazu et al. 2008: 124).

regulatory independence mattered little in the post-crisis period because governors and their ministers tended to negotiate directly with firm owners regarding contractual revisions.

DOMESTIC INVESTORS WITHOUT LOCAL HOLDINGS STRUGGLE

Domestic investors without additional diverse local operations served as lead investors in concessions in the provinces of Formosa, Santiago del Estero, and La Rioja. In the province of Salta, the concession was controlled by a joint venture partnership between a domestic investor with diverse local operations and one without a significant local presence. We would expect relations between investors and concessionaires to be smoother than in the preceding cases, given that domestic investors were less likely to have taken on debts outside the country to finance investment and were reluctant to enter legal conflicts with host governments (Table 6.A.II, chapter appendix). However, they should not perform as well as domestic investors with diverse local holdings, who had incentives to be patient and possessed access to additional negotiating strategies because of their other assets. This section reviews the post-crisis trajectories of these contracts, and shows that most results conform to expectations. The concessions in Formosa and La Rioja languished, and systems were eventually taken over by the state. In Salta, the joint venture partners managed to secure a full contract renegotiation, but infighting made it difficult for them to adapt to a less supportive gubernatorial administration. The Santiago contract, contrary to expectations, continues, buoyed by a supportive governor and less pressing investment needs.

Mixed Performance by Domestic Investors in Formosa, Santiago and La Rioja

Among the three contracts held by domestic investors *without* additional local holdings in provinces with low and moderate political hurdles, a workable post-crisis equilibrium emerged only in Santiago del Estero. In contrast, firm-government negotiations were drawn-out and ultimately unsuccessful in Formosa and La Rioja; systems were taken over by the government by the end of the decade. Importantly, these failures occurred even under relatively propitious political circumstances: in both cases, political hurdles were modest for the post-crisis period (Figure 5.1; Table 6.A.II, chapter appendix). The contracts in Formosa and Santiago were both held by Sagua, which was in turn owned by the Argentine Sielecki Group. This Buenos Aires–based business group operated in a number of sectors in Argentina, including pharmaceuticals, petrochemicals, banking, and viticulture. It did not, however, have a significant local presence in Formosa or Santiago del Estero prior, or subsequent, to obtaining water concessions in these provinces.[53]

The Formosa concession had been operating at a low-level equilibrium characterized by low levels of investment and only modest improvements in service quality during the second half of the 1990s, and the situation worsened considerably with the economic crisis. The provincial government became so strapped for cash that it paid its employees in provincial bonds that traded at 70 percent of the value of the peso in 2002 and early 2003. The government obliged Aguas de Formosa to accept customer payment in bonds. At the same time, net sales dropped dramatically from AR$9.7 million in 2002 to AR$7.9 million in 2003.[54] The provincial government also blocked service cutoffs that might have improved payment rates among middle- and upper-class consumers between 2000 and 2002.[55] Most importantly, inflation for producer inputs was 78 percent during 2002 alone.[56]

In spite of these difficulties, the Sielecki Group wanted to maintain a role in the country's water sector;[57] yet it was unwilling to subsidize a concession that had already been disappointing prior to the crisis in a province where it possessed no additional operations. This led Sielecki to recoup as much income as possible within the policy constraints imposed by the provincial government. Aguas de Formosa allowed customers to use provincial bonds not only to pay their current bills but also to pay back debts to the company, taking advantage of the fact that the bonds had limited purchasing power for households with other vendors.[58] Meanwhile, the company scaled back on investment.[59] In spite of these efforts and the province's phaseout of provincial bonds in 2003, however, Aguas de Formosa reported that it continued to lose money: its return on sales was −55 percent for 2002 and remained negative through 2005. Although the Sielecki Group desired a contract renegotiation that would address the concessionaire's financial situation, it did not push for one through legal channels or public threats of exit, which might hurt its domestic holdings outside the province.

53 According to firm representatives, there would have been political barriers to entry in related sectors, such as construction, at the provincial level.

54 Figures in Argentine pesos. Data in this section from Aguas de Formosa and EROSP, the regulatory agency.

55 According to Aguas de Formosa managers, the use of service cutoffs was limited to middle- and upper-income groups.

56 The cost of electricity, one of the firm's two most important inputs, rose with tariff adjustments after the crisis, for instance.

57 The Sielecki Group's 2004 purchase of Azurix's stake in the Mendoza concession, and efforts up until 2007 to purchase Saur's shares in the concession, reflected its continuing interest in the Argentine water sector after the crisis.

58 According to Sagua's president, the firm was able to collect more back payments this way than it would have been able to otherwise.

59 Investment as a percentage of net sales was negative during 2002 (reflecting depreciation), and the rate in 2003 was under 3 percent. (Data from Aguas de Formosa and EROSP. Ratios calculated by author.)

As the crisis subsided, Governor Gildo Insfrán enjoyed a high degree of political security and privileged access to federal funds because of his early support for Néstor Kirchner's 2003 presidential campaign. This gave him the political and financial flexibility to conclude contract renegotiations, including tariff increases or provincial contributions to the concessionaire's investment program, if he desired. Responding to comparatively modest improvements achieved by Aguas de Formosa during the 1990s and the immediate post-crisis period, however, Insfrán instead chose to orchestrate a transition back to state management. His main policy concession to Aguas de Formosa occurred in 2005, providing state subsidies for poor households struggling to pay their bills.[60] Although helpful, this measure did not adequately address the major problem of increasing costs: tariffs had been left at the same level for fourteen years, despite high rates of inflation following the crisis. As a result, the firm was not even covering operating costs through tariff revenue.[61] In comparative terms, the Formosa government was relatively unresponsive to firm concerns (Table 6.1).

Whereas some governors secured federal funding for projects to be built by or handed over to concessionaires, Insfrán used his federal connections to obtain federal funding for a project that would lay the groundwork for a transition back to state management. He secured AR$80 million for a new water treatment plant for the capital city of Formosa that would triple existing capacity, thereby addressing long-standing problems of low water pressure.[62] The company was essentially cut out of planning for integration of the new plant into the existing system, even though the plant promised to increase the utility's operating costs by a factor of three.[63] The governor approved a comprehensive review of the service in November 2006, with the stated aim of evaluating whether the company should continue to run it.[64] In the meantime, the head of the provincial housing bureau lashed out at the firm for withholding investments, arguing that "the investment is being done by the state after observing that the private sector has done nothing."[65]

The firm and government finally reached an accord at the end of 2008 under which the government purchased the concession from Sagua, while leaving the

[60] Gubernatorial decree 91, 2005.

[61] Statement based on data from Aguas de Formosa and EROSP. In a press statement, Aguas de Formosa general manager Alfredo Gusberti argued that even if the firm collected 100% of the amount billed, it would still not cover operating costs with tariff revenue. "Aguas de Formosa 'da pérdidas hace cinco años' y este sería el ultimo que podría soportar." FormosaYa.com.ar. April 12, 2007.

[62] "El Nuevo servicio de agua demandará una inversion de 110 millones de pesos." *La Mañana*. April 7, 2006. For more detail, see Post (2008).

[63] "Aguas de Formosa: la facturación está 40% por debajo de los costos operativos." *El Comercial*. Sept. 14, 2006.

[64] "Realizan estudios técnicos sobre Aguas de Formosa." Formosaahora.com. April 27, 2007.

[65] Translation by author. "Muraccioli criticó a Aguas de Formosa y aseguró que no hicieron inversiones." FormosaYa.com.ar. Jan. 9, 2007.

management team in place – a friendly transfer of ownership in comparative terms, albeit on a time frame that suited the government. After the transfer, the regulator approved an immediate tariff increase of 70 percent and a staged tariff increase of 24 percent, the latter to coincide with the improvements in service quality that could be achieved after the new water treatment plant had been completed.[66] A negotiated exit of this sort – even if late in coming – was more appealing to Sagua than a legal battle in federal court, which might ensue if the firm were to cancel the contract and argue that the provincial government was at fault for noncompliance.

The Sielecki Group's concession in the province of Santiago del Estero, where it also did not have a diversified presence, fared far better following the crisis despite significant political tumult in the first part of the decade. Aguas de Santiago, like other concessionaires, struggled with the immediate effects of the devaluation and consumers' reduced ability to pay their bills. On top of these usual difficulties, the concessionaire faced a rapidly changing political environment. Whereas before the crisis, a well-entrenched political boss, Carlos Juárez, administered the province with an almost authoritarian level of control, after the crisis the province was rocked by large-scale public protests, and the political regime was toppled (Table 6.A.II, chapter appendix).[67] The president sent federal appointees to run the province temporarily during a one-year federal "intervention" beginning in November 2003.[68] Within a year, the temporary administration held elections; Juárez's longtime competitor, the opposition mayor of the province's capital city, assumed power in March 2005. Following this change, Sagua's pre-crisis efforts to build political support by incorporating close associates of the Juarez regime as minority stakeholders became a liability.[69] Still hopeful about the medium-run prospects for the water sector – and especially opportunities to purchase concessions being abandoned by foreign investors – Sagua repositioned itself politically by purchasing these minority stakes.

Governor Gerardo Zamora proved to be much more supportive than his predecessor Juarez – or Insfrán in Formosa. Zamora and the concessionaire moved forward with contract renegotiations that yielded results exceeding those achieved by foreign investors but not as advantageous as those achieved by domestic investors with diverse local assets, as in Corrientes and Córdoba. The firm pursued an informal negotiating strategy and pushed for modest, staged tariff increases. The provincial government and firm reached a tariff accord in 2007, with a subsequent increase of 42 percent authorized in August

66 "Aumenta la tarifa del agua en Formosa." *La Nación*. Sept. 1, 2008; "La suba impacta más porque tendría que haberse implementado de manera gradual en tres años." *FormosaYa.com.ar*. Sept. 24, 2008; "El Gobierno autorizó incrementos del 24% en facturas de Aguas de Formosa." *La Mañana*. Aug. 10, 2009.

67 On Juarez's quasi-authoritarian regime, see Gibson (2005).

68 Dargoltz et al. (2006: 66–76).

69 See Chapter 4 and Post (2008) for further documentation.

2009.[70] Under an informal accord, the state came to control and execute almost all investment for the system, while the concessionaire provided an operational service.[71] Typically, Aguas de Santiago proposed particular projects, and the provincial government chose which it wanted to pursue. Zamora then lobbied the national government for funds to complete the infrastructure projects; his good relationship with the Kirchners has helped him secure such funds. For example, in April 2011, the national government secured an AR$800 million World Bank loan to fund water infrastructure in northern Argentina, which included a sewage treatment plant and sewage trunk lines for Santiago's capital.[72] (Such an informal accord assigning the state most investment responsibilities was easier to reach in Santiago than in Formosa because investment requirements were lower in Santiago.)[73] This reliance on government funds left Santiago's concessionaire with far less control over the sequencing and quality of projects undertaken than it had had when it had funded infrastructure investment out of tariff revenue. Given the provincial government's improved access to funds and reluctance to raise consumer rates to cover the full costs of the desired investment program, however, passing investment obligations to the state proved to be the politically palatable way forward in the post-crisis context that also allowed the concession to make money for its owners. It yielded improvements, such as an increase in sewerage coverage from 30 percent of the population in 1997 to 57 percent in 2011.[74] The arrangement, however, is fragile because it requires the governor's ongoing support. While the governor could afford to support Aguas de Santiago because of the lack of a viable political opposition,[75] Sagua has little reason to stay on if rising political competition prompts the governor to become less supportive of the concessionaire, given that it has no other holdings in the province and is increasingly pessimistic about the domestic water sector.

The concession in La Rioja Province, where a domestic investor with few additional provincial holdings secured similar concessions from the provincial government, finally collapsed by the end of the decade. The lead investor in the La Rioja concession, Latinaguas, was owned by the Chamas Group, a small but diversified economic group based in Corrientes Province. Latinaguas, its water

[70] "El gobierno acordó con Aguas de Santiago obras y una suba de tarifas." www.diariopanorama.com. July 14, 2007; "Aumento en las tarifas de Aguas de Santiago." www.nuevodiarioweb.com.ar. Aug. 31, 2009. In a June 2010 interview, Sagua president Federico Qüerio reported that total increases had reached 70%.

[71] Interview with Federico Qüerio, president, Sagua, June 2010.

[72] "El banco mundial aprobó un crédito por $800 millones para obras de infraestructura urbana." www.primerafuente.com.ar. April 6, 2011.

[73] Not-for-attribution interview with engineer familiar with both systems.

[74] Data from Aguas de Santiago. This figure approaches original contractual goals for municipalities in the concession area (Anexo V).

[75] Zamora won more than 85% of the provincial vote when he ran for reelection in 2008.

and sanitation firm, also controlled the Corrientes concession and jointly controlled the Salta concession. As discussed in Chapter 4, the La Rioja concession only began in 2002, following a three-year management contract that served as a trial period for both the company and the government.

In the short run, the concession's post-crisis start improved its bargaining position. The post-crisis timing of the negotiations regarding the conditions under which the firm would stay gave it the opportunity to stress challenges posed by the post-crisis environment *before* agreeing to sign the contract. In addition, the concessionaire had three years to develop an extensive knowledge of the system and investment necessities prior to negotiations. This helped it secure a contract that placed most infrastructure investment responsibilities with the state – similar to the revised contracts ultimately achieved following years of negotiations by water concessionaires in Corrientes, Santiago del Estero, Misiones, Salta, and Córdoba.[76] Governor Ángel Maza, who had overseen the 1999 management contract award to Latinaguas, remained in power through the first five years of the 2002 concession contract and enjoyed high levels of political security until the last period of his time in office (Table 6.A.II, chapter appendix).[77] With a reputational stake in the project, he supported the firm's efforts to improve its revenue stream in the difficult post-crisis environment. Because of this state backing, the concessionaire's finances recovered more than those of Aguas de Formosa: while the return on equity for the Formosa concession was –9 and –15 percent in 2004 and 2005, respectively, the return on equity in La Rioja was 7 and 4.6 percent in 2004 and 2005.[78] Maza also successfully lobbied the central government for funding for important water and sanitation infrastructure, including an AR$18 million sewage treatment plant.[79]

The concessionaire's vulnerability only became visible when a new governor, Luís Beder Herrera, took office in March 2007. Beder Herrera saw little rationale for privatization if the province secured funding for needed infrastructure. He rebuffed the firm's requests for rate increases, despite high rates of inflation, arguing that it should invest in exchange for assistance. The firm's financial situation worsened in the meantime, the concessionaire slipping into negative equity.[80] Following conflict between the union and the concessionaire regarding

[76] Regarding provincial funding for the concessionaire's investment program, see the *Plan de Obras*, published November 2005: http://www.aguasdelarioja.com (accessed October 30, 2008). In particular, see the descriptions of funding for wells and network expansion in the "POE Emergencia 2004," "POE Expansión 2004," and works completed in 2005.

[77] Maza's vice governor and successor, Luís Beder Herrera, led a successful effort to impeach Maza following his promotion of a measure that would have removed gubernatorial term limits.

[78] Return on net sales was 0.04% in La Rioja compared with –13% in Formosa in 2005 (ADERASA 2006).

[79] The licitation process for the sewage treatment plant is described at www.enohsa.gov.ar (accessed October 28, 2008).

[80] "Confirman manejo poco eficiente de la empresa Aguas de la Rioja S.A." www.nuevarioja.com.ar. Aug. 25, 2009.

salary increases and fights between the mayor of the capital city and the firm regarding street repairs in August 2009, Beder Herrera issued a decree providing for an audit of the concessionaire's books and monitoring of its expenditures.[81] With few local social ties, or additional holdings that instilled patience or provided opportunities for compensation in less political areas, the firm failed to reach a political settlement with the new administration. Shortly after the eruption of the conflict, the governor issued a decree formalizing the "intervention," or temporary takeover, of the firm.[82] The conflict escalated; both parties cancelled the contract, alleging noncompliance by the other party, and the state took over services.[83] While passing investment responsibilities on to the state had been meant to help the firm weather the crisis, it became a political liability once the privatizing governor left office. The contrast between the Chamas Group's experiences in La Rioja and Corrientes (discussed in Chapter 5) is telling: the group survived gubernatorial turnover in Corrientes Province, its historical base – where it possessed a much broader set of operations, and where its owners lived and interacted regularly with political elites – yet proved unable to manage similar transitions in contexts where it had fewer ties and operations.

There are a number of commonalities among these three cases in which domestic investors without diverse local operations held controlling stakes in their concessions. Investors' lack of integration in the local economy made them less willing to fund investment out of concern for other holdings. They instead focused on obtaining revised contractual arrangements that allowed for tariff increases and passed a large fraction of investment obligations to the state. The lead investors in La Rioja and Santiago managed to secure such agreements. As the La Rioja case testifies, however, such agreements – which approximate management rather than concession contracts – can be fragile, especially following political turnover.

A Domestic Joint Venture Does Better, Then Collapses

The concessionaire in Salta Province, a joint venture between a subsidiary of the Corrientes-based Chamas Group, Latinaguas, and another Corrientes-based investor with diverse local operations, was able to secure contractual amendments addressing the main effects of the crisis within a particularly propitious political environment. In the long run, however, coordination difficulties between the two partners made it difficult to respond to a new political administration beginning in 2008.

81 "El Gobierno condiciona asistencia financiera a Aguas de la Rioja." www.nuevarioja.com.ar. Aug. 19, 2009.

82 "El Gobierno intervino el servicio de aguas y cloacas por 90 dias." www.nuevarioja.com.ar. Sept. 22, 2009.

83 "Aguas de la Rioja inició el proceso para rescindir el contrato." www.nuevarioja.com.ar. Dec. 21, 2009; "La Provincia rescindió el contrato de Aguas de la Rioja." www.nuevarioja.com.ar. Jan. 14, 2010.

The Salta concession had gotten off to a promising start prior to the 2001–2002 crisis in a relatively receptive political context: Juan Carlos Romero, the governor who privatized, remained in power throughout this period and faced no immediate political threats. Chapter 4 describes how the concessionaire, controlled by Corrientes-based Latinaguas – the technical operator – and JCR (formerly Necon), another Corrientes-based economic group with significant operations in the province, maintained constructive relations with the provincial authorities. At the governor's behest, the concessionaire had invested heavily in network expansion, incorporated loss-making municipal systems into its network, and delayed contractually stipulated rate increases. Governor Romero, who had a personal stake in the success of his privatization program, contributed to the financing of investments and provided political cover for the firm as it implemented controversial revenue-enhancing measures such as consumer database updates.

The concessionaire and provincial administration proceeded to work out a mutually agreeable, more ambitious set of accords under difficult economic but politically auspicious circumstances in the years following the Argentine crisis. As in other provinces, the crisis created serious difficulties for the concessionaire, including lower rates of bill payment, inflation, and higher input costs.[84] At the same time, the concessionaire was expected to keep assuming control of additional, loss-making municipal systems in the interior of the province that could no longer survive on their own.[85] Although the Salta regulator finally authorized a 20 percent tariff hike originally scheduled for year two of the contract in July 2002 – and did not retract it following public protests – the investors desired a comprehensive contract renegotiation.[86]

The investors were able to reach a series of agreements with the Romero administration very quickly. The first accord, in June 2003, provided for a state subsidy for poor households and the transfer of funding for water meters from individual users to the state and company, so that installation would present fewer political problems.[87] A second accord, in June 2004, provided for a 20 percent rate increase (helping compensate for the 41 percent inflation experienced in 2002), increased the province's contribution to the investment program for the 2004–2008 period to 33.4 percent, postponed fines for the concessionaire, and incorporated twenty-seven additional loss-making municipal

[84] According to data from Aguas de Salta S.A., the rate of collection dropped from 81% in 2001 to 75% in 2002.

[85] The contract stipulated that the concessionaire would serve the entire province. Governor Romero wanted to transfer small municipal systems to the concessionaire because they were plagued with problems and ran deficits. See sections 1.2.2 and 1.2.3 of the contract and "Es precaria la provisión de agua en varias localidades." *El Tribuno*. July 11, 2002.

[86] See Post (2008).

[87] "Acta Acuerdo" of June 20, 2003, ratified in October by decree 1841. See Post (2008) for more detail.

systems.[88] Importantly, the regulatory agency and provincial government defended the rate increases and the introduction of water metering in the face of public criticism during the months immediately following the agreement.[89] An additional agreement at the end of 2005 ushered in another 19 percent rate hike and compensated the firm for part of the difference between the anticipated and actual costs of investments completed in the preceding year.[90] These measures returned the concessionaire to financial health: by 2004, its return on net sales was up to 8 percent.[91]

The structure of the investors' portfolios and Romero's secure political position made it feasible to reach these agreements. JCR possessed numerous, diverse operations in the province, which extended its time horizons in the jurisdiction and positioned it to benefit from policy concessions in other areas, while Latinaguas was very interested in maintaining its profile as a water specialist in Argentina.[92] This meant that both investors were willing to run short-run losses to invest, betting that this would eventually pay off. Rather than file for a large tariff increase all at once, a common strategy of foreign investors, the investors pushed for small incremental tariff hikes that could be tied to continuation of its investment program in a given year and the assumption of individual loss-making municipalities into the system.[93] Options were discussed on an informal basis before formal applications for tariff increases were made. Aguas de Salta invested 18 percent of its revenues stream in 2003 and 36 percent in 2004 – much more than its foreign-owned counterparts in Buenos Aires, Mendoza, and Santa Fe. Meanwhile, both partners – and JCR in particular because of its ongoing presence in the provincial construction sector – obtained contracts for related projects. JCR received the contract to construct the new AR$59 million southern aqueduct for the concession,[94] while Aguas de Salta contracted with Urbanoa, a joint JCR-Latinaguas subsidiary, for "complementary works" for the northern aqueduct, for approximately half of the AR$50 million budget.

88 The June agreement was approved via law 7,178 on July 1, 2004, and ratified via decree 1301. The new provincial contribution to the investment program represented a stark increase over previous years. For years one and two of the concession, for instance, the province committed to funding 20% of programmed investments (Saltiel 2003, 10).

89 "El En.Re.S.P. reglamentó el sistema medido de agua." *El Tribuno*. Aug. 8, 2004; "Salta tiene una tarifa social real." *El Tribuno*. Aug. 25, 2004; "Movilización en el centro por las tarifas del agua." *El Tribuno*. Aug. 27, 2004; "Hubo incidentes en la marcha contra el aumento de tarifas." *El Tribuno*, Sept. 9, 2004.

90 Decree number 2523, issued on December 20, 2005, approved the second agreement.

91 Data from Aguas de Salta S.A. and En.Re.S.P. (the regulatory agency); ratio calculated by author.

92 Chapter 4 provides more detail on how these firms' Salta holdings fit into larger, sectorally diverse portfolios.

93 A firm director described this approach in not-for-attribution interviews.

94 The licitation and contract for the southern aqueduct are described at www.enohsa.gov.ar (accessed October 28, 2008).

Negotiations were also eased because Romero had the political space to accede to firm requests during this period: he presided over a unified government, and having won the 2003 gubernatorial race by a 2:1 margin, faced no immediate threats to his power (Table 6.A.II, chapter appendix). Despite the political outcry over the 2005 agreement, the government supported the concessionaire, allowing the regulatory agency head rather than the firm to take the political fall for the rate increase. Concrete improvements in the system also made it easier for the governor to support the concessionaire. The percentage of customers receiving services twenty-four hours a day reportedly increased from 68 percent in 1998 to 94 percent in 2005.[95] In addition, a new aqueduct construction program allowed the company to phase out the use of contaminated wells, which improved water quality considerably.[96] The various accords reached make clear that the government's responsiveness to the concessionaire under the Romero administration was relatively high in comparative terms, as Table 6.1 shows: while the Salta case scores 90 percent – almost as high as domestic investors with diverse local assets in Córdoba – government responsiveness for contracts majority controlled by domestic or foreign investors in low- to moderate-hurdle provinces score between 25 percent and 75 percent.

Despite the conclusion of contract renegotiations in the first half of the decade, the concession ultimately faltered following the election of Juan Manuel Urtubey as governor. Urtubey, an ally of President Kirchner, challenged Romero's handpicked candidate, Walter Wayar, with a statist campaign, in which he stressed that he would review privatizations completed by the Romero administration. In January 2008, the new governor formed a commission to review all public services contracts with private companies.[97] Urtubey's new regulatory agency president pressured the firm to renegotiate the terms of the contract, arguing that it had not met its investment obligations under the 2004 agreement. The agency fined the firm and threatened to legislate that the state's contribution to the investment program be "capitalized" into shares in the concession.[98] The joint owners of the concession had difficulty coordinating a common response, and negotiations regarding an increased state role in management broke down. The provincial government cancelled the firm's

95 Data from Aguas de Salta S.A. In addition, the percentage of users reporting problems with water pressure reportedly decreased from 45% to 11%, and the percentage of users experiencing problems of turbidity from 43% to 27% between July 1998 and August 2005.

96 Water quality evaluations by the regulatory agency suggest that services in only a few residential areas did not meet the contractually stipulated quality standards and that aqueduct projects underway would address those problems. Documentation from the water quality department, En.Re.S.P.

97 "Se Revisará la Totalidad de los Contratos de Servicios Tercerizados." *La Hora de Salta*. Jan. 4, 2008.

98 See, for instance, "Se complica la situación de Aguas de Salta en la renegociación del contrato." *Nuevo Diario de Salta*. April 8, 2008.

contract and took over management of the service in May 2009.[99] The inability of JCR to broker a deal is surprising, given the owner's local ties and his close connection with the Kirchner administration.[100] This being said, the joint venture arrangement made negotiations much more complicated, as in Mendoza. So while JCR and Latinaguas were able to conclude contract renegotiations that stabilized the concessionaire's financial situation in a short time frame, they were ultimately unable to secure the concession's stability in the long run.

INVESTORS WITH DIVERSE LOCAL ASSETS PULL AHEAD AGAIN

In the one case in which a domestic investor with diverse local holdings held a majority stake in a concession in a low- to moderate-hurdle political environment, it fared much better than peers in similar contexts. An earlier section of this chapter recounted the French investor Suez's failed attempt to secure an accord with the province of Córdoba, including a substantial tariff increase and a revised set of investment commitments for the concessionaire. Although the provincial administration initially signed on to an agreement, it retracted its support following a campaign by the political opposition that rendered the ambitious accord politically unviable. Over the next few months, De la Sota's vice governor worked out an alternative contract under which one of Suez's minority partners, the Roggio Group, would be willing to assume control of the concession.[101] In spite of the upcoming gubernatorial elections and street protests, the government managed to push through the ownership transfer.[102]

The Roggio Group had grown from a small, Córdoba-based firm into one of the largest Argentine conglomerates, active in areas such as construction, rail and highway concessions, and garbage collection – all while maintaining a significant local presence.[103] Like the Chamas Group in Corrientes, the Roggio Group was confident it could handle the political side of concession operations more effectively than its predecessor.[104] The new contract included important

99 "El Gobierno rescindió el contrato con Aguas de Salta." *El Tribuno*. May 21, 2009; "Urtubey rescindió el contrato con Aguas de Salta, que pasará a ser estatal." *Nuevo Diario de Salta*. May 22, 2009.

100 On the long-standing relationship between Juan Carlos Relats and the Kirchners, see "Ámbito dice que con la estatización de Aguas de Salta Urtubey enojó a Kirchner y De Vido." *Nuevo Diario de Salta*. June 1, 2009; "Crisis, tierras fiscales, y amigos, claves de la fortuna de Kirchner." *La Nación*. July 19, 2009; "El ex titular de Aguas de Salta le paga los alquileres a Kirchner." *El Tribuno*. July 21, 2009; "El inquilino que multiplica la fortuna de los Kirchner." *La Nación*. Aug. 23, 2009.

101 Roggio had previously only held 16% of the concession's shares.

102 "Aprobaron el contrato con Aguas Cordobesas en un clima de tensión." *La Voz del Interior*. Nov. 29, 2006.

103 "Roggio asume la conducción de Aguas Cordobesas." *La Voz del Interior*. Dec. 22, 2006.

104 Because it started later than many of the concession contracts controlled by foreign investors, the concessionaire contracted less debt in foreign currency before the crisis. This made it more attractive to local buyers than some other concessions held by foreign investors.

changes, such as the conversion of the firm's AR$9.8 million canon payment into a fund that could be used for investments, a government-financed AR$500,000 annual subsidy scheme for low-income consumers, and a graduated set of rate increases to be instituted starting in 2008.[105] In other words, it had achieved a revised contract similar to those negotiated in Corrientes and Salta.

On assuming control, the Córdoba-based firm pursued a very different negotiating strategy than that of its foreign predecessor. More committed to the province and interested in maintaining a foothold in the concession market, it has eschewed highly public, brinksmanship-like negotiating strategies that might negatively affect its other operations. In contrast to its predecessor – and like most domestic investors – the Roggio Group pushed for a series of small rate increases that helped the firm cope with inflation while investing almost twice as much as its predecessor did during the post-crisis period.[106] Whereas Suez made formal, written appeals to the regulator, the Roggio Group pursued informal conversations.[107]

Roggio's more gradual and informal approach to renegotiations yielded results that were workable financially and politically. It negotiated a series of small tariff increases between December 2007 and March 2010 totaling 80 percent for residential consumers and 124 percent for commercial and industrial users, against approximately 200 percent inflation for the 2002–2010 period. Importantly, the provincial government allowed the firm to implement these graduated rate increases – which returned the concession to profitability– within an increasingly contentious political environment in which the opposition frequently drew attention to rate hikes and the majority of the respondents to a referendum had voiced their disapproval of the contract (Table 6.A.II, chapter appendix).[108] The provincial government and the concessionaire also worked together to launch a controversial water meter installation program in the wake of severe water shortage in 2008, funded through a surcharge on user bills.[109] At the behest of the governor, the concessionaire also agreed to reschedule network expansion into unserved areas in the provincial capital before the upcoming gubernatorial elections, if the province would provide financial assistance for the effort.[110] Although the concession was not an

105 "Aguas: no habrá aumentos hasta 2008." *La Voz del Interior*. July 17, 2006; "Roggio se hace cargo de Aguas Cordobesas." *La Voz del Interior*. July 18, 2006.

106 Investment data from Aguas Cordobesas.

107 Not-for-attribution interview, June 2010.

108 Regarding the firm's profitability, see "La Provincia financió la ganancia de Aguas Cordobesas." *La Voz del Interior*. Sept. 17, 2007. Regarding applications for the new inflation adjustments, see "Hoy, audiencia por aumentos." *La Voz del Interior*. April 14, 2008; "La Provincia analiza subir tarifas de agua." *La Voz del Interior*. April 13, 2009; "2010 llegará con aumentos de agua y luz." *La Voz del Interior*. Nov. 10, 2009. Regarding the citizen referendum, see "Consulta por el agua: el 'No' acumula el 78%." *La Voz del Interior*. Sept. 3, 2007.

109 "Rige el cargo fijo para medidores de agua." *La Voz del Interior*. Sept. 2, 2010.

110 "Cumplirán acuerdo de agua para barrios." *La Voz del Interior*. Feb. 22, 2011.

important profit center for the group by the end of the decade, it did allow the conglomerate to demonstrate the continuing viability of the concession model on its home turf and keep a foothold in the market for periods when the state no longer has sufficient funds to manage infrastructure investment on its own.[111] The concessionaire continued to invest in infrastructure throughout the decade, and remained in place in late 2012.[112]

Overall, this set of four contracts controlled by domestic investors suggests that even in provinces characterized by low to moderate levels of political hurdles, investors with diverse assets in their contract jurisdiction have important advantages in the regulatory arena. The new Córdoba concessionaire negotiated much more effectively with the provincial administration than domestic investors in provinces with similar levels of political contention, such as Formosa and La Rioja. Although a domestic investor with few local operations has achieved a good working relationship with the Santiago del Estero provincial government, it remains to be seen if it will outlast the current administration. In Salta, coordination problems between the concessionaire's partners prevented investors from reaching a stable, post-crisis settlement. As a general rule, domestic investors refrained from court cases and other highly public means of pushing host governments to negotiate, but those with diverse local holdings possessed both greater patience and opportunities for exchange because of their diversified presence in the provincial economy.

Examining all cases of domestic investor controlled contracts in provinces characterized by high or low to moderate political hurdles shows that the comparative advantage of investors with diverse local holdings occurs under a variety of conditions that alternative approaches suggest would contribute to contract durability and investment. They performed well in provinces characterized by strong state capacity and checks and balances, such as Córdoba, as well as in the more patrimonial and less affluent provinces with weak regulatory agencies, such as Corrientes. The difficulties faced by domestic investors without local holdings compared with their peers with diverse local operations occurred where regulators enjoyed relatively high levels of formal independence, such as Córdoba and Salta, and where formal regulatory independence was far more limited, such as La Rioja and Formosa.[113] Also, domestic investors with diverse local assets prevailed not only in relatively propitious political contexts, such as Córdoba, but also in the most difficult

111 Not-for-attribution interviews, June 2010.

112 Investments by the firm amounted to approximately 10% of net sales between 2007 and 2009. (Calculated from data from Aguas Cordobesas.)

113 Enabling legislation for regulatory agencies allowed firms to appeal regulators' decisions through administrative channels in La Rioja and Formosa, while formal appeals were prohibited in Córdoba and Salta (Azpiazu et al. 2008: 124).

provincial political environment according to the political hurdle index: Corrientes.

CONCLUSION

Although the Argentine crisis of 2001–2002 may have been particularly pronounced in comparison with economic downturns in other emerging markets, crises are common. Argentina's rate of inflation during the post-crisis recovery has been significant but is not unusual. For long-term contracts to be viable in emerging economies, they must survive challenges of this sort. For this reason, it is important to examine the circumstances under which some concession contracts have been able not only to survive a crisis of this magnitude but also adapt to the new post-crisis reality in ways that are workable for both firms and host governments.

This chapter has compared the respective negotiating relationships and exit patterns of investors with different portfolio structures in provinces with low to moderate political hurdles. Even in these relatively calm political environments, the case analyses suggest, domestic investors with diverse local holdings still enjoy important advantages. Of the four contracts controlled by foreign firms, only one managed to negotiate and secure a workable post-crisis settlement sufficiently generous to make it worthwhile to continue operating in the local market. In this case, substantial World Bank and national government support bolstered the firm's bargaining position and the sorts of infrastructure improvements the concessionaire could deliver. Of the three projects led by domestic investors with few local holdings, two ultimately failed, with local governments resuming control over services. The joint venture between domestic investors with and without diverse local assets controlling the Salta concession secured important early gains, yet ultimately proved unable to work effectively with the provincial administration in the long run – at least in part because of coordination difficulties between partners. Only the investors in Córdoba Province, which possessed a diverse portfolio there, managed to secure a workable post-crisis settlement. Furthermore, they did so where a foreign concessionaire had blatantly failed. The investor, Roggio, chose to enter the concession in 2006 fully aware of the difficulties the French Suez had encountered; the Córdoba-based conglomerate had previously controlled 16 percent of the concession shares and followed Suez's renegotiation efforts from the inside. These patterns, and their conformance with theoretical expectations, are summarized in Table 6.A.I (chapter appendix). The concession trajectories are similar to those observed in provinces with higher levels of political competition, divided government, and political instability, as shown in Chapter 5. Domestic investors' ongoing interest in entering concessions in jurisdictions where they already have a strong presence suggests that these investors are not trapped; the concessions offer opportunities in the long run.

CHAPTER APPENDIX

TABLE 6.A.1. *Post-Crisis Expectations and Findings in Provinces with Low to Moderate Political Hurdles*[a]

	Investor portfolio structure					
	Foreign		*Domestic* without *diverse holdings*		*Domestic* with *diverse holdings*	
	Expect	*Observe*	*Expect*	*Observe*	*Expect*	*Observe*
Contractual outcomes						
Investor exit	High	Santa Fe: Yes Córdoba 2002–2005: Yes Catamarca: Yes Misiones: No	Medium	Formosa: Yes Santiago del Estero: No La Rioja: Yes	Low	Córdoba 2006–2011: No Salta:[b] Yes
Full contract renegotiation	Low	Santa Fe: No Córdoba 2002–2005: No Catamarca: No Misiones: Yes	Medium	Formosa: No Santiago del Estero: Yes (informal) La Rioja: No[c]	High	Córdoba 2006–2011: Yes Salta: Yes
Indicators of health of the negotiating process						
Government addresses concessionaire financial concerns (in and outside of contract renegotiation)	Low	Santa Fe: Low Córdoba: Medium Catamarca: Low Misiones: High	Medium	Formosa: Medium Santiago del Estero: Medium La Rioja: Medium	High	Córdoba 2006–2011: High Salta: High
Concessionaire finances stabilize	Low	Santa Fe: Low Córdoba: Medium Catamarca: Low Misiones: Medium	Medium	Formosa: Low Santiago del Estero: Medium La Rioja: Medium	High	Córdoba 2006–2011: High Salta: High

TABLE 6.A.1. (*cont.*)

	Investor portfolio structure					
	Foreign		*Domestic* without *diverse holdings*		*Domestic* with *diverse holdings*	
	Expect	*Observe*	*Expect*	*Observe*	*Expect*	*Observe*
Firm employs legalistic retaliatory measures	High	Santa Fe: High Córdoba: High Catamarca: Low Misiones: Medium	Low	Formosa: Low Santiago del Estero: Low La Rioja: Low	Low	Córdoba 2006–2011: Low Salta: Low
Firm invests significant fraction of revenues	Low	Santa Fe: Low Córdoba: Low Catamarca: Low Misiones: Medium	Low	Formosa: Low Santiago del Estero: Low (investment by state) La Rioja: Low (investment by state)	Medium	Córdoba 2006–2011: Low (although almost twice predecessor) Salta: Medium

[a] Case coding is based on less information than cases for which separate charts exist in this chapter, and should therefore be viewed as less precise. Consult the case narratives in this chapter for the empirical details on which coding is based.
[b] The Salta concession was controlled by a joint venture between two domestic investors, only one of which possessed diverse local holdings.
[c] Latinaguas received a concession contract for the La Rioja system in 2002 that resembled renegotiation accords in other provinces. However, the contract was not respected by Governor Beder Herrera, who was elected in 2007.

TABLE 6.A.11. *Political Hurdle Index Components for Post-Crisis Period (Low- to Moderate-Hurdle Provinces)*

Year	***Competition for governor***	***Competition for legislature***	***Divided government***	***Governor did not privatize***	***Federal intervention***	***Hurdle index***
Córdoba						
2002	–	–		Not privatizer		1.5
2003	Low	Medium		Not privatizer		1.92
2004	–	–		Not privatizer		1
2005	–	–		Not privatizer		1
2006	–	–		Not privatizer		1
2007	High	Low		Not privatizer		2
2008	–	–		Not privatizer		2
2009	–	–		Not privatizer		1.75
Santiago del Estero[a]						
2002	Low	Low				1.33
2003	–	–				1
2004	–	–		Not privatizer	Yes	3
2005	High	High		Not privatizer		2.75
2006	–	–		Not privatizer		2
2007	–	–		Not privatizer		1.75
2008	Low	Low		Not privatizer		1.83
2009	–	–		Not privatizer		1.25
Santa Fe						
2002	–	–		Not privatizer		1.5
2003	High	Low		Not privatizer		2.25
2004	–	–		Not privatizer		2
2005	–	–		Not privatizer		1.75
2006	–	–		Not privatizer		1.5

TABLE 6.A.II. (*cont.*)

Year	*Competition for governor*	*Competition for legislature*	*Divided government*	*Governor did not privatize*	*Federal intervention*	*Hurdle index*
Misiones						
2002	–	–		Not privatizer		1.5
2003	Low	High		Not privatizer		2.25
2004	–	–		Not privatizer		1
2005	–	Low		Not privatizer		1.33
2006	–	–		Not privatizer		1
2007	Medium	Low		Not privatizer		1.67
2008	–	–		Not privatizer		1
2009	–	Low		Not privatizer		2.08
Catamarca						
2002	–	–				0
2003	Medium	Low				0.67
2004	–	–		Not privatizer		2
2005	–	Low		Not privatizer		2.08
2006	–	–		Not privatizer		2
2007	Low	Low		Not privatizer		1.5
2008	–	–		Not privatizer		1.58
Formosa						
2002	–	–		Not privatizer		1
2003	Low	Low		Not privatizer		1.33
2004	–	–		Not privatizer		1
2005	–	Low		Not privatizer		1.33
2006	–	–		Not privatizer		1
2007	Low	Low		Not privatizer		1.33
2008	–	–		Not privatizer		1

La Rioja[b]				
2002	–	–		0
2003	–	–		0.33
2004	–	–		0
2005	–	Low		0.33
2006	–	–		0
2007	High	High	Not privatizer	1
2008	–	–	Not privatizer	1
2009	–	–	Not privatizer	2.08
Salta				
2002	–	–		0
2003	Low	Low		0.33
2004	–	–		0
2005	–	Low		0.33
2006	–	–		0
2007	High	Medium		1
2008	–	–	Not privatizer	2
2009	–	Low	Not privatizer	2.08

Formula for index: Max(Legislative, Gubernatorial Competition)/3 + Divided government + Governor did not privatize + Governor not allied with Menem and not privatizer (for 1999 and earlier) + Federal intervention + Effect of turnover score (–0.25*years since turnover for 4 years following turnover).

[a] Although power turned over in Santiago del Estero before 2004, Carlos Juarez and his wife essentially maintained control through proxies until 2004. For the purposes of the hurdle index, therefore, turnover is not registered.

[b] The 2007 elections in La Rioja are coded as very competitive to capture the factional struggles between Governor Ángel Maza and his vice governor, Luís Beder Herrera, in the year preceding the election. (Maza was impeached before the election and did not run for reelection.)

7

Explaining Contractual Resilience in Low- and Middle-Income Countries

This chapter provides an initial assessment of the book's argument in a broader set of developing countries. It also evaluates arguments presented in Chapter 1 that cannot be explored fully in Argentina, including the contention that investor access to "substitutes" for property rights protections – such as international arbitration – makes contracts more fragile. Examining a larger set of countries also makes it possible to assess whether the relationship between investor portfolio structure and contractual resilience is strongest within political systems with competitive elections and when contracts are structured so as to assign investment obligations to firms.

In evaluating the book's claims within a more wide-ranging set of countries, this chapter considers two types of data. It first presents the results of statistical models of premature contract cancellation in the water and sanitation sector in low- and middle-income countries. Because contract termination is just one way investors exit contracts, however, the chapter also considers additional information about investor exit through equity sales, MNCs' public statements regarding their strategy in developing countries, and market entry statistics.

Overall, the material presented here suggests that domestic investors have found it more viable to hold water and sanitation contracts in the long run than foreign investors. In addition, access to international arbitration is associated with higher, rather than lower, rates of premature contract cancellation – despite the fact that arbitration access is more common in countries with stronger domestic property rights protections. Finally, the data analyzed offers little support for alternative explanations of variation in privatization program outcomes in the developing world, which focus on state capacity, property rights protections, and partisanship.

INVESTOR PORTFOLIOS AND PREMATURE CONTRACT CANCELLATION IN LOW- AND MIDDLE-INCOME COUNTRIES

To assess whether contractual resilience varies with investor organizational structure in weak institutional environments, this section examines patterns of premature contract cancellation in the water and sanitation sector in low- and middle-income countries. It provides a justification for – and explanation of – the data used to measure contract cancellation and investor structure, compares the incidence of exit among foreign and domestic investors, and uses event history models of contract duration to evaluate support for the book's primary argument.

The most comparable cross-national indicator available reflecting whether particular infrastructure contracts are evolving to the satisfaction of both investors and firms is the rate of premature contract cancellation. Patterns of contractual failure can be analyzed by drawing on a dataset developed and maintained by the World Bank: the Private Participation in Infrastructure (PPIAF-World Bank) database, which documents private sector participation in low- and middle-income countries – a population characterized by institutions weaker than those in developed countries. As of May 2008, the dataset contained 617 contracts in the water and sanitation sector, the first of which began in 1991 (PPIAF-World Bank: 2008). It includes information regarding the investors participating in the projects, the year of financial closure, contract type, and whether a project was canceled before term (and if so, when). Although the dataset is fairly complete, I have updated and obtained missing data on investor characteristics for Latin American projects. In the process, I was able to assess the accuracy of the Latin American data; its quality speaks well of the accuracy of the entire dataset.[1] Instances of contract cancellation recorded in the database are "premature" in that they occurred before the twenty to thirty years that is the usual legal length of an infrastructure privatization contract. Premature cancellation indicates that one or both parties are unhappy with the arrangement. This is, of course, an imperfect indicator. Investors may also exit through sales of equity stakes. For this reason, the statistical analysis of contract cancellation in this section is complemented in the final section of the chapter by information on sales of stakes in existing projects. Alternative quantitative measures of whether a contractual relationship is evolving to the satisfaction of one or both parties are, unfortunately, fraught with problems. Reliable cross-national data on annual investment levels simply does not exist.[2] Data that reflects realized

[1] It was necessary to correct only one start date and one cancellation date for the Latin American contracts.

[2] The PPIAF-World Bank database contains information on "investment commitments" at the time of contract award, but data on promised investments is a far cry from data on realized investments, given levels of contractual noncompliance by both firms and governments in infrastructure sectors. In addition, this data is available for just one year – which does not allow one to examine investment trajectories over time.

investment, such as statistics on improvements in service access, raises equally serious concerns about comparability. Census bureaus vary from country to country (and even project to project) in terms of how they measure service access, and improvements (or lack thereof) in access may reflect many other factors, such as subdivision approvals that impose service access requirements on developers, or simply rural-to-urban migration.[3]

The main independent variable of interest, investor organizational structure, must also be measured more crudely in a cross-national setting. One would ideally differentiate between domestic investors *with* and *without* diverse holdings in their contract jurisdiction and foreign investors, but this is impractical; the geographic dispersion of individual investors' business activities within their home market is rarely observable for projects in large sets of developing countries. Language barriers and uneven press coverage impede the collection of systematic data on this variable for the hundreds of water and sanitation projects in low- and middle-income countries. However, because a subset of domestic investors will have significant and diverse holdings in the subnational jurisdiction that awarded their contract, examining differences in patterns of market exit and contract longevity between foreign and domestic investors will suggest whether the patterns observed in the Argentine case hold more generally.[4]

Table 7.1 compares the relative frequency of premature contract cancellations among *concession contracts* and *divestitures* with foreign and domestic owners between 1990 and 2008, thereby providing a sense of trends in the data. This initial analysis focuses on these two types of privatizations, which conform to the scope conditions outlined in Chapter 1: both require firms to invest and both place investors in direct contact with consumers. In Latin America, where the privatization wave first took off, we see a stark difference in cancellation rates between projects with significant participation by foreign firms and those operated purely by domestic firms: 27 percent and 2 percent, respectively – almost a fourteenfold difference ($p < 0.0004$). Given the reasonable number of projects in each category, these differences are striking. Similar differences between groups, although not quite as stark, can be observed for the full set of low- and middle-income countries included in the World Bank's database. Fifteen percent of foreign-owned contracts

[3] Percentage coverage figures can be particularly misleading if one is unfamiliar with the cases in question. Coverage ratios vary in meaning depending on the percentage of the jurisdiction actually considered to fall in the company's service area. Coverage expansion can also be undertaken at the expense of service quality if sufficient investments in basic infrastructure are not made. Finally, data that is comparable across jurisdictions simply does not exist; see UN-Habitat (2001: 122–123) for a description of inaccuracies within standard international datasets that report percentage coverage at the country level. With respect to data on service quality, it is important to observe numerous indicators in parallel and also to examine the methodology used by the companies and regulators to calculate indicators.

[4] The PPIAF-World Bank database records investor information for a single point in time. Given that there has been limited turnover in projects, however, the information included is a reasonable proxy for the investors involved over the life of the project. (Sectors such as electricity have witnessed far greater turnover.)

TABLE 7.1. *Foreign Ownership and Contract Cancellation in Low- and Middle-Income Countries, 1990–2008*

	Latin America	*Worldwide*
Cases with ≥ 25% foreign ownership	27% (13/48) (0.03 Rule of law score[a])	15% (18/118) (−0.03 Rule of law score)
Cases with < 25% foreign ownership	2% (1/53) (−0.16 Rule of law score)	5% (5/105) (−0.09 Rule of law score)

Source: Base data from PPIAF-World Bank (2008 and World Bank Governance Indicators).
[a] Scale runs from −2.5 to 2.5. See the online appendix for variable definition.
Note: Latin American contracts: 120 in database, 101 after eliminating observations with missing values for ownership. Overall percentage cancelled: 14%. Average lifespan: 8 years; average start year: 1999. Contracts in low- and middle-income countries: 263 in database, 222 when projects missing values for foreign ownership or arbitration protection are eliminated. Overall percentage canceled: 10%. Average lifespan: 6.3 years. Average start year: 2001. No cancellations were omitted when observations with missing values were excluded.

ended prematurely, while only 5 percent of projects led by domestic investors were canceled ($p < 0.007$). The cancellation rate among Latin American contracts is higher than in other developing countries at least in part because the average start date is earlier, so projects have had more of a chance to be canceled. Higher rates of cancellation among contracts held by foreign investors appear not to stem from differences in levels of domestic property rights protections: average scores are actually higher for contracts held by foreign investors.

The raw data in this table, while compelling, does not present the whole story. It lumps together projects that were started in different years and hence does not adequately adjust for the fact that some have had more opportunity to be canceled than others. Also, we would like to compare cases that are similar with respect to other factors that might increase the probability of cancellation, such as low per capita income. To address these gaps, I model the expected life span of the population of concessions and divestitures using Cox proportional hazard regressions. The Cox proportional hazard model, a semiparametric approach, allows one to estimate the extent to which particular explanatory variables are associated with the risk of "failure," in this case premature contract cancellation, and thereby with longer or shorter duration times. Like other duration models, the Cox can accommodate censoring, or the fact that a portion of the contracts observed have not yet "failed" by the end of the observation period. The advantage of the Cox over other types of duration analyses is that we need make fewer assumptions regarding the functional form of duration dependence than are required for parametric models.[5] Cox results

[5] Another reason the Cox is appropriate is that the nature of duration dependence is not in and of itself of interest. Meanwhile, graphs of the estimated hazard function taken from Cox regressions with the contract data suggest that the assumptions regarding the shape of the hazard function consistent with

are straightforward to interpret for concession contracts and divestiture because all privatization arrangements – the first of which was entered in 1991 – were scheduled to last more than twenty years and had yet to reach that point by 2008, when the dataset was constructed. All "failures," then, amount to premature contract cancellations.

The statistical analysis of the association between investor type and contract lifespan has two stages. I begin with the entire population of 263 concessions and divestitures – the population of contracts for which the argument should hold – taking each contract as a unit of analysis or observation. A first set of regressions assesses the extent to which foreign ownership is associated with shorter contract life spans because of premature contract cancellation. I do not include time-varying covariates that occur after my "treatment" of interest: foreign ownership. This allows me to avoid what statisticians call "post-treatment bias."[6] (Regressions including time-varying covariates will be considered subsequently.) Regressions include a dummy variable for majority foreign ownership, which indicates that foreign investors own at least 50 percent of the project shares. Another set of regressions is run using a 25 percent threshold.[7] Regressions are stratified by the type of project (divestiture or concession), which allows for the accommodation of a different baseline hazard rate for each type. Models include control variables for GDP per capita, the extent of democratization of the host country,[8] project size, the level of property rights protections enjoyed in the host country,[9] and whether the contract has been granted by a subnational or national government. These control variables are measured before the start of the contracts. Standard

standard parametric approaches (such as the Weibull) do not match the data generation process under study.

[6] Statistics scholarship on causal inference argues that in order to obtain good statistical estimates of the influence of a factor measured at the beginning of the study period, one must not include factors occurring later in one's models, as these may be an outgrowth of the explanatory variables of interest. See Ho (2005) for an intuitive explanation and Rosenbaum (1984) for a technical treatment.

[7] The 50% cutoff was chosen on theoretical grounds: it corresponds to majority ownership, and formal decision-making power residing with the foreign investor. The alternative, 25% cutoff corresponds to the break below which there is very little foreign participation. Utilizing dummy variables corresponding to the two cutoff points also allows for the inclusion of many more cases (233 and 225 projects rather than 190); during coding of the dataset, it was often possible to deduce whether a contract fell in one of these binomial categories but not possible to ascertain an exact foreign ownership percentage due to missing data about investors possessing small equity stakes.

[8] As noted earlier in the chapter, we would expect there to be stronger opposition to tariff increases and other policies supportive of utilities in democratic settings. This independent variable captures that effect. A later section assesses empirical evidence regarding the claim that the relationship between foreign ownership and premature contract cancellation will be stronger in democracies than in autocracies.

[9] The online appendix contains definitions of, sources for, and the distributions of all variables used in the analysis. As Kurtz and Schrank (2007a, 2007b) stress, the World Bank's "rule of law" measure and other indexes designed to capture cross-country differences in levels of property rights protection are problematic and should be interpreted with care.

errors are clustered by country following Primo et al. (2007).[10] Regressions evaluating whether the relationship between foreign ownership and premature contract cancellation varies by contract type or by political regime type will be considered later in the chapter, as will regressions examining the extent to which factors such as international arbitration access are associated with greater contractual fragility for foreign investors.[11]

Table 7.2 displays the results of Cox proportional hazard regressions for all concessions and divestitures in low- and middle-income countries. In models 1 to 4, majority foreign ownership is strongly associated with premature cancellation.[12] When the coefficient for the 50 percent foreign ownership variable is 1.28 (as in model 1), this implies that projects with majority foreign ownership are 3.7 times more likely to fail than projects without 50 percent foreign ownership at a given contract age, holding other variables at their means.[13] This is similar to the ratio in the raw data from Table 7.1.

Inspection of the dfbeta residuals confirms that observations exerting the greatest influence on the coefficients for the foreign ownership variables are depressing rather than augmenting the coefficients, suggesting that the strong estimated effects are not the result of outliers.[14] Results of tests for nonproportionality also do not suggest problems with the regressions.[15] Among the control variables, the coefficient for the "rule of law" is somewhat surprising, suggesting that contracts in countries with stronger property rights protections have proven to be slightly more vulnerable to premature cancellation.[16] This result, however, reflects the inclusion of Chinese projects in the

[10] Note that there are a number of control variables at the country level, so country fixed effects are inappropriate given that analysis is cross-sectional.

[11] While the standard way to evaluate condition hypotheses is through the utilization of interaction terms, that is not possible for this dataset given the small number of contracts. I instead examine relationships within subsets of the data.

[12] Comparing models 1 and 2, note that the majority foreign ownership, rather than the 25% threshold, provides a better model fit.

[13] This mean hazard ratio was calculated using simulations in Zelig for model 1 in Table 7.2. The standard deviation for the hazard ratio is 2.1, and the 95% confidence interval runs from 1.1 to 9.1. For the purposes of the simulation, the values for the other covariates were held at their means: 2.3 for the Polity variable, –0.05 for the rule of law, and US$3,556 for GDP per capita in 1991.

[14] Visual inspection of dfbeta residuals was conducted using the R procedures suggested by Therneau and Gambsch (2000: 155). Results are almost as strong when we exclude the Argentine contracts from the regressions and if we stratify the regression by region.

[15] The tests for nonproportionality of hazards involving scaled Schoenfeld residuals are implemented utilizing R procedures described by Therneau and Gambsch (2000: 135–136).

[16] Results are comparable when one substitutes alternative measures for property rights protections, such as Heritage Foundation and International Country Risk Guide (ICRG) scores. Presumably, this means that the levels of property rights protection achieved in low- and middle-income countries are insufficient to protect investments in politicized sectors such as public utilities.

TABLE 7.2. *Foreign Ownership and Contract Duration in Low- and Middle-Income Countries, 1990–2008*

Variable	*Model 1*	*Model 2*	*Model 3*	*Model 4*	*Model 5*
50% Foreign	1.28**	1.86***	1.92***		1.25**
	(0.53)	(0.54)	(0.55)		(0.55)
25% Foreign				1.94**	
				(0.82)	
GDP per capita	−0.0004*	−0.0004	−0.0003	−0.0002	−0.0004*
(1991)	(0.0002)	(0.0003)	(0.0002)	(0.0002)	(0.0002)
Rule of law	0.73*	1.18**	0.78	1.18**	0.74*
(1996)	(0.43)	(0.58)	(0.69)	(0.60)	(0.44)
Polity (score for	0.06	0.19*	0.15	0.16	0.06
year of contract award)	(0.05)	(0.11)	(0.14)	(0.11)	(0.05)
Project size		0.68***	0.36	0.67***	
category (1–4)		(0.21)	(0.45)	(0.17)	
Contract with			0.42		
national government?			(1.28)		
Multilateral					0.21
bank participation					(0.46)
Observations	229	154	110	147	229
Log-likelihood	−99.14	−49.84	−36.74	−50.26	−99.08
Wald test	12.8 on 4 df, p=0.013	31.5 on 5 df, p=7.44e-06	61.8 on 6 df, p=1.93e-11	24.3 on 5 df, p=0.000188	13.8 on 5 df, p=0.0166

Note: Cox proportional hazard regressions with 229 contracts and 23 cancellations. Robust standard errors in parentheses;
* significant at 10% level; ** significant at 5% level; *** significant at 1% level. Regressions are stratified by the type of project: concession or divestiture. Standard errors are clustered by country. Results obtained using R (version 2.10.1) and Zelig (Version 3.4–5).

dataset; when they are removed, the rule of law variable loses statistical significance.[17] Larger projects also appear more vulnerable to premature cancellation, but due to missing data, the results here are based on a much smaller

[17] Results for other variables do not change significantly when the Chinese cases are dropped. China has a relatively low score for property protection measures and a relatively low proportion of contracts cancelled prematurely, which presumably reflects investor desires not to escalate tensions with regulatory authorities in the interest of maintaining a foothold in an extremely important, and growing, market. The results suggest that low- and middle-income countries with reputations for higher level of property rights protections may still be unable to protect investments in politicized sectors like public utilities.

set of observations.[18] The level of democracy appears not to be associated with shorter contract life spans – at least within the full population of contracts. Overall, these results suggest that contracts with significant stakes held by foreign investors have been more vulnerable to premature cancellation, even after taking into account how long we have observed each project and adding time-invariant controls for country- and project-level variables that we would expect to influence this risk.[19] After running the same regressions for the subset of the data from Latin America, the results are even stronger.[20] This is particularly suggestive, as the privatization wave occurred earlier in Latin America and contracts have therefore had a greater opportunity to be canceled; trends in this region may presage developments in other regions.[21]

As stressed in Chapter 1, the observed relationship between cancellation and foreign ownership is likely to be more pronounced under some circumstances than under others. This section concludes by considering the extent to which (1) the relationship between foreign ownership and premature contract cancellation is more visible when projects involve contact with the public and significant investment responsibilities, and (2) relationships are stronger in political systems that allow some degree of political competition. Results reported earlier in the chapter hold for concession contracts and divestitures: privatization arrangements in which private firms have direct contact with retail consumers and that place significant investment burdens on the private sector. In equivalent analyses of greenfield projects (contracts for the construction and management of individual new plants rather than existing distribution systems) and management and lease contracts (in

18 Project size refers to a categorization based on the size of the population receiving services from the private provider (see the online appendix for coding). In some cases, especially in China, the PPIAF-World Bank database only reports size in terms of the cubic meter capacity of associated treatment plants. These observations have not been coded and therefore do not enter into the regressions. The results for models 2–4 are comparable if one substitutes log(thousand connections) for the ordinal variable. I have presented the results including the ordinal variable because diagnostics with the regression residuals suggest that the ordinal variable provides a fit that is closer to linear. Similar diagnostic procedures suggest log(thousand connections) is far preferable to including the raw connection figures in the regression. The diagnostic techniques were conducted utilizing R routines described by Therneau and Gambsch (2000: 87–92).

19 It is, admittedly, difficult to rule out additional country-level factors that might affect cancellation rates. When one stratifies the regressions by country, rather than stratifying by region and clustering the standard errors by country, the p value for the foreign ownership variable rises to 0.11. This occurs because there are not enough cancellations within each country to estimate with precision separate hazard rates. In the models presented in Table 7.2 I have included country-level control variables instead. As a robustness check, I also estimate models stratified by region and by the income level of the host country (low, middle, and upper-middle income, according to World Bank classifications). The results are robust to stratification by both income level and region (and both at the same time).

20 Regression results available on request.

21 The average start year for the population of Latin American concessions and divestitures was 1999, whereas the average start year outside of the region was 2002. This means that Latin American projects have had more years in which they could have been canceled.

which investment responsibilities remain with the public sector), the strong relationship between foreign ownership and shorter contract duration disappears.[22]

This book also suggests that the relationship between foreign ownership and premature contract cancellation would be stronger in countries with contested elections, as political hurdles would appear with more regularity, and conflict, once begun, would be harder to contain given the greater number of actors involved. When we conduct the same regressions reported in Table 7.2 with the subset of the projects not located in authoritarian countries (i.e., where the Polity variable is > 0), the association between foreign ownership and cancellation is indeed stronger.[23] The Polity variable is not statistically significant, suggesting that the main differences are between authoritarian and democratic regimes.

SUPPORT FOR ALTERNATIVE EXPLANATIONS OF CANCELLATION AMONG *ALL* CONTRACTS

The literatures on foreign direct investment, regulation, and development suggest other factors that may account for variation in the resilience of privatization contracts. This section evaluates empirical support for alternative explanations already considered in Argentina to see if they are supported in other contexts, as well as arguments that suggest country-level factors may be important sources of variation. It considers, first, explanations that are most effectively operationalized as time-invariant variables, then explanations that emphasize factors that vary over time.

In Table 7.2, we find little support for alternative explanations best measured as time-invariant factors. Arguments stressing the ability of governments with greater "state capacity" to regulate private providers would suggest that privatization arrangements in countries with more able and stronger states would be less fragile. When we include the World Bank's "government effectiveness" score for the host country in the cross-sectional regressions, it is difficult to parse the respective effects of property rights protections and state capacity, since the two variables are highly correlated.[24] That being said, when the least correlated of the three property rights indexes is included in the regressions alongside the government effectiveness score, government effectiveness is actually associated with higher rates of premature contract

[22] Greenfield and management and lease contracts tend to involve shorter contracts, sometimes as short as three to five years. Projects of either type that are concluded on schedule rather than terminated prematurely are treated as censored in this analysis, following King et al. (1990).

[23] These results are left out of this chapter because of space considerations but are available on request. When the standard cutoff of Polity > 6 is used to only include full democracies in the sample, the results for the half-foreign variable are still strongly significant but due to the smaller sample size are not quite as strong as for the Polity > 0 cutoff.

[24] State capacity is measured at the time of contract award, as the state's ability to structure and manage the privatization process presumably exercises an ongoing influence on privatization outcomes.

cancellation.[25] This suggests that for low- and middle-income countries, high levels of state capacity have not been sufficient to institutionalize privatization in controversial sectors such as utilities.

Scholars have also argued that the involvement of multilateral institutions such as the World Bank and IMF in privatization programs can work against institutionalization (Henisz and Zelner 2004). To assess the extent to which IFI involvement in water and sanitation contracts contributed to contract fragility, I add a variable indicating whether a multilateral institution such as the World Bank or one of the regional development banks has participated in the privatization via a loan, syndication, equity stake or guarantee.[26] In this new model (Table 7.2, model 5), the multilateral participation variable is insignificant.[27] These results do not indicate that multilateral participation contributes strongly to contract fragility.

We might instead attribute the observed variation in patterns of premature contract cancellation to alternative factors that vary over time. The presence or absence of crisis and the ideology of the executive, for instance, fall in this category. To assess the extent to which these and other time-varying factors are associated with differences in contract life span, I add the covariates to time series versions of the baseline models that treat each project year as a separate observation. Although the coefficients for our original variable of interest – foreign ownership – will no longer indicate the full extent to which it contributes to or detracts from contract longevity, the coefficients on the time-varying covariates in these new models will suggest whether these factors are also associated with contractual fragility or resilience.

We first examine the extent to which the observed variation in patterns of premature contract cancellation is correlated with differential exposure to economic crises. In the utilities and infrastructure sector, a crisis characterized by shocks to consumer incomes or the exchange rate, or an episode of high inflation, will complicate the task of regulation greatly. Projects may be thrown off course by crises but not canceled for several years while negotiations proceed. Within the utilities sector, three types of economic shock or crisis are of particular importance: large, negative shocks to the foreign exchange rate; large drops in GDP growth; and bouts of severe inflation. I label a period as a crisis year when a country's GDP growth dips below −5 percent, the consumer price index rises by more than 50 percent, or the bilateral exchange rate with the U.S. dollar falls more than 25 percent. This is a more limited definition than that employed by Henisz

[25] Results are again omitted because of space constraints, but are available on request.

[26] This dummy variable is also coded from project profiles in the Private Participation in Infrastructure database. Variable descriptions are included in the online appendix.

[27] In these new regressions, the coefficients for the foreign ownership and control variables could be misleading, as multilateral participation could occur at various points in the life of the contract and are therefore post-treatment variables. In other words, one should not interpret the coefficients for treatment variables if post-treatment variables are also included in the model.

and Zelner (2005: 370), but it is tailored to the utility sector and allows us to code crisis years from publicly available macroeconomic data. To capture the lingering effect of crisis, and the fact that post-crisis negotiations about tariff increases or other regulatory changes can drag on for many years, I code a dummy variable that reflects whether a particular project has lived through a crisis.[28]

Scholars such as Murillo (2009) and Flores-Macías (2010) have highlighted the importance of the ideology of the party in power for regulatory relations. Murillo has argued that "right wing true believers" are more likely to provide companies with supportive regulatory policy than left-leaning politicians,[29] while Flores-Macías (2010) argues that shifts to the left in economic policy are likely to be more significant in weakly institutionalized party systems. As other scholars have noted, the ability of the executive branch to overcome "veto players" will of course temper the effects of ideology and other factors that may influence executive preferences (Henisz 2002). Therefore, to assess the extent to which ideology is associated with contract cancellation, I have created an interaction term using a left government variable and a measure of the strength of institutional checks and balances on the executive in a particular country.[30]

Table 7.3 compares results from the baseline model, designed to assess the extent to which foreign ownership is associated with greater contract fragility, with results from models designed to examine the influence of time-varying covariates. In the latter, the property rights and Polity variables are excluded because they substantively overlap with the checks and balances variable included in these models. The Polity variable is replaced by the Freedom House Civil Liberties variable, the definition of which also does not overlap with the checks and balances measure.[31]

When we include an after crisis variable in time series regressions with the full set of contracts, the coefficient is small and statistically insignificant (Table 7.3, model 4). Differential experience of crisis, in other words, does not appear to explain observed patterns of premature contract cancellation. Models 3 and 4 also evaluate support for the proposition that left-leaning governments, especially when unfettered by strong checks and balances, are more likely to oversee privatization reversals. The effect of left government at all levels of the checks variable is statistically insignificant.[32] This analysis is, of course, preliminary given the limited number of contract cancellations. It is consistent, however, with the case evidence

[28] I have also run regressions with only crises years coded, and these do not yield statistically or substantively significant coefficients for crisis variables. In addition, I have run regressions with GDP growth and inflation rates included separately, with similar results.

[29] Murillo argues this effect is likely to be particularly strong during less competitive periods.

[30] The party ideology coding and "checks" variable come from the World Bank database on Political Institutions.

[31] Regression results are comparable if the Freedom House press freedom variable is utilized instead.

[32] Unfortunately, the checks and ideology data was not available for 2007 and 2008, which constrains the number of observations available for these regressions. The statistical significance of the left government variable was assessed by calculating the standard error for the conditional effect at each level of the checks variable.

TABLE 7.3. *Foreign Ownership and Contract Duration in Low- and Middle-Income Countries, 1990–2008 (Annual Observations)*

Variable	*Model 1 (BASELINE)*	*Model 2 (BASELINE)*	*Model 3 (+ Time-varying covariates)*	*Model 4 (+ Time-varying covariates)*
Majority foreign	1.26***	2.06**	1.44***	1.50**
	(0.43)	(0.98)	(0.44)	(0.59)
GDP per capita (1991)	−0.0004**	0.0001	−0.0006***	−0.0006***
	(0.0002)	(0.0003)	(0.0002)	(0.0002)
Rule of law (1996)	0.73*	−0.55		
	(0.39)	(0.52)		
Polity (for year of contract award)	0.06	0.87***		
	(0.05)	(0.30)		
Checks on executive			0.05	0.02
			(0.40)	(0.38)
Civil liberties			−0.57*	−0.55*
			(0.32)	(0.29)
Project size category (1–4)		0.75***		
		(0.24)		
Executive branch controlled by left party			1.05	0.97
			(2.40)	(2.27)
Left executive* Checks on executive			−0.32	−0.31
			(0.55)	(0.53)
After crisis				0.33
				(0.68)
After crisis* Half-foreign				0.32
				(1.01)
Observations	1721	992	1078	1078
Log-likelihood	−99.3	−32.46	−63.50	−63.40
Wald test	17.6 on 4 df, p=0.002	25.6 on 5 df, p=0.0001	40.9 on 6 df, p=3.008e-0	37.7 on 7 df, p=3.48e-06

Note: Cox proportional hazard regressions with 229 contracts and 23 cancellations. Robust standard errors in parentheses; * significant at 10% level; ** significant at 5% level; *** significant at 1% level. Standard errors clustered by contract. All models stratified by type of project: concession or divestiture.

from Argentina presented in earlier chapters. Additional case study work on other regions, such as Southeast Asia, would add further support to this analysis.

Finally, we might suppose that the observed association between contract cancellation and foreign ownership stems from selection effects – for example, that domestic firms with superior knowledge of local markets secured more favorable contracts, and that this pattern would explain higher cancellation rates among contracts held by international firms. The contract award processes in

Argentina described in Chapter 2, however, suggest that the pattern, if any, was the reverse: jurisdictions sought international investors and settled for domestic firms if they could not attract consortia led by MNCs. Domestic firms, meanwhile, endeavored to enter all concessions, including those that eventually failed.

ACCESS TO INTERNATIONAL ARBITRATION AND PREMATURE CONTRACT CANCELLATION

All foreign investors holding majority stakes in Argentine water and sanitation concessions had access to international arbitration through their home country's bilateral investment treaties (BITs) with Argentina. This means that it was impossible to provide satisfying empirical support for the proposition that access to arbitration is associated with *greater* – rather than lesser – contractual fragility. This section evaluates support for this argument, drawing on the same dataset of concessions and divestitures in low- and middle-income countries.

Investor access to international arbitration for each of the contracts in the dataset is determined based on a careful examination of the BITs, other treaty-like instruments, and domestic investment laws that would affect particular cases, following Yackee (2007, 2008). The analysis distinguishes between two cases: (1) contracts protected by any provision for international arbitration; and (2) those protected by what Yackee terms "strong" arbitration clauses that involve explicit state preconsent to arbitration, do not restrict the scope of application to expropriation, and are contained within treaties (and hence less vulnerable to change than provisions within domestic investment law). A detailed description of the coding process is included in the online appendix.[33]

Table 7.4 compares rates of cancellation for contracts held by foreign investors with and without strong legal provisions for access to international arbitration. The difference in cancellation rate between the groups is striking: 39 percent as opposed to 6 percent in Latin America ($p < 0.003$), and 30 percent as opposed to 7 percent in low- and middle-income countries ($p < 0.003$). (Note that foreign investors without access to arbitration may still be exiting at a higher rate than is reflected by the data, as there are strong incentives to sell shares rather than go to the local courts under such circumstances. Sales to other private investors will not register as contract cancellations.) Importantly, the difference in the failure rates between projects with arbitration provisions and those without appears not to reflect differences in the level of property rights protections enjoyed in the host county: the projects where investors have the option of arbitration score higher on average on the World Bank's rule of law measure than those where investors have no arbitration protection. The fact that

[33] BIT data is from the United Nations Conference on Trade and Development (UNCTAD) International Investment Agreements Database (2008), additional treaties from the World Trade Organization, and arbitration provisions enacted through domestic law from ICSID/Oceana (2009).

TABLE 7.4. *International Arbitration Access and Contract Cancellation among Foreign Investors[a], 1990–2008*

	Latin America	*Worldwide[c]*
Strong international arbitration protection	39% (12/31) (0.27 rule of law score[b])	30% (13/43) (0.19 rule of law score)
Weak or no international arbitration protection	6% (1/17) (−0.42 rule of law score)	7% (5/75) (−0.14 rule of law score)

Source: Base data from PPIAF-World Bank (2008) and World Bank Governance Indicators. This chart contains a subset of the data in Table 7.1.

[a] Foreign ownership ≥ 25%.

[b] Scale runs from −2.5 to 2.5. See the online appendix for variable definition.

[c] The chart distinguishes between contracts that do and do not enjoy protection of "strong" arbitration protections. If we instead examine the respective cancellation rates of foreign-held contracts that enjoy all types of arbitration provisions versus no arbitration provisions, the cancellation rates are 17% (15/88) and 10% (3/30), respectively.

cancellation rates are higher in Latin America, as was previously mentioned, reflects the fact that the privatization wave began in the region.

The cancellation rates displayed in the table, while striking, do not present the whole story. The table lumps together contracts from different years, and important predictors of cancellation may vary between groups. To assess the extent to which otherwise equivalent projects with foreign investor participation are associated with higher risks of premature contract cancellation if protected by arbitration provisions, I conduct a second set of regressions that contain just the projects with foreign participation. Table 7.5 reports Cox regression results with foreign investor-held contracts in low- and middle-income countries. Standard errors are again clustered by country.[34] These regressions include a variable that reflects whether primary investors enjoyed access to international arbitration. In the first model, this variable reflects all forms of access, including weak provisions in BITs and domestic investment law. In the remaining models, the arbitration variable reflects strong access, or instances in which host governments offered explicit preconsent to international arbitration for a wide range of dispute types through international investment agreements or domestic investment law.

The positive and highly significant coefficient for the arbitration variable suggests that access to arbitration is strongly associated with shorter contract life spans. The regression coefficients for the arbitration variable in model 2

[34] The standard approach would be to stratify by country in this type of analysis. In addition to the estimation problems cited for that approach for the models in Table 7.2, BITs, other treaties providing for arbitration, and domestic investment laws are in almost all cases country-level variables in this dataset. Countries, after all, tend to sign series of agreements or eschew preferential trade agreements.

TABLE 7.5. *International Arbitration Access and Contract Duration for Foreign Investors in Low- and Middle-Income Countries, 1990–2008*

Variable	*Model 1 (Arbitration variable includes both weak and strong protections)*	*Model 2 (Strong version of arbitration variable)*	*Model 3 (Strong version of arbitration variable)*	*Model 4 (Strong version of arbitration variable)*	*Model 5 (Strong version of arbitration variable)*	*Model 6 (Strong version of arbitration variable)*
Arbitration protection	1.43**	1.58***	1.81**	1.24*		1.61***
	(0.68)	(0.51)	(0.75)	(0.64)		(0.54)
Joint venture with domestic firm					0.36	
					(0.57)	
GDP per capita (1991)	−0.0004**	−0.0004**	−0.0004**	−0.0003	−0.0002	−0.0004**
	(0.0002)	(0.0002)	(0.0001)	(0.0002)	(0.0002)	(0.0002)
Rule of law (1996)	0.20	0.33	0.64*	0.11	0.61*	0.30
	(0.46)	(0.43)	(0.57)	(0.54)	(0.36)	(0.45)
Polity (score for year of contract award)	0.19***	0.11***	0.17*	0.09**	0.12***	0.11***
	(0.04)	(0.03)	(0.10)	(0.04)	(0.04)	(0.03)
Project size category (1–4)			0.51***			
			(0.17)			
Contract with national government				1.41***		
				(0.49)		

BIT* national				−1.09* (0.55)		
Multilateral bank participation						−0.21 (0.40)
Observations	115	115	79	96	96	115
Log-likelihood	−59.52	−58.7	−40.11	−45.65	−44.74	−58.63
Wald test	50.9 on 4 df, p=2.32e-10	43.6 on 4 df, p=7.9e-09	34.2 on 5 df, p=2.2e-06	139 on 6 df, p=0	52.6 on 4 df, p=1.02e-10	42.9 on 5 df, p=3.97e-08

Note: Cox proportional hazard regressions with 115 contracts and 8 cancellations. Robust standard errors in parentheses; *significant at 10% level; ** significant at 5% level; *** significant at 1% level. Regressions are stratified by the type of project: concession or divestiture. Standard errors are clustered by country.

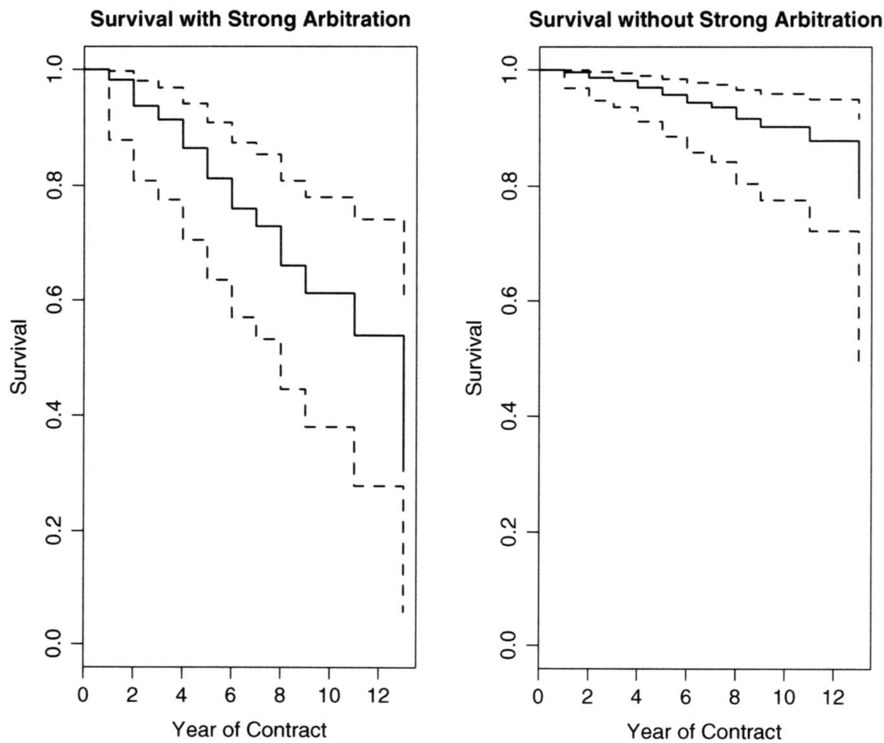

FIGURE 7.1. Estimated Survivor Curves for Projects with Foreign Owners in Low- and Middle-Income Countries, 1990–2008

Notes: Survivor curves correspond to Table 7.5, model 1. Covariate settings: polity = 6 (typical value for a democracy); rule of law = -0.02 (mean); GDP per capita (1991) = US$4,092 (mean). Difference between the two curves is not as large when Polity is set to the mean (1.74). Graph includes 95% confidence intervals.

suggests contracts with arbitration options are five times more likely to fail at a given contract age than foreign-led contracts without arbitration protection, holding other variables at their means.[35] Figure 7.1 presents estimates of the respective survival functions for contracts held by foreign investors with and without strong arbitration protections, holding other variables at typical values; the lower survival rates in the cases of arbitration protection come across dramatically. The implication is that access to international arbitration not only fails to make regulatory policy more favorable, it also makes exit easier.

Coefficients for our control variables, meanwhile, for the most part match expectations. Projects in countries with higher levels of GDP per capita tend to

[35] This mean hazard ratio was calculated using simulations in Zelig for model 1 in Table 7.5. The standard deviation for the hazard ratio of 5.7 is 3.3, and the 95% confidence interval runs from 1.6 to 14.3. For the purposes of the simulation, the values for the other covariates were held at their means.

last longer. A more democratic environment is associated with a higher probability of cancellation at a given contract age. The rule of law variable helps account for the fact that countries that score lower on standard measures of property rights protections may be more likely to adopt arbitration provisions in BITs or other international agreements in order to attract investment, and that this might account for higher rates of contract cancellation in countries that have provided arbitration options. The coefficient, however, is insignificant, and likelihood ratio tests suggest that it does not add explanatory power to the models, indicating that contract cancellation is not associated with subjective evaluations of property rights protections in low- and middle-income countries.[36] Larger projects – which, because water and sanitation systems tend to be geographic monopolies, tend to occur in larger metropolitan areas – are again associated with earlier contract termination. As before, inspection of the dfbeta residuals suggests that the observations that exert the strongest influence on the coefficient for the arbitration variable depress rather than inflate the coefficient, and global tests do not suggest problems of nonproportionality. And, consistent with expectations, strong arbitration provisions are even more strongly associated with premature contract cancellation when we exclude autocracies from the dataset.[37]

Model 4 (Table 7.5) tests a related, conditional hypothesis: that the effect of arbitration protection depends on whether contracts have been granted by subnational or national governments. As Chapter 1 stresses, the potential sanctions associated with international arbitration awards under BITs should prove more effective at bringing national than subnational governments to the bargaining table, as national governments usually bear the financial and reputation costs of arbitration awards. The results of the interactive model (model 4) suggest that this may indeed be the case. The coefficient for the arbitration variable, which reflects the effect of strong arbitration protections when the national government variable is equal to 0 – or in other words, the effect of strong arbitration protection when a subnational government granted the infrastructure contract – is positive and statistically significant. Meanwhile, the conditional effect of arbitration protection when a national government has signed the contract is close to zero (1.24 + (−1.09)) and insignificant.[38] Although these results must be interpreted with caution given the small set of cases, the respective raw cancellation rates of contracts with and without strong arbitration protections held by local and national governments, respectively, are certainly consistent with the regression results; the relative frequencies are presented in Table 7.6. Among contracts granted by local governments with strong arbitration protection, 26 percent of those held by foreign investors have been canceled whereas only 6 percent of those

[36] One obtains similar results when one substitutes alternative measures for property rights protections, such as the Heritage Foundation Property Rights index and the ICRG rule of law score.

[37] These results hold when one examines only countries with Polity scores > 0 or > 6.

[38] Project size is not included in this regression because of the strong correlation between national government participation and large project size.

TABLE 7.6. *Contract Cancellation Rates for Foreign Investors by Level of Government, 1990–2008*

	Strong arbitration option	***Weak or no arbitration option***
Local government holds contract (85 total)	26% (6/23)	6% (4/62)
National government holds contract (11 total)	33% (3/9)	50% (1/2)

Source: Base data from the PPIAF-World Bank (2008). International arbitration categorizations by author; see the online appendix for the coding procedure.

without strong arbitration provisions have been canceled. On the other hand, for contracts granted by national governments, there is no clear trend.

SUPPORT FOR ALTERNATIVE EXPLANATIONS OF CANCELLATIONS AMONG FOREIGN-LED CONTRACTS

The duration analyses presented in Table 7.5 also allow us to assess empirical support for a first set of alternative explanations of premature cancellations among foreign-led projects. There is little evidence that joint venture partnerships in the water sector are less vulnerable to premature cancellation than other foreign-led contracts. When we substitute a joint venture dummy variable[39] for the arbitration variable in the set of foreign contracts, the coefficient is not statistically significant (model 5), suggesting that joint ventures do not enjoy systematic advantages over other ownership arrangements. Similarly, multilateral bank participation is not associated with lower probabilities of cancellation at a given contract age (model 6).[40] As in the analysis of contract cancellation among all types of investors, it is difficult to parse the respective effects of property rights protections and state capacity, since most measures for both are highly correlated. This being said, when the less correlated of the three property rights indexes is included in the regressions alongside the

[39] The joint venture variable was coded using ownership data from the PPIAF-World Bank database. As mentioned previously, ownership information dates from the latest updates to the database. This means that while the joint venture variable provides a rough indication of whether a joint venture has been in place for much of a project's life span, ownership arrangements may in some cases have changed over time. Note, however, that changes in lead investors are relatively infrequent in these types of privatizations, as it is usually necessary to secure regulatory approval before selling shares.

[40] In these new regressions, the coefficients for the arbitration and control variables could be misleading, as multilateral participation could occur at various points in the life of the contract and is therefore a post-treatment variable.

government effectiveness score, government effectiveness is actually associated with higher rates of premature contract cancellation.[41]

A second set of alternative explanations of premature contract cancellation among foreign-led projects emphasize factors that vary over time. Table 7.7 compares a baseline model with models designed to examine the influence of time-varying covariates.[42] Among contracts with significant foreign participation, left government is again not associated with higher probabilities of contract cancellation: the conditional effect of left government at low levels of the checks variable is insignificant in models 2 and 3; the effect of left government becomes negative and significant above checks = 3, or in country environments where there are greater checks and balances.[43] (In other words, in systems with significant checks and balances, left-leaning governments have proven less likely to preside over contract cancellations than center or right-wing governments.) Differential experience of crisis also does not appear to explain observed patterns of premature contract cancellation (Table 7.7, model 2). These results are of course preliminary, given the limited number of contract failures in the sector; as stated previously, further case study work on other regions could provide additional empirical support.

Finally, we might worry that the association between access to arbitration and premature contract cancellation reflects a selection process: that foreign investors only entered projects in countries with weak property rights protections when they had access to international arbitration. There are a number of reasons, however, to suspect that this is not the case. First, the association between arbitration access and a higher probability of cancellation remains strong and significant when regressions include a control variable for the rule of law or checks and balances (Table 7.5). Second, the average level of property rights protections is actually lower among contracts where foreign investors have access to arbitration than in contracts where they do not have access (Table 7.4). Finally, an influential quantitative study of BIT adoption reports that strong property rights protections are associated with *greater* rather than lower probabilities of BIT adoption (Elkins et al. 2006).

In summary, this event history analysis finds no support for alternative explanations of premature contract cancellation among contracts held by foreign investors. Instead, we would be advised to focus on characteristics of the

[41] Results are again omitted because of space constraints but are available on request.

[42] As in Table 7.3, the property rights and Polity variables are excluded because they substantively overlap with the checks and balances variable that is included in these models. The Polity variable is again replaced by the Freedom House Civil Liberties variable, the definition of which does not overlap with the checks and balances measure. Regression results are comparable if the Freedom House press freedom variable is utilized instead.

[43] Global tests for nonproportionality reveal that there are problems with the left government/checks interaction term in models 2–4, so these coefficients and standard errors should be viewed as less reliable.

TABLE 7.7. *International Arbitration Access and Contract Duration for Foreign Investors in Low- and Middle-Income Countries, 1990–2008 (Annual Observations)*

Variable	*Model 1 Baseline model*	*Model 2 + Time-varying covariates*	*Model 3 + Time-varying covariates*	*Model 4 + Time-varying covariates*
Arbitration (access to strong protections)	1.64*** (0.44)	2.13*** (0.60)	2.25*** (0.71)	1.92*** (0.56)
GDP per capita (1991)	−0.0005*** (0.0001)	−0.0006*** (0.0002)	−0.0005*** (0.0002)	−0.0005*** (0.0002)
Rule of law (1996)	0.09 (0.39)			
Polity score (for year of contract award)	0.13*** (0.03)			
Civil liberties		−0.30 (0.22)	−0.30 (0.23)	−0.35* (0.21)
Executive branch controlled by left party		0.42 (.82)	0.51 (0.80)	0.76 (0.79)
Checks and balances		0.08 (0.16)	0.09 (0.16)	0.08 (0.15)
Left executive* checks		−0.32 (0.25)	−0.35 (0.42)	−0.42 (0.25)
After crisis		−0.25 (0.43)	0.03 (0.42)	−0.23 (0.39)
Arbitration* After crisis			−0.36 (0.55)	
Multilateral bank participation				0.41 (0.44)
Observations	901	609	609	609
Log-likelihood	−711	−594.3	−594	−592.8
Wald test	41.3 on 4 df, p=2.29e-08	183 on 7 df, p=0	242 on 8 df, p=0	198 on 8 df, p=0

Note: Cox proportional hazard regressions with 115 contracts and 8 cancellations. Robust standard errors in parentheses; *significant at 10% level; ** significant at 5% level; *** significant at 1% level. Standard errors clustered by project. Models stratified by project type: divestiture or concession.

international institutional framework for investment – that is, whether primary investors enjoy arbitration protection – and investor characteristics, such as whether consortia are led by foreign or domestic investors. These "primary" project characteristics appear to help determine the extent to which projects can surmount crises, political turnover, and other types of routine hurdles that are inevitable in developing countries.

ADDITIONAL SIGNS OF FOREIGN INVESTOR EXIT FROM EMERGING MARKETS

This section considers several other types of data suggesting that observed patterns of contract cancellation reflect foreign investors' dissatisfaction with their concessions and divestitures in developing countries – particularly countries with contested elections – following crises. This data includes corporate statements by the largest MNCs working in the sector, market entry statistics following the Asian and Argentine crises, and press coverage of share sales. Taken together, the information provides further support for the argument that MNCs will find it difficult to negotiate mutually agreeable adaptations to their contracts with host governments, even in cases when an arbitration option should, theoretically, provide them with greater leverage. The data also shows that the regressions in the preceding section underestimate the rate of exit by foreign investors from contracts in Latin America.

As the Introduction stresses, infrastructure contracts in the developing world will inevitably encounter crises, given the inherent volatility of such markets and the long-term nature of privatization agreements. It is therefore important to examine the respective ability of different types of investors to negotiate workable responses to the most recent, large-scale crises in the developing world. After the Asian and Argentine crises, the difficulties of maintaining infrastructure concessions and divestitures in developing countries became very clear. In high-profile cases in both contexts, concessionaires that had inherited or incurred high levels of debt in foreign currency saw their debt-equity ratios skyrocket. The most prominent example among Asian cases is the Manila West (Maynilad) concession in the Philippines, in which the French MNC Suez played a supporting role.[44] The concessionaire inherited a dollar-denominated $800 million debt from the former state provider and had trouble extracting tariff adjustments from the government that would allow it to cope with ballooning interest payments after the crisis. In Latin America, the Argentine government froze the rates that privatized utilities could charge consumers following the crisis of 2001. In prominent cases, foreign investors' threats to take host governments into international arbitration if they were not allowed to raise tariffs (as was often stipulated through exchange rate guarantees in their contracts) or delay investments had little effect.[45]

MNCs responded to these difficulties by announcing that they would not be taking on new projects in emerging markets. The largest player in the international water and sanitation market, Suez, signaled such a shift to investors in

[44] "Government Set to File Counter Claim Against Maynilad." *Manila Bulletin*. Jan. 6, 2003.

[45] The Manila West concession ultimately entered bankruptcy after losing an international arbitration case against the Philippine government in 2003 (Wu and Malaluan 2008: 217); a domestic investor was granted a new, replacement concession in the territory. In Argentina, threats to file arbitration cases did not yield revised concession agreements either, as Chapters 5 and 6 show.

January 2003, announcing it would refocus on the Franco-Belgian domestic market, the EU, and North America – and reduce its exposure to developing countries.[46] Vivendi Environnement, its main competitor, also announced its intention to concentrate future expansion in developed countries.[47] Saur International, the third largest French firm in the industry, also declared that it would withdraw from the sector in Latin America.[48] Agbar, one of the main Spanish players in the sector, publicly voiced its commitment to the relatively safe Chilean market and a public-private partnership in Cuba but announced plans to withdraw from its remaining contracts in the region.[49]

Patterns of market entry and sales of stakes in existing projects following the two crises show that firms have been acting in line with these public statements. International operators in the water sector virtually stopped bidding for new contracts involving investment commitments in Latin America and Southeast Asia. For the twenty-nine concession contracts and divestitures on offer in Latin America between the Argentine economic crisis (2001–2002) and 2008, only two winning consortia included investor participation from outside the region.[50] This ratio is minuscule compared with the forty-six out of eighty-four projects (55 percent) with foreign participation prior to the crisis. Although foreign MNCs appeared reluctant to enter concessions and divestitures that required both substantial investment and contact with retail customers, as expected, they have proven more willing to enter greenfield projects and management contracts in the region: whereas 45 percent (26/58) of the pre-crisis greenfield and management or lease contracts had or have foreign investor participation, 39 percent (7/18) of the post-crisis projects do.

Market entry trends in Southeast Asia following the Asian financial crisis have been similar. Before the crisis, the large European and North American water and sanitation firms entered concession contracts and divestitures in what were then democracies, including Malaysia, Thailand, and the Philippines. After the crisis, however, dominant industry players such as Suez, Veolia, and RWE concentrated new investments in the region in China. Of the eighty-six concessions awarded in China since 2000, forty-eight involve the large European or North American companies as major shareholders.[51]

International operators' dissatisfaction with their prospects in developing country markets – and particularly their frustration regarding stalled negotiations with host governments following crises – becomes even more apparent in sales of stakes

[46] "Suez Introduces Its 2003–2004 Action Plan." Suez press release. Jan. 9, 2003.

[47] "Q4 2004 Veolia Environnement SA Earnings Conference Call – Final." *FD (FAIR DISCLOSURE) WIRE*. Aug. 20, 2005.

[48] "Los franceses de OSM de retiran y desisten de demanda millonaria." *Diario UNO*. April 8, 2007.

[49] Pinsent Masons Water Yearbook (2008: 272); "Spanish Agbar to Quit Latin American Market, Except Chile." *Latin America News Digest*. Sept. 13, 2005.

[50] Ratio calculated from PPIAF-World Bank (2008).

[51] Figures calculated from PPIAF-World Bank (2008).

in existing concessions and divestitures. Patterns in Latin America serve as a case in point. Following the Argentine crisis, as previous chapters illustrate, foreign investors in the country's concessions tried to sell their stakes in existing concessions before carrying out their threats to register arbitration claims. Since the 1990s, MNCs have also been gradually selling their stakes in existing projects in other Latin American countries characterized by roughly similar levels of property rights protections, especially in cases where foreign investors had no access to international arbitration.[52] For instance, in Brazil and Colombia, two countries that did not sign BITs and have not otherwise provided international firms with access to international arbitration, share sales have been the main avenue for market exit. In Brazil, foreign investors sold their stakes in all twelve water and sanitation concessions they held to domestic investors. Suez sold its shares in the Manaus and Limeira concessions to domestic construction firms in 2006, and Agbar sold its holdings in the Aguas Guariroba concession to local investors.[53] Aguas de Portugal, meanwhile, sold controlling stakes in its bundle of five concessions in the state of Rio de Janeiro to a Brazilian firm in 2007.[54] The American firm Tyco found domestic buyers for its Ourinhos and Nova Friburgo concessions.[55] Finally, Veolia (formerly Vivendi), the other major French player in the market, sold its stake in the Sanepar concession to a state-owned power utility.[56] In Colombia, two prominent projects with international investors have been canceled, and international investors have conspicuously announced the fact that they are not committed to staying in the market.[57]

Brazilian economic groups have entered the water and sanitation market both through purchases of stakes in projects being abandoned by foreign investors and through bids for new contracts. Their water and sanitation arms have typically taken on contracts within specific geographic areas – usually clusters of municipal contracts within states where the parent firms have operations in other sectors.[58] The geographic focus of these investments suggests that similar processes may be at work as in Argentina. Moreover, profit data aggregated and

[52] These three countries' respective scores for three different indexes of property rights protections are presented in Table 7.8. Note that these measures draw on some common elements and are correlated.

[53] Pinsent Masons Water Yearbook (2008: 224). "Agbar Considers Pulling Out of Potable Water Business." *Expansión*. Jan. 3, 2006.

[54] "Empresas multinacionais reduzem presença no sector." *Valor Econômico*. Feb. 23, 2007. "Brasil: Águas de Portugal conclui venda da concessionária Prolagos por 58 ME". Agência Lusa-Serviço Economia. Dec. 17, 2007.

[55] "Brazil: Water & Sewage Business Not So Hectic as Expected." *Valor Econômico*. June 24, 2009.

[56] "Empresas multinacionais reduzem presença no sector." *Valor Econômico*. Feb. 23, 2007. "Brazil's Copel Buys 30 Pct Stake in Domino Holdings." *Latin America News Digest*. Jan. 15, 2008.

[57] Agbar announced that it had withdrawn from the Argentine, Uruguayan, and Brazilian markets and that other holdings in Latin America – except those in Chile and Cuba – were under review. Pinsent Masons Water Yearbook (2007–2008: 256).

[58] Odebrecht has amassed a cluster of water and sanitation concessions in the states of São Paulo, and has acquired isolated contracts in Bahia, Espíritu Santo, and Rio de Janeiro. The company – one of the largest construction firms in Brazil – has important projects in other sectors in each of these

TABLE 7.8. *Property Rights Protections in Selected Latin American Countries*

	Heritage property rights			*International country risk guide*			*World Bank rule of law*		
	1996	*2002*	*2004*	*1996*	*2002*	*2004*	*1996*	*2002*	*2004*
Argentina	70	50	30	5	4	1.5	+0.12	−0.89	−0.71
Brazil	50	50	50	2	3	1.5	−0.20	−0.34	−0.33
Chile	90	90	90	5	5	5	1.24	1.18	1.18
Colombia	50	30	30	2	2	1	−0.65	−0.89	−0.80
Mexico	50	50	50	3	2	2	−0.48	−0.37	−0.40

reported by the Brazilian government suggests that in most cases, domestic firms are earning positive returns on their investments.[59]

Within Latin America, the only country in which international investors continued to enter concessions or divestitures between the Argentine crisis and 2008 was Chile, which scores significantly higher across the board on various property rights indexes (Table 7.8). Specialized international operators are staying in Chile, and pension funds from advanced industrial markets are actually buying into the water sector, suggesting that Chilean concessions offer stable and predictable income streams on par with utilities in home markets.[60]

Taken together, patterns of market exit from Latin America suggest that MNCs have not been able to make the concession or divestiture model work in weak institutional environments – regardless of whether firms have access to international arbitration, which presumably gives them greater leverage. Moreover, domestic firms have shown themselves willing to take over these

states. Águas do Brasil, co-owned by a group of Brazilian engineering, construction, and property development companies, has clustered its water and sanitation holdings in the states of São Paulo and Rio de Janeiro, where its owners also have construction, highway, metro, and railroad projects. Carioca Christini-Nielsen Engenharia has also clustered its water and sanitation holdings in the states of Rio de Janeiro and São Paulo; material posted on the firm's web site and local press coverage suggests it has railroad and "urbanization" projects in Rio. CAB, a subsidiary of Galvão Engenharia, has entered numerous concessions in both São Paulo and Mato Grosso; Galvão Engenharia also works on housing, metro, highway, and airport projects in São Paulo. Bertin acquired the Águas Guariroba concession in Mato Grosso do Sul, where it also has important sugar and ethanol holdings. In addition, in partnership with Grupo Equipav, it assumed control of a cluster of five municipal contracts in Rio de Janeiro. Finally, Empresa Sul-Americana de Montagens S.A. acquired a set of six concessions in the state of Pará, and then another in Tocantins, where the firm also has completed bridge, highway, and construction projects.

59 SNIS (www.snis.gov.br) and Ministry of Cities (2008) report profitability data for 8 out of 22 of the water and sanitation distribution system concessions controlled by domestic investors for the 2004–2006 period. Positive (and in most cases, high) returns were reported for seven out of the eight cases.

60 The Ontario Teachers' Pension Plan submitted successful takeover bids for two utilities, Essbio and Aguas Nuevo Sur Maule. "Paper: Japanese Cos vie for Esval, Now Estimated at US$700 million." *Business News Americas*. Aug. 1, 2007.

same projects – as long as not too much debt has been accumulated – suggesting that they see their projects as potentially profitable if government relations can be managed effectively.

From all these various types of evidence, it is clear that contract cancellation figures for concessions and divestitures underrepresent the shift of foreign operators away from investment in developing country water and sanitation markets. International operators appear unable to make the projects work financially in the long run in the face of political and economic turmoil. Entry patterns suggest MNCs have recognized their weaknesses in such markets and have shifted their strategies accordingly. It could, of course, be argued that domestic firms are now more competitive in bidding processes, having had the chance to amass experience during the 1990s through partnership with foreign firms. However, given that foreign companies are actively leaving existing projects and making public statements regarding their lack of interest in Latin America in particular and developing countries more generally, it seems fair to interpret the data as reflective of declining foreign interest. For foreign operators, international arbitration simply offers an additional exit option if projects do not evolve as planned. For the host countries, arbitration clauses for projects carry an additional, unanticipated effect: the private provision model may survive less often, as projects taken into international arbitration may become so politicized that the state must take them over rather than putting them out to tender again.

CONCLUSION

This chapter provides an empirical assessment of the extent to which the argument advanced in this book – that domestic firms with significant local holdings are better placed to maintain mutually beneficial negotiating relationships with host governments – applies outside Argentina within low- and middle-income countries, which tend to be characterized by weak institutions. Presenting empirical evidence regarding the conditions under which the argument applies, it first analyzes differential patterns of premature contract cancellation – in particular, how long contracts held by different types of investors have lasted before being canceled. Cox proportional hazard regressions find strong associations between domestic investor control over a project and lower probabilities of premature cancellation at a given contract age. Contrary to existing theory, measures of the strength of domestic property rights protections are not associated with contract cancellation within emerging markets. Regressions for the subset of contracts with foreign investors show strong associations between access to international arbitration and premature cancellation. Policy substitutes for strong property rights protections, in other words, are associated with contractual fragility rather than durability. These findings are particularly strong for democracies and when contracts place investors in direct contact with consumers and involve investment obligations.

Patterns of market exit and shifts in corporate strategy among MNCs working in the sector provide further evidence that international firms have proven less able to maintain effective negotiating relationships with host governments: international investors have only infrequently entered new contracts following the Asian and Argentine crises, whereas domestic firms are entering contracts at higher rates in their home markets. Moreover, even when not canceling their contracts, MNCs are often attempting to sell shares in existing projects in developing countries.

This broad-brush picture of trends within low- and middle-income countries suggests that the solution to infrastructure deficits in developing countries marketed widely during the 1990s – investment by MNCs with superior access to international finance, encouraged by a new set of international property rights protections – has not worked as promised in the water and sanitation sector. Rather, a set of new entrants into infrastructure markets – investors from developing countries – has proven more politically and financially successful in the long run. Although MNCs continue to exit the sector, these conglomerates continue to enter new contracts, seeing them as profitable business opportunities.

Conclusion

Dominant approaches to economic development stress the importance of institutions. Where strong institutions provide checks and balances within a polity, policy is more predictable, and property rights are more secure.[1] As a result, the private sector invests more readily. The leading scholarly approach to studying the regulation of investment in privatized infrastructure and utilities is based on a similar logic and suggests there will be little investment in developing countries with weak institutions because regulatory policy is unpredictable. Complementary scholarship in international political economy argues that countries with weak institutions can attract investment by instituting international legal substitutes for domestic property rights protections, such as guaranteeing investors access to international arbitration through bilateral investment treaties or domestic investment law.

In stressing the importance of formal institutions, however, these approaches neglect important *informal* contractual supports that firms have developed to cope with the economic volatility and weak institutions so commonly found in developing countries. In this book, I have examined how the cross-sector organizational form commonly adopted by developing country firms in their home market buttresses long-term contracts with the state in the infrastructure and utilities sector. Because developing country firms tend to hold a range of businesses in their contract jurisdiction, they will be more patient, entertain a wider range of bargaining outcomes, and have better access to informal bargaining strategies than will foreign firms. This allows them to negotiate more effectively with host governments, reaching agreements that ensure contracts stay economically and politically viable as circumstances change. Because private and public sector parties to contracts are able to resolve differences over time, neither is likely to cancel them prematurely. As

[1] This literature is reviewed in the Introduction and Chapter 1.

a result, privatization is more likely to become institutionalized. Firms without these characteristics may invest heavily in the short run – particularly in stable periods – but their relationships tend to be knocked off track during periods of economic or political change. When contracts are awarded at the subnational level, this argument suggests, only domestic investors with diverse holdings in the jurisdiction awarding their contract will enjoy these advantages.

In making this argument, the book provides explicit microfoundations for the classic obsolescing bargain hypothesis, which stresses that foreign investors in sectors with immobile assets are vulnerable once upfront investments have been made. This vulnerability stems in large part from multinationals (MNCs)' tendency to invest in particular sectors rather than amass diverse portfolios within developing countries. As a result, they do not have access to many informal negotiating strategies and exhibit less patience than their domestic counterparts. The book also outlines the circumstances under which investors' "bargains" are most likely to obsolesce: when firms stop investing or governments obtain resources to invest on their own, or when the political environment shortens leaders' time horizons or increases the political transaction costs of reaching settlements acceptable to firms and host governments. The wave of international property rights protections enacted during the 1980s and 1990s has not shielded MNCs from the obsolescing bargain because the sanctions imposed through international arbitration are further off than the immediate political threats or economic problems that could prompt developing country governments to push for contractual revisions in the short run. Lodging international claims with public bodies such as the International Centre for Settlement of Investment Disputes (ICSID) also makes firm-government conflicts more salient, thereby pushing governments to take a harder line with firms. Rather than helping governments "commit credibly" to foreign investors, then, international legal protections simply provide foreign investors with easier exit options.

The book also contributes to a growing literature on informal protections for property rights in weak institutional environments.[2] One source of insights is scholarship on "crony capitalism" that seeks, for instance, to identify the circumstances under which corruption coexists with productive investment, albeit at rates below or less stable than those observed in countries with well-established, universalistic systems of property rights. Existing work argues that investment is more likely when corruption is more predictable (Khan and Sundaram 2000), when a balance of power exists between cohesive groups of political and economic elites (Kang 2002), under resource constraints or security threats that limit corruption (Doner 2009), or when the state enforces property rights for a select group of government officials and members of the

[2] The proponents of analyzing "informal institutions" make a similar critique of institutionalist approaches to the analysis of weak institutional environments in the developing world (Helmke and Levitsky 2006).

ruling family (Haber 2002). A second, very recent literature on transition economies suggests that firms develop "bottom-up" strategies to protect their assets when legal protections for property rights are nonexistent or ineffective: providing local public goods or other corporate social responsibility programs can improve relations with authorities and the public (Frye 2006; Jones Luong and Weinthal 2010: 15), and forming strategic alliances allows firms to bring popular and/or international pressure to bear during disputes (Markus 2012). This book's focus on firm organizational structure – domestic ownership, and cross-sector diversification that increases investor patience and access to informal bargaining strategies – thus represents an important departure. Moreover, it shows that although efforts to draw attention to disputes may help firms protect their assets under some circumstances, in the infrastructure and utilities sectors, outside attention tends to create political fallout and actually makes it more difficult to negotiate effectively with host governments.

KEY FINDINGS

This book finds strong support for this argument regarding the importance of firm structure through within-country and cross-country comparisons. Studying a set of similar contracts within Argentina, which privatized at the provincial level, allowed for the comparison of firm-government relations held by investors with different organizational structures: MNCs, and domestic investors with and without long-standing, diverse holdings in their contract jurisdiction. The correlation between domestic ownership and diverse local holdings, and the long-run financial and political viability of private sector management, is clear in the Argentine case. Concessionaires controlled by domestic investors with significant, diverse local holdings successfully concluded contract renegotiations following the Argentine economic crisis of 2001–2002, ushering in significant consumer rate increases, in the vast majority of the cases. In contrast, only half of the domestic operators without local holdings and a quarter of foreign investors successfully concluded renegotiations. And while almost all foreign investors with controlling stakes in contracts exited their contracts, the respective rates of exit were lower for domestic firms (78 percent), and very low for domestic firms with local holdings (33 percent). Tellingly, Argentine conglomerates appear to have learned the advantages of diversification over time. Those that made bids for the stakes of firms exiting the market already had operations in other sectors in the contract jurisdiction.

Case studies of the negotiation processes between Argentine provincial governments and firms presented in Chapters 3–6 illustrate the reasons domestic investors with diverse local holdings could sustain constructive relationships with the political establishment – even in periods when politician time horizons shortened or government leverage increased. Firms asked for fewer policy concessions at a time because they had other operations at stake, which in turn decreased the probability of public backlash. They did not need to earn high rates of return in the utility sector itself at every point in time; returns could be earned in other, often related, operations, if necessary. And they could take advantage of opportunities for issue linkage – that is, linking policy benefits in one sphere of operations to those in other sectors during negotiations. Importantly, differences in contract trajectories were visible in many cases well before the Argentine crisis, which suggests that these outcomes are not just a product of the crisis and the subsequent devaluation – although long-term infrastructure contracts must be able to surmount such hurdles to be viable in developing countries.

To assess whether contractual resilience is associated with investor portfolio structure outside of Argentina, as well as whether legal substitutes for strong domestic property rights protections detract from rather than contribute to contractual durability, Chapter 7 examines patterns of market entry and exit from the water and sanitation sector in low- and middle-income countries. Cox proportional hazard regressions find strong associations between domestic investor control over a project, the best available proxy for diverse local holdings, and lower probabilities of premature contract cancellation at a given contract age for concessions and divestitures throughout the developing world. Patterns of market exit and shifts in corporate strategy among MNCs working in the sector provide further evidence that international firms have proven less able to maintain long-term agreements with host governments: international investors entered new contracts infrequently following the Asian and Argentine crises, whereas diversified, developing country conglomerates entered contracts at higher rates in their home markets than they had previously. Even when their contracts remained in force, MNCs often attempted to sell their stakes in existing projects in developing countries. Most strikingly, contrary to the expectations of many international political economy scholars and consistent with this book's expectations, regressions analyzing the subset of contracts with foreign sponsors show strong associations between access to international arbitration and premature contract cancellation. Trends in low- and middle-income countries, then, suggest that the Argentine experience is anything but unique.

In the water and sanitation sector, variation in the resilience of privatization contracts is *not* associated with factors emphasized by alternative approaches to the study of regulatory politics and foreign direct investment (FDI). Analysis of patterns of premature contract cancellation in low- and middle-income countries did not yield support for institutionalist explanations of regulatory outcomes, which would attribute variation to the levels of checks and balances in the domestic political environment and international investment treaty protection. Within Argentina, contracts did not prove more durable in provinces with greater checks and balances. In addition, formal regulatory independence was unassociated with contractual resilience. The case studies also showed that regulatory agencies were repeatedly constrained or overruled – regardless of whether they were formally independent.

In the cross-national data set, left-wing control of government also did not serve as a good predictor of contract cancellation, as arguments stressing the importance of executive branch ideology would lead one to expect. And in the Argentine cases, domestic investors with diverse local holdings negotiated effectively with governors from across the party spectrum, while foreign investors failed to secure politically workable post-crisis agreements even with governors ideologically predisposed to support private providers. This study also found little support for arguments stressing the importance of state capacity. Not only did the cross-country regressions find no association between state capacity and patterns of premature contract cancellation, but the case studies also showed that formally independent and technically competent regulatory agencies were often overruled by government ministers, and technically competent but ideologically motivated regulators could focus on battling with private providers rather than arbitrating between consumer and provider interests.[3]

The observed relationship between diverse local holdings and contractual resilience appears not to stem from selection effects. In Argentina, consortia led by MNCs secured the most desirable contracts, suggesting that contracts held by foreign firms did not fail at a higher rate because domestic investors secured better contracts. Meanwhile, governments in almost all cases only took over services after giving up on finding replacement private operators – they did not rush to nationalize the contracts of firms servicing more affluent urban markets. In the cross-national analysis, contracts held by foreign and domestic investors were located in countries with almost identical average scores on standard rule of law indexes, suggesting that higher cancellation rates among foreign-held contracts do not stem from entrance into riskier institutional environments. Among contracts held by foreign investors, those protected by provisions for international arbitration were located, on average, in countries with *higher* levels of property rights protections according to the standard international indexes.

The association between domestic ownership, diverse local holdings, and contractual resilience might seem to reflect either firm capture of local governments or governmental capture of firms, rather than negotiated settlements acceptable to both parties. Chapter 1 stresses that the benefits derived from negotiations will vary with the leverage of both parties, which depends on their respective abilities and willingness to invest. This being said, the empirical evidence presented here clearly shows that domestic investors are neither simply trapped nor making out like bandits. In Argentina, the domestic investors still holding contracts have earned low, albeit positive, rates of return since the crisis, despite the fact that tariff adjustments have only partly compensated for inflation. Moreover, provincial governments have shown themselves to be perfectly capable of cancelling contracts when dissatisfied with investment levels or service quality: the Tucumán and Azurix contracts are cases in point. And in

[3] The Santa Fe and Mendoza cases in Argentina are striking in this regard.

Argentina and throughout the developing world, domestic investors have continued to bid for new contracts imposing investment commitments.

HOW FAR DOES THE ARGUMENT TRAVEL?

This book presents both a fine-grained analysis of Argentine contracts and a broader survey of trends in the water and sanitation sector in developing countries, and in so doing begins to examine how extensively the argument developed applies. This section summarizes the book's evidence that the argument can be extended to countries of different income levels and regime types, as well as to other types of infrastructure. It also proposes lines of future research that would provide greater certainty.

Is the relationship between diverse local holdings and contractual resilience evident in all low- and middle-income countries? One might question whether domestic firms in very poor countries possess the technical expertise and financial capacity to manage urban water and sanitation systems or highway concessions. Alternatively, one might argue that the greater prevalence of organized civil society groups in middle-income countries would make it difficult for host governments and firms to engage in the sorts of informal negotiations regarding contractual adaptations preferred by domestic conglomerates. Chapter 7's analysis of patterns of contract cancellation in low- and middle-income countries finds a strong association between higher per capita income and stronger probabilities of contract cancellation at a given contract age, including for the subset of contracts held by foreign investors. This suggests that the politics of utilities management becomes more difficult to navigate in middle-income countries relative to low-income countries. The Argentine provincial case studies, meanwhile, show that domestic investors with diverse local holdings in their contract jurisdiction were able to maintain more durable contracts than other types of investors in both low- and higher-income provinces. Comparatively small, albeit still diverse, firms such as the Chamas Group proved just as able to manage the complicated politics involved with running a water system as a larger business, such as the Roggio Group. In-depth case studies of contracts in low-income countries with fewer and less sophisticated indigenous business groups would provide further insights into the viability of system management by domestic firms in countries of varying income.

The theoretical approach advanced here also posits that the relationship between investor structure and contractual resilience should be strongest in democracies and hybrid regimes allowing for electoral contestation. Chapter 7 provides initial empirical support for this proposition, showing that the association between domestic ownership and lower rates of premature contract cancellation is stronger in the subset of low- and middle-income countries regarded as democracies. These findings would be buttressed by detailed case studies of the politics of utilities regulation in autocracies – and especially those where foreign investors continue to vie for new contracts, such as China and Middle Eastern nations.

Future research should also explore the extent to which domestic investors with diverse portfolios in their contract jurisdictions preside over more durable contracts in other infrastructure sectors. The superior ability of diversified, domestic conglomerates to navigate the politics of long-term contracting with the state should be observed in many other infrastructure sectors – particularly when industries are bundled so that investors handle relations with consumers as well as investment in basic infrastructure for supply. For sectors that are more profitable over time than water and sanitation, such as electricity and natural gas, these differences may not be captured with measures as crude as rates of contract cancellation. Differences may only become visible when considering rates of exit through equity sale or analyzing the terms of renegotiation agreements.

BROADER IMPLICATIONS

My findings in this study can inform policy debates about infrastructure finance and management in the developing world – an important foundation for economic and social development – by leading policy makers to reframe the debate about infrastructure privatization. They also contribute to a growing set of evaluations suggesting that investors and states should view with caution the international investment regime that has emerged over the last thirty years.

The first, and perhaps most basic, lesson from this book is that privatization does not depoliticize the provision of infrastructure services. Proponents of privatization assumed it would depoliticize charging for services and raising consumer rates.[4] Institutional analyses of regulatory politics have long cautioned, however, that privatization on its own cannot bring about these changes in the absence of institutions that impose checks and balances on executive discretion (Levy and Spiller 1994, 1996). I go further on to contend that privatization actually *increases* politicization by raising the visibility of the policy area and giving politicians electoral incentives to champion consumer interests. The Argentine cases illustrate the "volatile politics of accountability" that emerged following privatization and show that for private sector management to be viable politically, conflict between firms and host governments must be kept within manageable boundaries.

This leads to the second takeaway point of the book: rather than debate the advantages and disadvantages of public and private sector service provision, it is important to consider the performance of different types of private sector

[4] Among others, see Kessides (1993: 27–30), World Bank (1994a: 39–40), and World Bank (1994b: 35–36).

providers. MNCs, the Argentine case studies suggest, invested heavily in the initial years of their concessions but failed to sustain even moderate rates of investment as soon as political or economic difficulties arose. Diversified domestic investors – and, when contracts were granted at the subnational level, domestic investors with diverse holdings in their contract jurisdiction – invested at lower rates but more steadily over time. Moreover, they have demonstrated a continuing interest in working in the sector while MNCs have been pulling out, except in cases where contracts involve few investment obligations or are located in autocracies. This means that when governments debate whether to privatize, the correct comparison may not be between status quo management of utilities by the public sector and management by a large MNC with specialized, foreign expertise and superior access to finance – as the comparison was typically framed during the 1990s. Rather, the choice may be between management by a state-owned firm and management by a domestic conglomerate, possibly able or willing to invest only limited amounts at a time. And as the Argentine case highlights, even contracts held by domestic investors with a diversified local presence can collapse. They simply do so less frequently than those held by other types of investors.

The picture painted here of resilient contractual relationships does not constitute a model of transparency and clean politics. Yet it does recall the cozy relationships between diversified firms investing in infrastructure and politicians in the nineteenth-century United States. Private investors holding monopoly franchise contracts built much of the period's urban infrastructure, often earning more through related operations than through the contracts themselves. For example, firms constructing urban streetcar networks often both made significant sums from real estate development along track lines and operated amusement parks at the end of rail lines to increase traffic.[5] Historians have even argued that investors expanded streetcar networks at a faster rate in the United States than in Europe because of greater opportunities for investment in related sectors (Sutcliffe 1988: 35). Such arrangements may not be as cost-effective or by the book as public *or* private service provision in contemporary Europe or America, but they represent second-best alternatives that are viable in the developing world.

Future research should explore sources of variation in the performance of domestic investors in infrastructure sectors, especially given the growing importance of developing country firms within their own countries and on the global stage. This study has stressed how diversification in a firm's contract jurisdiction facilitates negotiations with host governments in the long run. In Argentina's water and sanitation sector, fruitful negotiations have been accompanied by steady, albeit modest, levels of investment – in the post-crisis period, often partly funded or even executed by the state. Still, Argentina has witnessed

[5] E.g., Warner (1962: 125); Bagwell (1982: 160–161); Jackson (1985: 91, 112–113); Fogelson (1993: 185); Brechin (2006: 65).

tragedies such as the 2012 Once station train crash, in which fifty-one people died. The commuter train that crashed was managed by a domestic conglomerate, the Plaza Group, and had fallen into a deplorable state of disrepair in the decade following the Argentine crisis (Mochkofsky 2012). In sectors other than water and sanitation, some domestic business groups have assembled large and diverse business empires through relationships with particular politicians, such as the Kirchners. We would expect such investors to be treated with leniency by their political patrons in the short run and be less able to survive political transitions than the long-standing diversified business groups discussed in this book.[6] A new wave of research on business groups in developing countries is needed to craft nuanced understandings of the circumstances under which domestic firms respond to informal incentives to invest and comply with basic health and safety standards – building on the insights presented here but incorporating additional factors.

Multilateral bank policies can be adapted to address weaknesses of some of the developing country conglomerates working in infrastructure, including low levels of technical capacity and a reluctance to borrow to fund significant investments. Exchange rate guarantees in loans, for instance, would decrease the risk and cost of borrowing substantially, especially where domestic capital markets are weak. Technical assistance programs could be designed for managers from such firms, as well as for the regulatory agencies established to oversee them.[7] Lenders could encourage adherence to standards set by private entities, such as the International Organization for Standardization. Lastly, the World Bank and other lenders can continue to disburse funds incrementally as projects are completed, thereby ensuring that most of the money is actually being used as originally intended. In other words, the development community can continue to innovate and find ways to improve the services offered by developing country conglomerates.

Finally, this book questions whether new legal substitutes for domestic property rights protections, such as international arbitration, really work. As Wells and Gleason (1995) stress, MNCs' rush to enter infrastructure markets of the developing world during the 1990s was based, at least in part, on a trust in new protections such as access to international arbitration and political risk insurance. It was assumed that these policies would discourage governments from violating contractual terms because of the financial and reputational costs they would impose. This book joins a small but growing body of scholarship suggesting that these protections do little to increase FDI, particularly in

6 Examples include Cristóbal López and Lázaro Báez. Schneider (2010) distinguishes between these two types of groups.

7 The World Bank did grant loans to finance regulatory capacity building during the 1990s. Unfortunately, some governments did not apply for or take up loans granted for this purpose, leaving regulatory agencies underfunded during their start-up phase.

the long run.[8] Rather, as the case studies and cross-national analysis here suggest, they provide simpler exit options for firms when projects do not evolve as investors had hoped. And as countries such as Argentina and Bolivia either fail to pay awards to firms or exit the Washington Convention, the value of these protections as insurance policies even comes into question.[9] Rather than focusing on legal safeguards, firms should consider how specific organizational structures confer informal supports for property rights in the developing world.

[8] See Hallward-Driemeier (2003) and Tobin and Rose-Ackerman (2005), who argue that there is no empirical relationship between bilateral investment treaty (BIT) adoption and FDI flows. See Wells and Ahmed (2007) for a general, critical view of international property rights protections.

[9] The Washington Convention, or the Convention on the Settlement of Investment Disputes between States and Nationals of Other States, is the 1966 international accord that established ICSID.

References

Acemoglu, Daron, Simon Johnson, James Robinson, and Yunyong Thaicharoen. 2003. "Institutional Causes, Macroeconomic Symptoms: Volatility, Crises and Growth." *Journal of Monetary Economics* 50(1): 49–123.

ADERASA. 2003, 2004, 2005, 2006. *Ejercicio Anual de Benchmarking*. Buenos Aires.

Albrieu, Ramiro, and José María Fanelli. 2008. "¿Stop-and-go o Go-and-fail? Sobre aceleraciones, crisis e instituciones en la Argentina." *Desarrollo Económico* 48:190–191, 235–268.

Alt, James, and Barry Eichengreen. 1989. "Parallel and Overlapping Games: Theory and Application to the European Gas Trade." *Economics & Politics* 1 (2): 119–144.

Amsden, Alice. 1989. *Asia's Next Giant: South Korea and Late Industrialization*. New York: Oxford University Press.

Amsden, Alice, and Takashi Hikino. 1994. "Project Execution Capability, Organizational Know-how and Conglomerate Corporate Growth in Late Industrialization." *Industrial and Corporate Change* 3(1): 111–147.

Andrés, Luis A., J. Luis Guasch, Thomas Haven, and Vivien Foster. 2008. *The Impact of Private Sector Participation in Infrastructure: Lights, Shadows, and the Road Ahead*. Washington, DC: The World Bank.

Arce, Moisés. 2005. *Market Reform in Society: Post-Crisis Politics and Economic Change in Authoritarian Peru*. University Park: Pennsylvania State University Press.

Armijo, Leslie and Philippe Faucher. 2002. "'We Have a Consensus': Explaining Political Support for Market Reform in Latin America." *Latin American Politics & Society*. 44(2): 1–40.

Artana, Daniel, Fernando Navajas, and Santiago Urbiztondo. 1998. *The Regulation and Contractual Adaptation of Public Utilities: The Case of Argentina*. Washington, DC: FIEL.

Artana, Daniel, Fernando Navajas, and Santiago Urbiztondo. 1999. "Governance and Regulation: A Tale of Two Concessions in Argentina." In *Spilled Water: Institutional Commitments in the Provision of Water Services*, eds. William Savedoff and Pablo Spiller, pp. 197–248. Washington, DC: Inter-American Development Bank.

Auyero, Javier. 2005. "Protest and Politics in Contemporary Argentina." In *Argentine Democracy: The Politics of Institutional Weakness*, eds. Steven Levitsky and María Victoria Murillo, pp. 250–268. University Park: Pennsylvania State University Press.

Azemar, Celine, Julia Darby, Rodolphe Desbordes, Ian Wooton. 2012. "Market Familiarity and the Location of South and North MNEs." *Economics & Politics* 24(3):307–345.

Azpiazu, Daniel. 2008. "Concentración y centralización del capital en el mercado eléctrico argentino." *Realidad Económica* 233: 86–110.

Azpiazu, Daniel, Nicolás Bonofiglio, and Carolina Nahón. 2008. Agua y energia: Mapa de situación y problemáticas regulatorias de los servicios públicos en el interior del país. Buenos Aires: FLACSO.

Azpiazu, Daniel, and Karina Forcinito. 2003. Historia de un fracaso: La privatización del sistema de agua y saneamiento en el Área Metropolitana de Buenos Aires. Buenos Aires: FLACSO.

Bagwell, Beth. 1982. *Oakland: The Story of a City*. Novato, CA: Presidio Press.

Baker, Andy. 2009. *The Market and the Masses in Latin America: Policy Reform and Consumption in Liberalizing Economies*. New York: Cambridge University Press.

Bakker, Karen. 2010. *Privatizing Water: Governance Failure and the World's Urban Water Crisis*. Ithaca, NY: Cornell University Press.

Banco Interamericano de Desarrollo (BID). 1996. *Estudio del sector de agua potable y saneamiento en Argentina*. Buenos Aires. Unpublished report commissioned from CETI consulting.

Bandelj, Nina. 2008. *From Communists to Foreign Capitalists: The Social Foundations of Foreign Direct Investment*. Princeton, NJ: Princeton University Press.

Barjot, Dominique. 2011. "Public Utilities and Private Initiative: The French Concession Model in Historical Perspective." *Business History* 53(5): 782–800.

Basañes, Federico, and Robert Willig, eds. 2002. *Second-Generation Reforms in Infrastructure Services*. Washington, DC: Inter-American Development Bank.

Bates, Robert. 1997. *Open Economy Politics: The Political Economy of the World Coffee Trade*. Princeton, NJ: Princeton University Press.

Bayliss, Kate. 2003. "Utility Privatization in Sub-Saharan Africa: A Case Study of Water." *Journal of Modern African Studies* 41(4): 507–531.

Beazer, Quitin. 2012. "Bureaucratic Discretion, Business Investment, and Uncertainty." *Journal of Politics* 74(3): 637–652.

Behrend, Jacqueline. 2011. "The Unevenness of Democracy at the Subnational Level: Provincial Closed Games in Argentina." *Latin American Research Review* 46(1): 150–176.

Behrman, Jere, and Barbara Wolfe. 1987. "How Does a Mother's Schooling Affect Family Health, Nutrition, Medical Care Usage, and Household Sanitation?" *Journal of Econometrics* 36: 185–204.

Boixadós, María Cristina. 2000. *Las tramas de una ciudad, Córdoba entre 1870 y 1895*. Córdoba, Argentina: Ferreyra Editorial.

Bordi de Ragucci, Olga. 1997. *El agua privada en Buenos Aires 1856–1892: Negocio y fracaso*. Buenos Aires: Editorial Vinciguerra S.R.L.

Brechin, Gray. 2006. *Imperial San Francisco: Urban Power, Earthly Ruin*. Berkeley: University of California Press.

Brooks, Sarah M. 2009. *Social Protection and the Market in Latin America: The Transformation of Social Security Institutions*. New York: Cambridge University Press.

Brown, J. David, John S. Searle, and Scott Gehlbach. 2009. "Helping Hand or Grabbing Hand? State Bureaucracy and Privatization Effectiveness." *American Political Science Review* 103(2): 264–283.

Brunstein, Fernando. 1986. "Población de bajos ingresos y agua potable en Argentina: un aspecto poco tratado de la acción del Estado sobre el habitat." In *Habitat Popular: Experiencias y Alternativas en Paises de America Latina*, eds. Nora Clichevsky, Beatriz Cuenya, and Susan Peñalva, pp. 147–162. Buenos Aires: Cuadernos del Centro de Estudios Urbanos y Regionales, 16.

Brunstein, Fernando, Sandra Grisotto, and Gabriela Peirano. 1988. "Saneamiento hídrico en el Gran Buenos Aires: Limite de la precariedad." In *Crisis y Servicios Públicos: Agua y Saneamiento en la Región Metropolitana de Buenos Aires*, ed. Fernando Brunstein, pp. 5–42. Buenos Aires: Cuadernos del Centro de Estudios Urbanos y Regionales, 23.

Budds, Jessica, and Gordon McGranahan. 2003. "Are the Debates on Water Privatization Missing the Point? Experiences from Africa, Asia, and Latin America." *Environment and Urbanization* 15(2): 87–113.

Büthe, Tim. 2002. "Taking Temporarily Seriously: Modeling History and the Use of Narratives as Evidence." *American Political Science Review* 96(3): 481–493.

Büthe, Tim, and Helen V. Milner. 2008. "The Politics of Foreign Direct Investment into Developing Countries: Increasing FDI through Trade Agreements?" *American Journal of Political Science* 52(4): 741–762.

Carvalho, Oscar Enrique. 2003. "Evaluación de algunos de los enfoques sobre la comercialización del servicio de agua potable y desagües cloacales, para el case del operador privado de este servicio público en la Provincia de Corrientes, República Argentina, desde el año 1998 al 2001." MA thesis. Universidad Tecnológica Nacional, Argentina.

Cebu Team. 1991. "Underlying and Proximate Determinants of Child Health: The Cebu Longitudinal Health and Nutrition survey." *American Journal of Epidemiology* 33(2): 185–201.

Chan, Henry, and Raymond E. Levitt. 2011. "To Talk or to Fight? Effects of Strategic, Cultural, and Institutional Factors on Renegotiation Approaches in Public-Private Concessions." In *Global Projects: Institutional and Political Challenges*, eds. W. Richard Scott, Raymond E. Levitt, and Ryan J. Orr, pp. 310–350. New York: Cambridge University Press.

Chong, Alberto, and Florencio López-de-Silanes. 2005. "La verdad sobre la privatización en América Latina." In *La privatización en América Latina*, eds. Alberto Chong and Florencio López-de-Silanes, pp. 1–76. Washington, DC: Banco Interamericano de Desarrollo.

Clifton, Judith, Francisco Comín, and Daniel Díaz-Fuentes. 2007. "Transforming Network Services in Europe and the Americas: From Ugly Ducklings to Swans?" In *Transforming Public Enterprise in Europe and North America: Networks, Integration, and Transnationalisation*, eds. Judith Clifton, Francisco Comín, and Daniel Díaz-Fuentes, pp. 3–15. Houndsmill, UK: Palgrave Macmillan.

Conca, Ken. 2006. *Governing Water: Contentious Transnational Politics and Global Institution Building*. Cambridge, MA: MIT Press.

Coriat, Benjamín. 2004. "Régimen de convertibilidad, acumulación, y crisis en la Argentina de los '90." In *La Economía Argentina y su crisis (1976–2001): visiones institutionalistas y regulacionistas*, eds. Robert Boyer and Julia Neffa, pp. 681–694. Buenos Aires: Ceil-Piette Conicet.

Corrales, Javier. 1998. "Coalitions and Corporate Choices in Argentina, 1976–1994: The Recent Private Sector Support of Privatization." *Studies in Comparative International Development* 32(4): 24–51.

Corrales, Javier. 2002. *Presidents without Parties: The Politics of Economic Reform in Argentina and Venezuela in the 1990s*. University Park: Pennsylvania State University Press.

Culpepper, Pepper. 2011. *Quiet Politics and Business Power: Corporate Control in Europe and Japan*. New York: Cambridge University Press.

Dargoltz, Raúl, Oscar Gerez, and Horacio Cao. 2006. *El Nuevo Santiagueñazo: cambio político y régimen caudillista*. Buenos Aires: Editorial Biblos (Colección Política, Estado y Administración Pública).

Davis, Cristina. 2004. "International Institutions and Issue Linkage: Building Support for Agricultural Trade Liberalization." *American Political Science Review* 98(1): 154–169.

Davis, Jennifer. 2005. "Private-Sector Participation in the Water and Sanitation Sector." *Annual Review of Environmental Resources* 30: 145–183.

Dixit, Avinash K., and Robert S. Pindyck. 1994. *Investment under Uncertainty*. Princeton, NJ: Princeton University Press.

Domínguez, Jorge I. 1997. *Technopols: Freeing Politics and Markets in Latin America in the 1990s*. University Park: Pennsylvania State University Press.

Doner, Richard. 1992. "Limits of State Strength: Toward an Institutionalist Approach to Economic Development." *World Politics* 44(3): 398–431.

Doner, Richard. 2009. *The Politics of Uneven Development: Thailand's Economic Growth in Comparative Perspective*. Cambridge: Cambridge University Press.

Ducci, Jorge. 2007. Salida de operadores privados internacionales de agua en América Latina. Washington, DC: Banco Interamericano de Desarrollo.

Eaton, Kent. 2004. *Politics Beyond the Capital: The Design of Subnational Institutions in South America*. Stanford, CA: Stanford University Press.

Eichengreen, Barry, and Jeffry Frieden. 1993. "The Political Economy of European Monetary Unification: An Analytical Introduction." *Economics & Politics* 5(2): 85–104.

Eichenwald, Kurt. 2005. *Conspiracy of Fools*. New York: Broadway Books.

Elkins, Zachary, Andrew T. Guzman, and Beth A. Simmons. 2006. "Competing for Capital: The Diffusion of Bilateral Investment Treaties, 1960–2000." *International Organization* 60(Fall): 811–846.

ENOHSA-COFES. 1999. *La cobrabilidad de los servicios sanitarios en Argentina*. Buenos Aires.

Esrey, S., J. Potash, L. Roberts, and C. Shiff. 1991. "Effects of Improved Water Supply and Sanitation on Ascariasis, Diarrhea, Dracunculiasis, Hookworm Infection, Schistosomiasis, and Trachoma." *Bulletin of the World Health Organization* 69(5): 609–621.

Estache, Antonio, Andrés Gómez-Lobo, and Daniel Leipziger. 2001. "Utilities Privatization and the Poor: Lessons and Evidence from Latin America." *World Development* 29(7): 1179–1198.

Etchemendy, Sebastian. 2001. "Constructing Reform Coalitions: The Politics of Compensations in Argentina's Economic Liberalization." *Latin American Politics and Society* 43(3): 1–35.

Evans, Peter. 1995. *Embedded Autonomy: States and Industrial Transformation*. Princeton, NJ: Princeton University Press.

Ferro, Gustavo. 2001. "Aguas del Aconquija: revisión a una experiencia fallida de privatización." Texto de Discusión No. 26. Buenos Aires: CEER.

Flores-Macías, Gustavo. 2010. "Statist vs. Pro-Market: Explaining Leftist Government's Economic Policies in Latin America." *Comparative Politics* 42(4): 413–433.

Fogelson, Robert. 1993. *The Fragmented Metropolis: Los Angeles 1850–1930*. Berkeley: University of California Press.

Foster, Vivien. 2005. "Ten Years of Water Service Reform in Latin America: Towards an Anglo-French Model." Water Supply and Sanitation Sector Board Discussion Paper Series, no. 3. Washington, DC: World Bank Group.

Franceys, Richard, and Esther Gerlach. 2008. *Regulating Water and Sanitation for the Poor: Economic Regulation for Public and Private Partnerships*. London: Earthscan.

Fridenson, Patrick. 2007. "Transforming Public Enterprise in France." In *Transforming Public Enterprise in Europe and North America: Networks, Integration, and Transnationalisation*, eds. Judith Clifton, Francisco Comín, and Daniel Díaz-Fuentes, pp. 65–76. Houndsmill, UK: Palgrave Macmillan.

Frieden, Jeffrey A. 1991. *Debt, Development & Democracy*. Princeton, NJ: Princeton University Press.

Frye, Timothy. 2006. "Original Sin, Good Works, and Property Rights in Russia." *World Politics* 58(4): 479–504.

Frye, Timothy. 2010. *Building States and Markets after Communism: The Perils of Polarized Democracy*. New York: Cambridge University Press.

Galiani, Sebastián, Paul Gertler, and Ernesto Schargrodsky. 2005. "Water for Life: The Impact of Privatization of Water Services on Child Mortality." *Journal of Political Economy* 113(1): 83–120.

Gassner, Katharina, Alexander Popov, and Nataliya Pushak. 2009. "Does Private Sector Participation Improve Performance in Electricity and Water Distribution? An Empirical Assessment in Developing and Transition Countries." PPIAF Trends and Policy Series. Washington, DC: World Bank.

Gavin, Michael. 1997. "A Decade of Reform in Latin America: Has It Delivered Lower Volatility?" Working Paper Green Series no. 349. Washington, DC: Inter-American Development Bank.

Gervasoni, Carlos. 2010. "Measuring Variance in Subnational Regimes: Results from an Expert-Based Operationalization of Democracy in the Argentine Provinces." *Journal of Politics in Latin America* 2(2): 13–52.

Giarracca, Norma, and Norma Del Pozo. 2005. "To Make Waves: Water and Privatization in Tucumán, Argentina." In *Opposing Currents: The Politics of Water and Gender in Latin America*, eds. Vivienne Bennett, Sonia Dávila-Poblete, and María Neves Rico, pp. 91–106. Pittsburgh: Pittsburgh University Press.

Gibson, Edward. 1996. *Class and Conservative Parties: Argentina in Comparative Perspective*. Baltimore: Johns Hopkins University Press.

Gibson, Edward. 1997. "The Populist Road to Market Reform: Policy and Electoral Coalitions in Mexico and Argentina." *World Politics* 49(3): 339–370.

Gibson, Edward. 2005. "Boundary Control: Sub-national Authoritarianism in Democratic Countries." *World Politics* 58(1): 101–132.

Gilbert, Alan. 1998. *The Latin American City*. London: Latin America Bureau.

Ginsburg, Tom. 2005. "International Substitutes for Domestic Institutions: Bilateral Investment Treaties and Governance." *International Review of Law and Economics* 25(1): 107–123.

Giraudy, Agustina. 2010. "The Politics of Subnational Undemocratic Regime Reproduction in Argentina and Mexico." *Journal of Politics in Latin America* 2(2): 53–84.

Gómez-Ibáñez, José. 2003. *Regulating Infrastructure: Monopoly, Contracts, and Discretion*. Cambridge, MA: Harvard University Press.
Gómez-Ibáñez, José. 2008. "Private Infrastructure in Developing Countries: Lessons from Recent Experience." Paper presented to the Commission on Growth and Development at the Workshop on Global Trends and Challenges, Yale Center for the Study of Globalization, New Haven, CT, September 28–29, 2007.
Gough, Ian, Geoff Wood, Armando Barrientos, Philippa Bevan, Peter David, and Graham Room. 2004. *Insecurity and Welfare Regimes in Asia, Africa, and Latin America*. Cambridge: Cambridge University Press.
Granovetter, Mark. 1985. "Economic Action and Social Structure: The Problem of Embeddedness." *The American Journal of Sociology* 91(3): 481–510.
Granovetter, Mark. 1994. "Business Groups." In *The Handbook of Economic Sociology*, eds. Neil J. Smelser and Richard Swedberg, pp. 453–475. Princeton, NJ: Princeton University Press.
Granovetter, Mark. 2005. "Business Groups and Social Organization." In *The Handbook of Economic Sociology*, 2nd ed., eds. Neil J. Smelser and Richard Swedberg, pp. 429–450. Princeton, NJ: Princeton University Press.
Green, Colin. 2003. *Handbook of Water Economics: Principles & Practice*. Chichester, UK: John Wiley & Sons.
Groom, Eric, Jonathan Halpern, and David Ehrhardt. 2006. "Explanatory Notes on Key Topics in the Regulation of Water and Sanitation Services." World Bank Water Supply and Sanitation Sector Discussion Paper No. 6. Washington, DC: World Bank.
Guarch, José Luis. 2005. "Concesión de Aguas de Salta, 91 localidades en 150.000 km2." Presentation presented at the AIDIS conference, Salta, Argentina.
Guasch, J. Luis. 2004. *Granting and Renegotiating Infrastructure Concessions: Doing It Right*. Washington, DC: World Bank Institute.
Guasch, J. Luis, Jean-Jacques Laffont, and Stéphane Straub. 2003. "Renegotiation of Concession Contracts in Latin America." Working Paper No. 3011. Washington, DC: World Bank Group.
Guasch, J. Luis, and Stéphane Straub. 2005. "Infrastructure Concessions in Latin America: Government-Led Renegotiations." Working Paper No. 3749. Washington, DC: World Bank Group.
Guillén, Mauro. 2001. *The Limits of Convergence: Globalization and Organizational Change in Argentina, South Korea, and Spain*. Princeton, NJ: Princeton University Press.
Guillén, Mauro. 2005. *The Rise of Spanish Multinationals: European Business in the Global Economy*. Cambridge: Cambridge University Press.
Haber, Stephen, ed. 2002. *Crony Capitalism and Economic Growth in Latin America: Theory and Evidence*. Stanford, CA: Hoover Institution Press.
Haggard, Stephan. 1989. "The Political Economy of Foreign Direct Investment in Latin America." *Latin American Research Review* 24(1): 184–208.
Haglund, Ladawn. 2010. *Limiting Resources: Market-Led Reform and the Transformation of Public Goods*. University Park: Pennsylvania State University Press.
Hallward-Driemeier, Mary. 2003. "Do Bilateral Investment Treaties Attract FDI? Only a Bit ... and They Could Bite." World Bank Policy Research Paper WPS 3121. Washington, DC: World Bank.
Hardoy, Jorge. 1988. "Prácticas urbanísticas europeas en América Latina." In *Repensando la ciudad en América Latina*, eds. Jorge Hardoy and Richard Morse. Buenos Aires: Grupo Editor Latinoamericano.

Harris, Clive. 2003. "Private Participation in Infrastructure in Developing Countries: Trends, Impacts, and Policy Lessons." World Bank Working Paper No. 5. Washington, DC: World Bank Group.

Haslam, Paul Alexander. 2010. "Foreign Investors Over a Barrel: Nationalizations and Investment Policy of the Latin American New Left." In *Left Turns*, eds. Eric Herschberg, Max Cameron, and Jon Beasly-Murray, pp. 209–230. Boulder, CO: Lynne Rienner.

Heller, William B., and Mathew D. McCubbins. 1996. "Politics, Institutions, and Outcomes: Electricity Regulation in Argentina and Chile." *Policy Reform* 1: 357–387.

Helmke, Gretchen, and Steven Levitsky. 2006. *Informal Institutions and Democracy: Lessons from Latin America*. Baltimore: The Johns Hopkins University Press.

Henisz, Witold J. 2000. "The Institutional Environment for Multinational Investment." *Journal of Law, Economics, and Organization* 16(2): 334–364.

Henisz, Witold J. 2002. *Politics and International Investment: Measuring Risks and Protecting Profits*. Cheltenham, UK: Edward Elgar Publishing.

Henisz, Witold J., Mauro Guillén, and Bennet A. Zelner. 2005. "The Worldwide Diffusion of Market-Oriented Infrastructure Reform, 1977–1999." *American Sociological Review* 70(6): 871–897.

Henisz, Witold J., and Bennet A. Zelner. 2001. "The Institutional Environment for Telecommunications Investment." *Journal of Economics & Management Strategy* 10(1): 123–147.

Henisz, Witold J., and Bennet A. Zelner. 2004. "Resistance to Illegitimate Multilateral Influence on Reform: The Political Backlash against Private Infrastructure Investments." Unpublished manuscript.

Henisz, Witold J., and Bennet A. Zelner. 2005. "Legitimacy, Interest Group Pressures, and Change in Emergent Institutions: The Case of Foreign Investors and Host Country Governments." *Academy of Management Review* 30(2): 361–382.

Ho, Daniel. 2005. "Why Affirmative Action Does Not Cause Black Students to Fail the Bar." *The Yale Law Journal* 114(8): 1997–2004.

Hogan, William, Federico Sturzenegger, and Laurence Tai. 2010. "Contracts and Investment in Natural Resources." In *The Natural Resources Trap: Private Investment without Public Commitment*, eds. William Hogan and Federico Sturzenegger, Cambridge, MA: MIT Press.

Holburn, Guy, and Bennet Zelner. 2010. "Political Capabilities, Policy Risk and International Investment Strategy: Evidence from the Global Electric Power Industry." *Strategic Management Journal* 21(12): 1290–1315.

Imai, Kosuke, Gary King, and Olivia Lau. 2008. "Toward a Common Framework for Statistical Analysis and Development." *Journal of Computational and Graphical Statistics* 17(4): 892–913.

International Centre for the Settlement of Investment Disputes (ICSID). 2009. *Investment Laws of the World, 1972–2009*. New York: Oceana Publications.

International Centre for the Settlement of Investment Disputes. 2009. *Investment Promotion and Protection Treaties, 1983–2009*. New York: Oceana Publications.

Jackson. Kenneth T. 1985. *Crabgrass Frontier: The Suburbanization of the United States*. New York: Oxford University Press.

Jalan, Jyotsna, and Martin Ravallion. 2003. "Does Piped Water Reduce Diarrhea for Children in Rural India?" *Journal of Econometrics* 112(1): 153–173.

Johnson, Jo, and Martine Orange. 2003. *The Man Who Tried to Buy the World: Jean-Marie Messier and Vivendi Universal*. New York: Penguin Group.

Johnstone, Nick, and Libby Wood, eds. 2001. *Private Firms and Public Water*. Cheltenham, UK: Edward Elgar.

Jones, Mark, Pablo Sanguinetti, and Mariano Tommasi. 2000. "Politics, Institutions, and Fiscal Performance in a Federal System: An Analysis of the Argentine Provinces." *Journal of Development Economics* 61: 305–333.

Jones Luong, Pauline, and Erika Weinthal. 2010. *Oil Is Not a Curse: Ownership Structure and Institutions in Soviet Successor States*. Cambridge: Cambridge University Press.

Jordana, Jacint, and David Levi-Faur. 2005. "The Diffusion of Regulatory Capitalism in Latin America: Sectoral and National Channels in the Making of New Order." *Annals of the American Academy of Political and Social Science* 598: 102–124.

Kang, David C. 2002. *Crony Capitalism: Corruption and Development in South Korea and the Philippines*. Cambridge: Cambridge University Press.

Karl, Terry Lynn. 1997. *The Paradox of Plenty: Oil Booms and Petro-States*. Berkeley: University of California Press.

Kaufman, Robert R. 2011. "The Political Left, the Export Boom, and the Populist Temptation." In *The Resurgence of the Latin America Left*, eds. Steven Levitsky and Kenneth M. Roberts, pp. 93–116. Baltimore: Johns Hopkins University Press.

Kerner, Andrew. 2009. "Why Should I Believe You? The Costs and Consequences of Bilateral Investment Treaties." *International Studies Quarterly* 53: 73–102.

Kessides, Christine. 1993. *Institutional Options for the Provision of Infrastructure*. Discussion Paper 212. Washington, DC: World Bank.

Khan, Mushtaq H., and Jomo Kwame Sundaram. 2000. *Rents, Rent-Seeking, and Economic Development: Theory and Evidence in Asia*. Cambridge: Cambridge University Press.

Khanna, Tarun, and Yishay Yafeh. 2007. "Business Groups in Emerging Markets: Paragons or Parasites?" *Journal of Economic Literature* 45(2): 331–372.

Kindleberger, Charles. 1969. *American Business Abroad: Six Lectures on Direct Investment*. New Haven, CT: Yale University Press.

King, Gary, James E. Alt, Nancy E. Burns, and Michael Laver. 1990. "A Unified Model of Cabinet Dissolution in Parliamentary Democracies." *American Journal of Political Science* 34: 846–871.

Kingstone, Peter. 1999. *Crafting Coalitions for Reform: Business Preferences, Political Institutions, and Neoliberal Reform in Brazil*. University Park: Pennsylvania State University Press.

Kobrin, Stephen J. 1980. "Foreign Enterprise and Forced Divestment in LDCs." *International Organization* 34(1): 65–88.

Kobrin, Stephen J. 1984. "Expropriation as an Attempt to Control Foreign Firms in LDCs: Trends from 1960 to 1979." *International Studies Quarterly* 28: 329–348.

Kogut, Bruce, and J. Muir MacPherson. 2004. "The Decision to Privatize: Economists and the Construction of Ideas and Policies." In *The Global Diffusion of Markets and Democracy*, eds. Beth A. Simmons, Frank Dobbin, and Geoffrey Garrett, pp. 104–140. Cambridge: Cambridge University Press.

Krause, Matthias. 2009. *The Political Economy of Water and Sanitation*. New York: Routledge.

Kurtz, Marcus, and Andrew Schrank. 2007a. "Growth and Governance: Models, Measurement, and Mechanisms." *Journal of Politics* 69(2): 538–554.

Kurtz, Marcus, and Andrew Schrank. 2007b. "Growth and Governance: A Defense." *Journal of Politics* 69(2): 563–569.

Laffont, Jean-Jacques. 2005. *Regulation and Development*. Cambridge: Cambridge University Press.

Laffont, Jean-Jacques, and Jean Tirole. 1993. *A Theory of Incentives in Procurement and Regulation*. Cambridge, MA: MIT Press.

Lam, Patrick. 2007. "coxph: Cox Proportional Hazards Regression for Duration Dependent Variables." In "Zelig: Everyone's Statistical Software," eds. Kosuke Imai, Gary King, and Olivia Lau. http://gking.harvard.edu/zelig.

Lavy, Victor, John Strauss, Duncan Thomas, and Philippe de Vreyer. 1996. "Quality of Health Care, Survival and Health Outcomes in Ghana." *Journal of Health Economics* 15(3): 333–357.

Lee, Lung-fei, Mark R. Rosenzweig, and Mark M. Pitt. 1997. "The Effects of Improved Nutrition, Sanitation, and Water Quality on Child Health in High-Mortality Populations." *Journal of Econometrics* 77(1): 209–235.

Leiras, Marcelo. 2007. *Todos los Caballos del Rey: La integración de los partidos políticos y el gobierno democrático de la Argentina, 1995–2003*. Buenos Aires: Fundación PENT and Prometeo Libros.

Lentini, Emilio J. 2004. "La participación privada en los servicios de agua y alcantarillado: la experiencia de la Concesión de Buenos Aires." Paper presented at the Fourth International Seminar CYTED-XVII, National University of Costa Rica, March 29–31, 2004.

Levitsky, Steven. 2003. *Transforming Labor-Based Parties in Latin America: Argentine Peronism in Comparative Perspective*. New York: Cambridge University Press.

Levitsky, Steven, and María Victoria Murillo, eds. 2005. *Argentine Democracy: The Politics of Institutional Weakness*. University Park: Pennsylvania State University Press.

Levitsky, Steven, and María Victoria Murillo. 2009. "Variation in Institutional Strength." *Annual Review of Political Science* 12: 115–133.

Levitsky, Steven, and Kenneth M. Roberts. 2011. "Introduction: Latin America's 'Left Turn': A Framework for Analysis." In *The Resurgence of the Latin America Left*, eds. Steven Levitsky and Kenneth M. Roberts, pp. 1–30. Baltimore: Johns Hopkins University Press.

Levy, Brian, and Pablo Spiller. 1994. "The Institutional Foundations of Regulatory Commitment: A Comparative Analysis of Telecommunications Regulations." *Journal of Law Economics and Organization* 10(2): 201–246.

Levy, Brian, and Pablo Spiller, eds. 1996. *Regulations, Institutions, and Commitment: Comparative Studies of Telecommunications*. New York: Cambridge University Press.

Lobina, Emanuele. 2005. "Problems with Private Water Concessions: A Review of Experiences and Analysis of Dynamics." *Water Resources Development* 21(1): 55–87.

Loftus, Alexander J., and David A. McDonald. 2001. "Of Liquid Dreams: A Political Ecology of Water Privatization in Buenos Aires." *Environment and Urbanization* 13(2): 179–199.

Lohmann, Susanne. 1995. "Linkage Politics." *Journal of Conflict Resolution* 41(1): 38–67.

Luna, Juan Pablo. 2010. "The Left Turns: Why They Happened and How They Compare." In *Latin America's Left Turns: Politics, Policies & Trajectories of Change*, eds. Maxwell A. Cameron and Eric Hershberg, 23–40. Boulder, CO: Lynne Rienner.

Macaulay, Stewart. 1963. "Non-Contractual Relations in Business: A Preliminary Study." *American Sociological Review* 28(1): 55–67.

Macneil, Ian R. 1978. "Contracts: Adjustment of Long-Term Economic Relations under Classical, Neoclassical, and Relational Contract Law." *Northwestern University Law Review* 72(6): 854–902.

Madrid, Raúl. 2003. *Retiring the State: The Politics of Pension Privatization in Latin America and Beyond*. Stanford, CA: Stanford University Press.

Manzetti, Luigi. 1999. *Privatization South American Style*. Oxford: Oxford University Press.

Manzetti, Luigi. 2009. *Neoliberalism, Accountability, and Reform Failures in Emerging Markets: Eastern Europe, Russia, Argentina, and Chile in Comparative Perspective*. University Park: Pennsylvania State University Press.

Marin, Philippe. 2009. *Public-Private Partnerships for Urban Water Utilities*. Washington, DC: World Bank-PPIAF.

Markus, Stanislav. 2012. "Secure Property as a Bottom-Up Process: Firms, Stakeholders, and Predators in Weak States." *World Politics* 64(2): 242–277.

McLean, Bethany, and Peter Elkind. 2003. *The Smartest Guys in the Room: The Amazing Rise and Scandalous Fall of Enron*. New York: Penguin Books.

Merrick, T. 1985. "The Effect of Piped Water on Early Childhood Mortality in Urban Brazil, 1970 to 1976." *Demography* 22(1): 1–24.

Ministry of Cities, Government of Brazil. 2008. "Examination of Private-Sector Participation in the Provision of Water Supply and Sewerage Services in Brazil." Final Report. October 30, 2008.

Minor, Michael S. 1994. "The Demise of Expropriation as an Instrument of LDC Policy, 1980–1992." *Journal of International Business Studies* 25(1): 177–188.

Mochkofsky, Graciela. 2012. *Once: Viajar y Morir Como Animales*. Buenos Aires: Grupo Editorial Planeta.

Montero, Alfred P. 1998. "State Interests and the New Industrial Policy in Brazil: The Privatization of Steel, 1990–1994." *Journal of Interamerican Studies and World Affairs* 40(3): 27–62.

Montinola, Gabriella, Yingyi Qian, and Barry R. Weingast. 1995. "Federalism, Chinese Style – The Political Basis for Economic Success in China." *World Politics* 48(1): 50–81.

Morgan, Bronwen. 2008. "Comparative Regulatory Regimes in Water Service Delivery: Emerging Contours of Global Water Welfarism?" CLPE Research Paper 33/2008.

Morgan, Bronwen. 2011. *Water on Tap: Rights and Regulation in the Transnational Governance of Urban Water Services*. Cambridge: Cambridge University Press.

Murillo, Maria Victoria. 2002. "Political Bias in Policy Convergence: Privatization Choices in Latin America." *World Politics* 54(4): 462–493.

Murillo, Maria Victoria. 2009. *Political Competition, Partisanship, and Policymaking in Latin America*. Cambridge: Cambridge University Press.

Murillo, Maria Victoria, Virginia Oliveros, and Milan Vaishnav. 2011. "Economic Constraints and Presidential Agency." In *The Resurgence of the Latin America Left*, eds. Steven Levitsky and Kenneth M. Roberts, pp. 52–70. Baltimore: Johns Hopkins University Press.

Neumayer, Eric, and Laura Spess. 2005. "Do Bilateral Investment Treaties Increase Foreign Direct Investment to Developing Countries?" *World Development* 33(10): 1567–1585.

Nickson, Andrew. 2001. "Building Municipal Capacity for Private Sector Participation." London: GHK International.

Nickson, Andrew, and Claudia Vargas. 2002. "The Limitations of Water Regulation: The Failure of the Cochabamba Concession in Bolivia." *Bulletin of Latin American Research* 21(1): 99–120.

North, Douglass C. 1990. *Institutions, Institutional Change, and Economic Performance*. New York: Cambridge University Press.

North, Douglass C., and Barry Weingast. 1989. "Constitutions and Credible Commitments: The Evolution of the Institutions of Public Choice in Seventeenth-Century England." *Journal of Economic History* 49(4): 803–832.

Ordoqui Urcelay, María Begoña. 2006. "Determinantes de la sostenibilidad de la prestación de los servicios de agua potable y saneamiento: el caso de la Ciudad de Buenos Aires, Argentina." Buenos Aires: ECLAC.

O'Rourke, Dara. 2004. *Community-Driven Regulation: Balancing Development and the Environment in Vietnam*. Cambridge, MA: MIT Press.

OPSM. 2003. *Los servicios públicos privatizados en el marco de la post-devaluación*. Buenos Aires: OPSM.

Paige, Jeffrey M. 1997. *Coffee and Power: Revolution and the Rise of Democracy in Central America*. Cambridge, MA: Harvard University Press.

Peltzman, Sam. 1993. "George Stigler's Contribution to the Economic Analysis of Regulation." *The Journal of Political Economy* 101(5): 818–832.

Peltzman, Sam, Michael E. Levine, and Roger Noll. 1989. "The Economic Theory of Regulation after a Decade of Deregulation." *Brookings Papers on Economic Activity, Microeconomics* 1989: 1–59.

Petrecolla, Diego, and Gustavo Ferro. 2003. "Tarifa Social en Agua y Saneamiento en Argentina." Texto de Discusión No. 47. Buenos Aires: CEER.

Pinsent Masons Water Yearbook: 2006–2007. 2006. London: Pinsent Masons.

Pinsent Masons Water Yearbook: 2007–2008. 2007. London: Pinsent Masons.

Post, Alison E. 2008. Liquid Assets and Fluid Contracts: Explaining the Uneven Effects of Water and Sanitation Privatization. PhD dissertation, Harvard University.

Post, Alison E., and Maria Victoria Murillo. 2011. "Infrastructure Investment in Weak Institutional Contexts: Exit Threats and Regulatory Bargaining in the Argentine Electricity and Water Sectors." Presented at the American Political Science Association Annual Meeting, Sept. 1–4, 2011, Seattle, WA.

PPIAF-World Bank. "Private Participation in Infrastructure Database." ppi.worldbank.org. (2006, 2007, 2008, 2010, 2011 downloads).

Prasad, Naren. 2006. "Privatisation Results: Private Sector Participation in Water Services after 15 Years." *Development Policy Review* 24(6): 669–692.

Primo, David M., Matthew L. Jacobsmeier, and Jeffrey Milyo. 2007. "Estimating the Impact of State Policies and Institutions with Mixed-Level Data." *State Politics & Policy Quarterly* 7(40): 446–459.

R Survival Package.

Rais, Jorge Carlos, María Esther Esquivel, and Sergio Sour. "Estudio de la concesión de Tucumán." Unpublished manuscript.

Ramamurti, Ravi, and Jitendra V. Singh, eds. 2009. *Emerging Multinationals in Emerging Markets*. Cambridge: Cambridge University Press.

Rey, Osvaldo. 2003. *El saneamiento en el área metropolitana: Desde el Virreinato a 1993*. Argentina: Aguas Argentinas.

Rhodes, Sybil. 2006. *Social Movements and Free-Market Capitalism in Latin America: Telecommunications Privatization and the Rise of Consumer Protest.* Albany: State University of New York Press.

Roitman, Mauricio, and Gustavo Ferro. 2003. "La concesión de Aguas Provinciales de Santa Fe." Texto de Discusión No. 43. Buenos Aires: CEER, UADE.

Roland, Gérard. 2008. *Privatization: Successes and Failures.* New York: Columbia University Press.

Rosenbaum, Paul R. 1984. "The Consequences of Adjustment for a Concomitant Variable That Has Been Affected by the Treatment." *Journal of the Royal Statistical Society Series A* 147(5): 656–666.

Saltiel, Gustavo. 2003. "La participación del sector privado en los servicios de agua y saneamiento en la provincia de Salta en Argentina." Washington, DC: Banco Interamericano de Desarrollo, Departamento de Desarrollo Sostenible.

Sanguinetti, Juan. 2001. "Determinantes políticos e institucionales ligados al desempeño fiscal: el caso de las provincias argentinas." *Revista Internacional de Presupuesto Público* 46: 79–114.

Savedoff, William, and Pablo Spiller, eds. 1999. *Spilled Water: Institutional Commitment in the Provision of Water Services.* Washington, DC: Inter-American Development Bank.

Schamis, Hector. 1999. "Distributional Coalitions and the Politics of Economic Reform in Latin America." *World Politics* 51(2): 236–268.

Schill, Stephan W. 2009. *The Multilateralization of International Investment Law.* Cambridge: Cambridge University Press.

Schneider, Ben Ross. 1998. "Elusive Synergy: Business-Government Relations and Development." *Comparative Politics* 31(1): 101–122.

Schneider, Ben Ross. 2008. "Economic Liberalization and Corporate Governance: The Resilience of Business Groups in Latin America." *Comparative Politics* 40(4): 379–397.

Schneider, Ben Ross. 2009. "A Comparative Political Economy of Diversified Business Groups, or How States Organize Big Business." *Review of International Political Economy* 16(2): 178–201.

Schneider, Ben Ross. 2010. "Business Groups and the State." In *Oxford Handbook of Business Groups*, eds. Aslie Colpan, Takashi Hikino, and James Lincoln, pp. 650–669. New York: Oxford University Press.

Schrank, Andrew. 2008. "Homeward Bound? Interest, Identity, and Investor Behavior in a Third World Export Platform." *American Journal of Sociology* 114(1): 1–34.

Schultz, Jim. 2008. "Water in Cochabamba after the Water Revolt: A Legend with Mixed Results." In *Dignity and Defiance: Stories from Bolivia's Challenge to Globalization*, eds. J. Schultz, and M. Draper, 9–34. Berkeley: University of California Press.

Scott, W. Richard. 2011. "The Institutional Environment of Global Projects." In *Global Projects: Institutional and Political Challenges*, eds. W. Richard Scott, Raymond E. Levitt, and Ryan J. Orr, pp. 52–85. New York: Cambridge University Press.

Seawright, Jason, and David Collier. 2010. "Glossary." In *Rethinking Social Inquiry: Diverse Tools, Shared Standards*, eds. Henry E. Brady and David Collier, pp. 313–361. Lanham, MD: Rowman & Littlefield Publishers.

Secretaria Nacional de Saneamento Ambiental Database (SNIS). www.snis.gov.br.

Serafinoff, Valeria. 2010. "La relación entre el estado y los empresarios de la construcción: el caso de las concesiones viales en Argentina." PhD dissertation. Universidad Nacional San Martín, Buenos Aires.

Shafer, D. Michael. 1994. *Winners and Losers: How Sectors Shape the Developmental Prospects of States*. Ithaca, NY: Cornell University Press.

Shirley, Mary, and Claude Ménard. 2002. "Cities Awash: A Synthesis of the Country Cases." In *Thirsting for Efficiency: The Economics and Politics of Urban Water System Reform*, ed. Mary Shirley, pp. 1–43. Oxford, UK: Elsevier Science B.V.

Sil, Rudra, and Peter J. Katzenstein. 2010. "Analytic Eclecticism in the Study of World Politics: Reconfiguring Problems and Mechanisms across Research Traditions." *Perspectives on Politics* 8(2): 411–431.

Sirtaine, Sophie, María Elena Pinglo, J. Luis Guasch, and Vivien Foster. 2005. "How Profitable Are Infrastructure Concessions in Latin America?: Empirical Evidence and Regulatory Implications." *Trends and Policy Options* 2, Public Private Infrastructure Advisory Facility, World Bank.

Snyder, Richard. 2001. *Politics after Neoliberalism: Reregulation in Mexico*. Cambridge: Cambridge University Press.

Spiller, Pablo, and Mariano Tommasi. 2007. *The Institutional Foundations of Public Policy in Argentina*. Cambridge: Cambridge University Press.

Stillwaggon, Eileen. 1998. *Stunted Lives, Stagnant Economies: Poverty, Disease, and Underdevelopment*. New Brunswick, NJ: Rutgers University Press.

Stokes, Susan. 2001. *Mandates and Democracy: Neoliberalism by Surprise in Latin America*. Cambridge: Cambridge University Press.

Sutcliffe, Anthony. 1988. "Street Transport in the Second Half of the Nineteenth Century: Mechanization Delayed?" In *Technology and the Rise of the Networked City in Europe and America*, eds. Joel A. Tarr and Gabriel Dupuy, pp. 22–39. Philadelphia: Temple University Press.

Teichman, Judith. 2001. *The Politics of Freeing Markets in Latin America*. Chapel Hill: University of North Carolina Press.

Tenti, María Mercedes. 2005. *La reforma del Estado santiagueño: la gestión política en los '90*. Santiago del Estero, Argentina: Ediciones Universidad Católica de Santiago del Estero.

Thacker, Strom. 2000. *Big Business, the State, and Free Trade: Constructing Coalitions in Mexico*. Cambridge: Cambridge University Press.

Therneau, Terry M., and Patricia M. Grambsch, 2000. *Modeling Survival Data: Extending the Cox Model*. New York: Springer Science and Business, LLC.

Thomas, Jonathan, and Tim Worrall. 1994. "Foreign Direct Investment and the Risk of Expropriation." *Review of Economic Studies* 61(1): 81–108.

Tobin, Jennifer, and Susan Rose-Ackerman. 2005. "Foreign Direct Investment and the Business Environment in Developing Countries: The Impact of Bilateral Investment Treaties." Yale Law School Center for Law, Economics, and Public Policy. Research Paper No. 293.

Treisman, Daniel. 2003. "Cardoso, Menem, and Machiavelli: Political Tactics and Privatization in Latin America." *Studies in Comparative International Development* 38(3): 93–109.

Tsebelis, George. 2002. *Veto Players: How Political Institutions Work*. Princeton, NJ: Princeton University Press.

United Nations Conference on Trade and Development. 1999. *World Investment Report: Foreign Direct Investment and the Challenge of Development*. New York and Geneva: United Nations.

United Nations Conference on Trade and Development. 2009. *World Investment Report: Transnational Corporations, Agricultural Production, and Development.* New York and Geneva: United Nations.

UN-Habitat. 2001. *Cities in a Globalizing World: Global Report on Human Settlements.* London: Earthscan.

United Cities and Local Governments. 2009. *Decentralization and Local Democracy in the World.* Barcelona: World Bank and United Cities and Local Governments.

Vernon, Raymond. 1971. *Sovereignty at Bay: The Multinational Spread of U.S. Enterprises.* New York: Basic Books.

Victor, David, and Thomas C. Heller, eds. 2007. *The Political Economy of Power Sector Reform: Experiences in Five Major Developing Countries.* New York: Cambridge University Press.

Villarino, Julio, and Carolina Sternberg. 2005. "La inestabilidad del sistema político correntino y el surgimiento de actors de base territorial (1993–2003)." *Revista SAAP* 2(2): 293–317.

Vogel, Steven K. 1996. *Freer Markets, More Rules.* Ithaca, NY: Cornell University Press.

von Klaudy, Stephan, Apurva Sanghi, and Georgina Dellacha. 2008. *Emerging Market Investors and Operators – A New Breed of Infrastructure Investors.* PPIAF Working Paper No. 7, 2008.

Warner, Sam Bass. 1962. *Streetcar Suburbs: The Process of Growth in Boston, 1870–1900.* Cambridge, MA: Harvard University Press

Weingast, Barry. 1995. "The Economic Role of Political Institutions: Market-Preserving Federalism and Economic Development." *The Journal of Law, Economics, and Organization* 11(1): 1–32.

Wells, Louis. 2001. "God and Fair Competition." In *Managing International Political Risk*, ed. Theodore Moran, pp. 15–43. Malden, MA: Blackwell.

Wells, Louis, and Rafiq Ahmed. 2007. *Making Foreign Investment Safe: Property Rights and National Sovereignty.* Oxford: Oxford University Press.

Wells, Louis, and Regina Garcia-Cuellar. 2005. "Arbitration between Foreign Investors and Host Governments." Cambridge, MA: Harvard Business School. Case N9-705-019.

Wells, Louis, and Eric Gleason. 1995. "Is Foreign Infrastructure Investment Still Risky?" *Harvard Business Review* 73(5): 4–12.

Wells, Louis, and Alexandra de Royere. 2007. "Aguas Argentinas: Settling a Dispute." Cambridge, MA: Harvard Business School. Case 9-705-019.

Wengle, Susanne A. 2012. "Post-Soviet Developmentalism and the Political Economy of Russia's Electricity Sector Liberalization." *Studies in Comparative International Development* 47(1): 75–114.

Weyland, Kurt. 2002. *The Politics of Reform in Fragile Democracies: Argentina, Brazil, Peru, and Venezuela.* Princeton, NJ: Princeton University Press.

Weyland, Kurt. 2005. "Theories of Policy Diffusion: Lessons from Latin American Pension Reform." *World Politics* 57(2): 262–295.

Weyland, Kurt. 2010. "The Performance of Leftist Governments in Latin America: Conceptual and Theoretical Issues." In *Leftist Governments in Latin America: Successes and Shortcomings*, eds. Kurt Weyland, Raúl Madrid, and Wendy Hunter, pp. 1–27. New York: Cambridge University Press.

Wibbels, Erik. 2004. "Decentralization, Democracy, and Market Reform: On the Difficulties of Killing Two Birds with One Stone." In *Decentralization and Democracy in Latin America*, eds. Alfred P. Montero and David J. Samuels, pp. 203–234. South Bend, IN: University of Notre Dame Press.

Wibbels, Erik. 2006. "Dependency Revisited: International Markets, Business Cycles, and Social Spending in the Developing World." *International Organization* 60(2): 433–468.

Wibbels, Erik. 2006. *Federalism and the Market: Intergovernmental Conflict and Economic Reform in the Developing World*. New York: Cambridge University Press.

Williamson, Oliver E. 1985. *The Economic Institutions of Capitalism*. New York: The Free Press.

Wilson, James Q., ed. 1980. *The Politics of Regulation*. New York: Basic Books.

Woodhouse, Erik. 2005–2006. "The Obsolescing Bargain Redux? Foreign Investment in the Electric Power Sector in Developing Countries." *NYU Journal of International Law and Politics* 38: 121–220.

World Bank. 1994a. *World Development Report: Infrastructure for Development*. Washington, DC: World Bank.

World Bank. 1994b. *A Strategy for Managing Water in the Middle East and North Africa*. Washington, DC: International Bank for Reconstruction and Development.

World Health Organization and United Nations Children's Fund Joint Monitoring Programme for Water Supply and Sanitation (JMP). [UNICEF-WHO]. 2008. *Progress on Drinking Water and Sanitation: Special Focus on Sanitation*. New York and Geneva: UNICEF and WHO.

Wu, Xun, and Nepomuceno A. Malaluan. 2008. "A Tale of Two Concessionaires: A Natural Experiment of Water Privatisation in Metro Manila. *Urban Studies* 45(1): 207–229.

Yackee, Jason Webb. 2007. *Sacrificing Sovereignty: International Dispute Settlement and Foreign Direct Investment*. PhD dissertation, Department of Political Science, University of North Carolina, Chapel Hill.

Yackee, Jason Webb. 2008. "Conceptual Difficulties in the Empirical Study of Bilateral Investment Treaties." *Brooklyn Journal of International Law* 33(2): 405–462.

Yadav, Vineeta. 2011. *Political Parties, Business Groups, and Corruption in Developing Countries*. New York: Oxford University Press.

Zaheer, Srilata. 1995. "Overcoming the Liability of Foreignness." *Academy of Management Journal* 38(2): 341–363.

Zelner, Bennet A., Witold J. Henisz, and Guy L.F. Holburn. 2009. "Contentious Implementation and Retrenchment in Neoliberal Policy Reform: The Global Electric Power Industry 1989–2001." *Administrative Science Quarterly* 54(3): 379–412.

Zukin, Sharon, and Paul DiMaggio. 1990. "Introduction." In *Structures of Capital: The Social Organization of the Economy*, eds. Sharon Zukin and Paul DiMaggio, 1–36. New York: Cambridge University Press.

Index

CPSIA information can be obtained at www.ICGtesting.com
Printed in the USA
BVOW04*1535290614

357662BV00002B/4/P

9 781107 048041